AF594159
15
16
17
18
19
21
21
9
CANAL STR
WASHINGTON CHANNEL
TIDAL RESERVOIR
ECKINGTON

THE HEART OF IT ALL:

A HISTORY OF HOGAN & HARTSON L.L.P.

BY ADRIAN KINNANE

Printed and Bound in the United States of America

Published by: Montrose Press
300 North Stonestreet Avenue
Rockville, MD 20850

ISBN 0-9728874-1-5
Library of Congress Control Number 2004109765

Cover design by Gina Dwyer

Contents

Foreword

J. Warren Gorrell, Jr. Bob Glen Odle

The year 2004 marks the 100th year of Hogan & Hartson. Particularly for those lawyers who joined Hogan & Hartson in the 1950s or earlier, when there were fewer than thirty attorneys all in one location in Washington, D.C., it is altogether astonishing that in its centennial year the firm has become one of the leading global law firms, with more than a thousand lawyers in over twenty offices around the world. How has this happened? The story that follows helps answer the question.

The beginnings in the early 1900s were certainly fascinating, with founding partner Frank Hogan facing off against the U.S. government in a number of the highest profile cases of the day. The firm's growth and expansion from those early days, in terms of lawyers, practice groups, offices, and support staff, is a tale of planning and hard work (and considerable good fortune).

But there are other threads, too, such as how the firm's governance evolved, which internal decisions had the greatest impact, the effects of the up-and-down national economy and globalization, the way recruiting was carried out, how remarkable successes in the courts were prepared for and achieved, and how the regulatory and corporate practices emerged and prospered as the firm evolved to meet the needs of its clients.

While a book of this size could not possibly do justice to the thousands of client representations undertaken by the firm in the hundred years since 1904, and while it is, regrettably, impossible to describe the contributions of all of the firm's lawyers and staff, the reader will find here a gratifying sample, and not just of the marquee variety. Perhaps the most important tale that this history tells so well is how the firm developed early on, and has since protected and enhanced, a feeling of camaraderie, respect, and interdependence among its people. The firm's partners over the years have consistently embraced the need for the highest quality lawyering, teamwork, integrity, and professionalism in the firm's practice, while at the same time recognizing that there is a life beyond the computers, courtrooms, and boardrooms, that experiences in areas outside the firm are important too, and that public service and private caring will be rewarded. H&H has been particularly proud of its Community Services Department, whose pro bono matters have been carried out by a large proportion of the firm's attorneys. It is this firm culture that is so important at H&H, and that we hope this book captures. Especially for a large and diverse organization in today's competitive world, this is no mean feat.

J. Warren Gorrell, Jr. Bob Glen Odle

Acknowledgments

This project owes its greatest debt to the many Hogan & Hartson partners, former and present, who, with unfailing graciousness, made time available for interviews. They provided much valuable source material as well as perspective. The project also is indebted to the many Hogan & Hartson partners, associates, and staff members whose work, if not specifically included in this narrative, nevertheless helped create the headwaters for the stream carrying the project to completion. Hogan & Hartson's E. Barrett Prettyman, Jr., Bob Glen Odle, and J. Warren Gorrell, Jr., provided valuable factual information and editorial feedback, while partners George W. "Sandy" Mayo and Robert J. Kenney, Jr., offered administrative and logistical support. Jennifer Seibert, Dianne Sams, and Lucy Walker kept the information flowing smoothly. Austin Doherty and Bernadette Maramba of the firm's Information Resources Center were instrumental in making archival material available continually throughout the project. Many persons in Hogan & Hartson's twenty offices around the world provided helpful and timely information.

The staff at several institutions provided photographs, illustrations, and other material. They include archivists at the Washingtoniana Division of the Martin Luther King, Jr. Memorial Library in Washington, D.C.; the National Archives and Records Administration; the Library of Congress; Georgetown University and the Georgetown University Law Center; the District of Columbia Bar and the Bar Association of the District of Columbia; and the Benjamin Cardozo School of Law at Yeshiva University. Photographers Doug DeMark, Patrice Gilbert, and Mike Flanery also made their work available, as did Bruce Blunck of Chase Photography, and several Hogan & Hartson partners and former partners. An additional thanks goes to attorney Jo Brooks, who helped the author navigate unfamiliar legal territory.

At History Associates Incorporated, historians Kate Belinski, now also a law student at George Mason University, and Garry Adelman, an accomplished photo historian, brought their expert research and organizational talents to the project. Ken Durr, director of HAI's History Division, gave helpful advice during the writing phase of the project. Historian Lee Sullivan brought a keen eye to the final proofs. Gail Mathews provided superlative proofreading and editorial guidance throughout the project. Carol Spielman coordinated the extensive oral history interview portion of the project, assuring timely and accurate transcripts.

Gina Dwyer of Graphcom Inc., who created the book's cover design and internal layout, expertly captured Hogan & Hartson's special blend of proud tradition and forward-looking innovation.

Introduction

One hundred and two years ago, young Frank Joseph Hogan represented his first client, an indigent burglar of a dress shop, in Washington, D.C.'s criminal court. Hogan had recently finished law school and passed the bar, but a baby daughter was taking her first steps at home, so he held onto his job as a secretary in the War Department for nearly two more years while building his practice part-time.

On September 4, 1904, Hogan woke up to his first day of full-time work as an attorney, marking the birthday of the law practice now known as Hogan & Hartson L.L.P. For a few years he shared offices with a law school classmate, Joseph Sheehy. Then Daniel Baker, a former assistant U.S. Attorney, joined them. Hogan's talents shone as his star rose rapidly over the District of Columbia's legal landscape. By 1913 he was busy enough to hire two assistants; by 1915 his reputation not only was secure but had spread nationwide; by 1920 he had left Sheehy and Baker and moved into his own quarters.

In 1925, Nelson Hartson, a prominent tax lawyer, joined Hogan's practice. In the 1930s the two men hired a few more attorneys to handle communications and commercial work, and in 1938 the practice organized formally as a partnership of seven. Hogan & Hartson grew apace with comparable firms until the late 1980s, when it surged into a new era of national and international expansion.

It is not likely that Frank Hogan, for all his ambition and enthusiasm, foresaw what would become of the seven-man partnership he left behind when he died in 1944. Some growth was predictable, of course, or at least expected. But every passing decade churned up fresh winds and sudden storms, challenging Hogan & Hartson in ways that often tested its leadership. The firm's response, guided by its legacy and inspired by the future's possibilities, kept Hogan & Hartson on course with its aims in the currents of its times. Still, the firm's soaring trajectory in the twentieth century's closing years startled even its contemporaries. How could all this have happened, and seemingly so fast?

This book offers a response, less by way of analysis and explanation than by telling the firm's story. The first chapter begins with Frank Hogan's inauspicious origins and describes his early career, first as a civilian employee of the War Department, then through law school and into private practice in Washington, D.C. By 1930 Hogan's victories in several highly challenging and well-publicized cases had earned him a national reputation as an ideal advocate.

Chapter 2 places Hogan's growing practice in the context of the Great Depression, World War II, and the expansion of the federal government that accompanied these momentous events. In 1938 the practice organized formally as a partnership, Hogan & Hartson. Many current partners or of counsel who shaped the firm in mid-century joined Hogan & Hartson in the postwar decades, during what some observers have called the "golden age" of law firms in the United States.

In chapter 3, the year 1968 marks the end of the "golden age" and the beginning of a new era of changing times. Americans struggled with a new sense of being divided — over the Vietnam War, the environment, racial and social justice, and rising anxiety about crime and civil order. Hogan & Hartson met those challenges in a variety of ways, including the establishment of a unique department dedicated to pro bono service. At the same time, the growing firm looked to new management models that would address issues of size and complexity while preserving its valued ethos of collegiality. In 1979 the naming of partner Bob Odle to the then six-year-old Administrative Partner position, precursor to the Managing Partner position he filled ten years later, set the stage for Hogan & Hartson's next era, one of initially ambivalent, then confident, expansion.

Chapter 4 describes how Hogan & Hartson resolved its desire to nurture traditional values of personal friendliness and cohesion with its need for more centralized control. Also important in this crucial decade, 1979 to 1989, was the firm's successful resolution of an initial uncertainty some partners felt about the wisdom of opening offices outside of Washington, D.C. Besides its reputation for first-rate trial and appellate work, Hogan & Hartson's expertise in all facets of federal regulation had helped establish its reputation as a premier Washington, D.C., firm. But Hogan & Hartson's corporate practice also was flourishing. And as business clients globalized, so too did their needs for legal services. Sharply increased competition within the legal profession, along with the natural trajectory of its own practice growth, led a now well-poised Hogan & Hartson into a whole new era of growth in the 1990s.

The final and fifth chapter describes Hogan & Hartson's phenomenal expansion to more than twenty offices around the globe between 1989 and its centennial year, 2004. The complexity and scope of the firm's many practice areas also increased. During the 1990s the firm's outstanding corporate practice capabilities helped anchor its reputation as uniquely situated to serve clients at the busy intersection of government and private enterprise.

Once more Hogan & Hartson adapted its management model to changing conditions. Warren Gorrell filled a newly created Chairman position, assisted by a team of several Managing Partners. The firm's broadened management structure addressed the challenges of international growth while maintaining a robust commitment to Hogan & Hartson's traditional values — mutual respect, individual initiative, relaxed collegiality, and total commitment to client service. These ideals, ingrained over a century of practice, formed the heart of the firm's singular longevity and success.

It was a long journey from Frank Hogan's early practice in a shared office in downtown Washington to the international presence of Hogan & Hartson L.L.P. But just as looking down suddenly may enhance one's sense of height, looking backwards may offer a panoramic view of the past — in this case linking Frank Hogan's fragile origins in nineteenth-century Brooklyn, New York, to the modern enterprise that bears both Hogan's name and the imprint of his remarkable character. This vantage point of history offers a stunning view, from the travails of a hard-pressed widow, Mollie Hogan, and her three surviving children to Hogan & Hartson L.L.P., one of the world's largest and most successful law firms.

PANY.

Chapter 1
The Ideal Advocate
1877-1930

Maurice Hogan's wiry frame, worn thin as his tailor's fingers, stiffened on the ice blocks preserving him for the morrow's service at St. Brigid's Catholic Church, Brooklyn, New York. Tuberculosis, the "wasting disease," had at last consumed him, as it had two of his and Mary's five children. Now Mollie, as he had affectionately called her, sat close by Maurice for their long, last night together. Five-year-old Frankie peered sleepily at her and at his older sister, just seven, and his little sister, still a baby. She mustn't worry them, Mollie thought. But what would she do? Brooklyn had been her husband's home, their home together, for so long. Her birthplace, South Carolina, was so far away. Should she stay, or go? And who might help her there? Heavy with the practicalities of new widowhood, Mollie's head dipped wearily into the balm of sleep, then out again, to fresh anguishes of wakefulness. Yes, she was alone now. Maurice was gone.

Frank J. Hogan, young, serious and self-assured

Frankie lay quietly nearby. Slight and sickly, he, too, bobbed in and out of sleep while two sounds soaked deep into his capacious memory. Fifty years later, in the middle of the 1930s' Great Depression, he could still hear them. "Drip, drip, drip," went Daddy's ice all night long, steady and regular, the soothing sound of slumber. From time to time Mother's crying broke the rhythm of the melting ice and its gossamer suggestion of regularity. Mother's was the sound of trouble. Maybe things wouldn't be all right, after all. Frankie had never seen her like this. She was very sad. Sister was sad. Frankie was sad, too. Thus the night passed slowly, pulling behind it the first dawn of their newly precarious lives.

Daddy never woke up. Mollie went to work as a seamstress, making children's clothes and hemstitching handkerchiefs. Soon the wasting disease took her baby daughter. Mollie labored on while neighbors looked after Frankie and his sister. Once Mother's heart got too heavy, and on a Sunday afternoon she took Frankie down to the orphanage to see if they might take him in. But he was weak and in poor health, so instead she sent him south to the warmer climate of Charleston, South Carolina, to stay with her sister, Elizabeth, and Elizabeth's son, Jimmy Byrnes, two years Frankie's junior. Not long afterward Mollie and her surviving daughter followed. The two widows took in sewing to keep their families going. Frankie and Jimmy became fast friends and thrived in school, encouraged by their mothers' keen interest. One day in 1888 the local paper noted eleven-year-old Frank's recitation of an Irish poem at St. Patrick's graduation ceremony and ventured that the boy "will probably become some day a noted orator."

Frank finished one more year of school, then went to work, first in a dry goods store, then as a telegraph messenger boy for the South Carolina Railway, adding to his small income by selling newspaper subscriptions after hours. There was one more tear in the fabric, when Frank's remaining sister died. But the kindness of strangers helped mend things. A woman at the railway, Miss Little, taught him shorthand, which opened doors to stenographer and clerk positions. Another railway employee, John Austin, supplied Frank with copies of Shakespeare and other English classics. The teenager could read as many as he wished — provided Austin made the selections.

Legal training changed dramatically in Frank Hogan's lifetime. Prior to the late nineteenth century, most lawyers were trained as Abraham Lincoln had been trained, by apprenticing in the office of an established attorney. By 1900, however, most aspiring lawyers went to law school. The majority were not college graduates, but that was not unusual in an age when fewer than 10 percent of Americans completed high school and only about 1 percent graduated from college.

In the twentieth century Americans increasingly looked to trained professionals to manage their institutions and solve their problems. Teachers, physicians, engineers, social workers, business managers, and lawyers were among the many groups that established new educational and credentialing requirements. In 1910, for example, the Flexner Commission set new standards for medical training. But the legal profession remained deeply divided between its wish to update educational requirements and its effort to keep its doors open to talented candidates who could not afford a college education. Law schools could barely keep up with the demand, even as they gradually raised admission standards. In 1890 there were 61 law schools in the United States, but by 1900, when the Association of American Law Schools was founded, that number had increased to 102. At that time only about half of U.S. law schools required a high school diploma for admission.

Change came slowly. In 1920 the American Bar Association tasked a committee, chaired by Elihu Root, former cabinet member in the McKinley and Roosevelt administrations and a U.S. senator from New York (1909-1915), with recommending new standards. The following year the ABA accepted the Root Committee's proposal that candidates for admission to the bar must complete three years of legal education in a law school whose entrance requirements included at least two years of college.

When the United States declared war on Spain in 1898, twenty-one-year-old Frank went to Savannah to enlist but failed the physical exam. But the next year, when the War Department asked for civilian volunteers to go to Cuba to assist the Army quartermaster and medical officers, Frank signed on. As a reward for his bravery in facing the yellow fever that decimated U.S. ranks, he was given a paid position as clerk to General J. B. Bellinger, chief of the Quartermaster Corps. Returning to South Carolina in 1899, Frank married Mary Cecile Adair and, with his new bride, moved to Washington, D.C., to take up his new career with General Bellinger, now Quartermaster General of the Army. Frank's mother traveled with the newlyweds and joined them in their Washington home. Hogan learned rapidly all he could about military supplies, government contracts, and bureaucratic channels in his new War Department job.

At the first opportunity Frank enrolled for evening classes at Georgetown University Law School. "In my day," he later told the Erie County, New York, bar, "every male stenographer

GEORGETOWN UNIVERSITY LAW SCHOOL, C. 1900, NOW KNOWN AS THE GEORGETOWN UNIVERSITY LAW CENTER.

in the Government departments at Washington tried to study law," and one out of five lawyers was a night school graduate.[1] Many went to Georgetown, which had opened its law school in 1870 with twenty-five students but which now, with more than a thousand, was the largest law school in the country. In contrast to the small number of exclusive schools that tended to train college-educated men for corporate work in law firms, schools such as Georgetown attracted ethnic immigrants, Catholics, Jews, and others who may have lacked formal educational background, but who were self-taught, bright, and seeking to advance themselves. These law graduates typically entered solo practice rather than corporate law practices, and handled criminal cases, wills and estate work, personal injury suits, and divorces. Most made do on meager fees.

Hogan, now the father of baby Dorothy, completed his courses in 1902 at the head of his class and in record time. He passed the bar exam and, with classmate Joseph Sheehy, rented an office in the National Union Trust Building at 918 F Street, N.W., just four blocks from the D.C. courthouses.[2] Hogan's practice at first consisted of "sundowning," representing clients after work or by using his annual leave. His friendly wit, diligent preparation, and sharp command of the law earned respect from the "5th Street lawyers" whose offices were located near the courthouses. He also attracted the attention of distinguished local practitioners like J. J. Darlington, who offered him guidance as well as cases.

Hogan's first client, however, was not referred by mentors but assigned by the court. Augustus "Gus" Wilson was a chronic petty criminal who had pled not guilty to charges of burglarizing a women's clothing shop where he had worked as a porter until being fired four days before the crime. When Wilson mumbled to the judge, "I don't have no lawyer and don't have no money to get no lawyer," Hogan got the case. It looked open-and-shut for the prosecutor, who presented three men the police had rounded up to testify that they had seen Wilson outside the shop on the night of the burglary. Wilson denied breaking into the shop but admitted to Hogan that on the evening he had been fired he had sold a couple of pilfered blouses to a woman friend. Hogan decided to keep him off the stand.

Wilson's prospects looked bleak. But Hogan's footwork revealed that two of the three prosecution "witnesses" had been in jail at the time they were supposed to have seen the defendant, while the third had been serving on a chain gang for a knife assault. They could not possibly have seen Wilson in front of the store, or anywhere else for that matter. And since burglary, with its element of

[1] Frank J. Hogan, Class of '02, Georgetown University Law School [2] Looking West on F St. towards the U.S. Treasury c. 1903. The offices of Sheehy & Hogan were in the fourth building on the left side of the street. [3] After graduating in 1902, Hogan and fellow Georgetown Law classmate Joseph Sheehy opened an office in The National Union Trust Building, 918 F St., N.W. The building still stands, just three blocks away from Hogan & Hartson's current D.C. office.

In 1905 Hogan successfully interceded with President Theodore Roosevelt to win fair consideration for the Herman Shoe Company in its Navy contract bid.

SHEEHY & HOGAN (Joseph C Sheehy and Frank J Hogan), lawyers, National Union bldg, 918 F nw

breaking and entering, not simple larceny, had been the only charge, the astonished Wilson was judged not guilty and set free.

In 1904 Hogan was ready, as he said, "to give up the certainty of a government salary for the well-established uncertainty of a law practice." He resigned from his War Department job effective August 31, and relocated with Sheehy to the Colorado Building, on the corner of 14th and G Streets, N.W. Three years later Daniel Baker, a former assistant U.S. Attorney, joined them there. Perhaps aided by former War Department contacts, Hogan soon landed a major client, the Herman Shoe Company of Boston, which had lost a Navy contract to a Pennsylvania competitor convicted just a few months earlier of selling "paper sole" shoes to the Army. Secretary of War William Howard Taft had banned the competitor from any further government contracts, but the company's officials asserted that Taft's ban had been only for Army contracts and therefore did not apply to the Navy.

Hogan went straight to the White House to complain to President Theodore Roosevelt but the President's secretary, William Loeb, deflected him. Just then Roosevelt walked in from an adjacent room. Hogan grabbed the moment to make his case. "I don't believe you!" the President bellowed. "Your story is preposterous." But Hogan persisted, putting his own future on the line. "Will you at least direct an investigation, Mr. President? If you find that the facts are not precisely as I state them, then I wish you would issue an order barring me out of the government departments!" Roosevelt agreed.

A few days later Loeb summoned Hogan back to the White House, where Roosevelt announced that he had confirmed Hogan's account and had ordered the Navy Secretary to cancel the Pennsylvania company's contract.

Samuel B. Wilson	Clk. 1600	Q.M. Dept, P.I.	June 25/04	Died
Edward C. Howe	Clk S&T $900	Q.M. Dept Jeffersonville, Ind	Aug 14/04	Resigned
Thomas Murphy	Marine Fireman $660	Q.M. Dept Boston, Mass, Str. "Henry Wilson"	" 2/04	"
Ralph Van Name	Clk $882	Ord. Dept. Sandy Hook P.G., N.J.	" 29/04	"
Frank J. Hogan	S&T $1800	Q.M. Dept. Wash. D.C.	" 31/04	"
Wm Krider	Cl 1600	Q.M. Dept San Francisco	Sept 3/04 (Pay to cease June 1/04)	Discharged
Noah Lohr	Watch 720	Q.M. Dept Schuylkill Ars. Pa	Aug 31/04	Resigned
A. M. Healy	Clk.	Q.M. Dept. P.I.	July 1/04	Discharged by Comdg Genl.
John Wilson	Foragemaster $600	Q.M. Dept. P.I.	Mar 31/04	Resigned
Edward Wyatt	Painter	Q.M. Dept Jeffersonville, Ind.	Sept 14/04	Discharged
James W. Stuckenbruck	Blksmith $720	Q.M. Dept.	Sept 10/04	Resigned

Government records show Frank J. Hogan's resignation from the War Department, effective August 31, 1904. The following Monday, September 4, he began full-time work as an attorney in private practice in Washington, D.C.

This first encounter between two spirited fighters revealed a special chemistry, for they developed a lasting friendship. Both had overcome sickly childhoods and both had seen service in the Spanish-American War, Hogan as a civilian. In the larger scheme of Roosevelt's life, saving the Herman shoe contract was a minor matter. But it meant the world to Hogan, a Republican, who remained a solid supporter of Roosevelt even when the former President bolted the party in 1912 to run as a Progressive against William H. Taft and the Democrat, Woodrow Wilson.

Hogan's practice grew steadily on a diet of wills, criminal cases, and tort claims. Washington's streetcar company, Capital Traction, was a favorite target for pedestrian ankle-twisters and errant carriage drivers. Hogan became the attorney of choice for injured citizens, establishing an unbroken string of successful suits against the company between 1904 and 1913. Such cases were his early bread and butter, while others, like his representation of a local city official, tax assessor Samuel T. Kalbfus, helped create new opportunities. In an age when advertising legal services was unethical for lawyers, Sam Kalbfus kept Hogan on the front page of local newspapers for months.

Kalbfus's troubles began in mid-July 1910 when "society man" and Metropolitan Club member F. Oden "Odie" Horstmann, following his physician's advice, took up gainful employment and joined the city's excise, or tax, department as a saloon inspector. Horstmann quickly proved to be a meddler for reform, even pointing out to Kalbfus, his boss, how Kalbfus should do his job. When his suggestions were ignored, Horstmann spread them more widely. At the club and on the golf greens he told the district commissioners of improprieties in the city's tax department, particularly some real estate-related loans made to Kalbfus by a brewer whose operations Kalbfus had assessed.

The commissioners took no action, however, in part because what the assessor had done was not officially prohibited. So Horstmann sallied over to Capitol Hill to visit Congressman William S. Bennett of New York, a member of the House District Committee. Soon stories about the brewer's loans appeared on the front pages of city newspapers, along with Congressman Bennett's denunciation of Sam Kalbfus from the House floor. On October 14, 1911, Horstmann was fired. When Congress

OLD SUPREME COURT ROOM AND LAW LIBRARY C. 1900 (LC).

There were sixty students in Frank Hogan's third-year class at the Georgetown University Law School, then located at 506 and 508 E Street, NW. Tuition for the 1902-1903 academic year was $80. Text books for the year cost about $30. Though the school offered no room and board, its catalog assured students that in Washington, D.C., "the cost of comfortable lodging, board, fuel, and gas varies from $20 to $30 per month, according to the location and appointments selected." The catalog noted the school's proximity to public resources such as the 100,000-volume Law Library at the United States Capitol, now called the Law Library of Congress, which had served the Supreme Court and members of Congress since 1832. The library opened to the public late in the nineteenth century and often was used by local law students, though they were not allowed to withdraw books.

[Above Left] Edmund "Nubby" Jones, Class of 1916, Georgetown Law School. [Above Right] Milton Kaufman, Class of 1913, Georgetown Law School. [Right] Hogan earned early fame in Washington with a successful challenge to the will of Washington Post founder, millionaire and local philanthropist, Stilson Hutchins. Among Hutchins's many gifts to the city was this statue of Benjamin Franklin, installed in 1889. It now stands in front of the Old Post Office Building at 12th St. and Pennsylvania Ave., N.W., just a block from Hogan & Hartson's D.C. office.

pressured the district commissioners to investigate Horstmann's allegations, Kalbfus hired Frank Hogan, who discounted the charges as "merely the grumblings of a disgruntled employee." However, the *Washington Times* and other papers took the opportunity to beat the drum for reform in the city's government.

On October 16, 1911, hearings began before the district commissioners. Hogan's task was to show there had been no conflict of interest when Kalbfus accepted a loan from the president of the brewing company to purchase a desirable tract of land in suburban Maryland. He called to the stand Michael Keane, the brewery's general counsel and the person who had delivered the loan. "Mr. Keane, are you not aware that all of the justices of the District Supreme Court hear cases pleaded by their bosom friends?" asked Hogan. "Why, of course," Keane answered. Hogan continued, "As a matter of fact, don't you know that Justice Barnard has two sons who are lawyers and who frequently have cases before the District Supreme Court?" "Why, certainly." "And what is your opinion of Justice Barnard as a jurist?" Keane quickly averred that Barnard was a jurist of the highest integrity. Hogan pressed on, reciting several more examples of esteemed judges who routinely heard cases argued by close friends or relatives, with no imputation of conflict of interest or bias. Why, then, must it be different for Sam Kalbfus? In a city where official and personal connections often were intertwined, Hogan's argument struck a chord. On November 3 the commissioners exonerated Kalbfus while advising him to avoid future real estate transactions that might cause suspicion.[3]

The outcome of the hearings displeased reformers but was a success for Hogan, and the publicity served him well. In 1912 he, Baker, and Sheehy moved to new quarters just one block north, in the Evans Building, at 1420 New York Avenue. A year later Hogan's practice had grown enough to warrant the hiring of an assistant, Milton Kaufman, a recent Georgetown Law School graduate. Just a few months later Hogan hired a clerk, Edmund "Nubby" Jones, a college track star whose nickname was never explained. Jones started law school on October 1, 1913, while working on what he dubbed "Mr. Hogan's scholarship." That year Capital Traction, having lost case after case to Hogan, offered to retain him. Thereafter Hogan continued his unbroken winning streak, though now for the transit company.

In 1915 Hogan's courtroom skill and his cultivation of veteran trial lawyers won him another high-profile case. Multimillionaire Stilson Hutchins, founder of the *Washington Post* and a generous city benefactor, had changed his will three times in ten years before he passed away. The last change displeased his youngest son, Lee, who hired J. J. Darlington to challenge the will. Darlington, a highly esteemed attorney in local practice, knew Hogan from frequent contacts in the D.C. courts and now engaged the younger man to help with the complicated case. Recognizing Hogan's talents,

Darlington soon turned the lead over to his younger colleague. Hogan's task was to convince a jury that Stilson had been mentally incompetent when he decided to give 35 percent of his $3 million to his wife, 35 percent to eldest son Walter, 10 percent to a granddaughter, and just 20 percent to Lee. The five-month trial turned out to be the longest civil proceeding up to that point in the city's history.

One day Hogan awed the jury with a question to a psychiatrist that may have been the longest ever asked in a courtroom. Hogan asked for a simple yes or no answer, but the question proved to be a three-hour-long, 27,000-word summary of every significant point made in the trial, delivered without notes and without interruption. All present, including a full complement of reporters, were awed by this feat of memory, which the witness capped with his single-word response. Darlington's prestige, combined with Hogan's mental agility and whatever merits his arguments contained, impressed the jury, which returned a verdict in favor of Hogan's client after only an hour's deliberation.

HOGAN'S REPUTATION AS A GIFTED TRIAL ATTORNEY SPREAD NATIONALLY DURING A SEQUENCE OF LAWSUITS BETWEEN RIGGS NATIONAL BANK (L) AND THE U.S. TREASURY (R) IN 1915-1916. THE TWO BUILDINGS FACED EACH OTHER ACROSS A SWATH OF PENNSYLVANIA AVE., N.W., JUST EAST OF THE WHITE HOUSE.

As Hogan's professional star rose in Washington, he was careful to credit those who had helped him. Years later he told how, in the jury selection phase of the Hutchins trial, a prospective juror had asked to be excused because he thought so highly of J. J. Darlington that he would favor any client he represented. Darlington leaned over to Hogan and whispered the firm command, "Get up and tell the judge to excuse him; I want that to come from our side." Through numerous such incidents the young litigator absorbed a courtroom etiquette of fair play that tempered his scrappy advocacy.

FIFTY-FIRST YEAR OF
BOYD'S
DIRECTORY
OF THE
DISTRICT OF COLUMBIA
FOR
1909
EMBRACING
An Alphabetical List of Business Firms and Private Citizens, Also Street and Congressional Directories and a Classified Business Directory,
AS WELL AS A COMPENDIUM OF

HOGAN FRANK J, Lawyer 810-819 Colorado Bldg, Tel Main 2007, h2320 Sheridan Circle, Tel North 10307 (See card in Legal Blue Book)

"TO FIND A NAME YOU MUST KNOW HOW TO SPELL IT"

R. L. POLK & CO.
PUBLISHERS AND PROPRIETORS
W. ANDREW BOYD, Special Mngr. Washington
810 F STREET, WASHINGTON, D. C.

The United States was still pondering the sobering news of a German U-boat's sinking of the passenger ship *Lusitania* on May 7, 1915, when a complicated case — a case within a case, really — launched Hogan from local to national prominence. The Treasury Department and Riggs Bank, whose classical porticos still face each other across a swath of Pennsylvania Avenue just east of the White House, were embroiled in a dispute. Riggs Bank officers charged that Treasury officials were conspiring for partisan reasons to wreck the bank by withdrawing its monetary lifeblood, federal deposits; moreover, they charged that these officials were abusing their regulatory authority by harassing the bank with ceaseless demands for reports that had kept shifts of clerks working overtime for months. The case within this case was a countercharge of perjury, brought by the government against bank officers, that eventually eclipsed the larger case and drew the entire affair to a dramatic close.

The change in national administration in 1913 formed the backdrop for the erupting conflict next door to the White House. Ever since the bank panic of 1907, the worst the country had yet experienced, bankers and politicians had struggled to find a system of monetary stabilization acceptable both to rural, mostly Democratic, interests and to urban, mostly Republican, financial interests exemplified by Wall Street. The Wilson administration had promoted, and a Democratic Congress had passed, the Federal Reserve Act in 1913. But bankers felt slighted by the composition of the Federal Reserve Board that the act established. Only one of the then seven Reserve Board governors was a private banker. The others were appointed or ex officio government officials. The Federal Reserve Act also included new monitoring and reporting requirements that bankers thought exceeded the federal government's authority.

FRANK HOGAN AT WORK

In the years after the Federal Reserve Act's passage, bankers continued their campaign against its requirements. In December 1915 Treasury Secretary William McAdoo read articles in the New York *Tribune* critical of him personally and of his department's policies. McAdoo suspected Riggs Bank and the National City Bank of New York of planting the articles. Additionally, he believed these banks had cooperated in using depositors' funds to engage in improper stock transactions. He summoned Riggs Bank president Charles Glover and other bank officers across the street and demanded an accounting.

The bank officers' heated but unconvincing denials about the Tribune stories not only angered McAdoo but unearthed personal grievances between Riggs vice president Milton E. Ailes and John Williams, Comptroller of the Treasury. The Treasury then increased the pressure on the bank, demanding report after report, further curtailing federal deposits, and imposing fines and deadlines that the bank could not meet. The bad publicity shook depositors' confidence, and Riggs Bank risked losing its license to hold federal deposits. The bank therefore brought suit in the District Supreme Court against McAdoo and Williams for conspiracy to wreck its business. Judge Walter T. McCoy granted a temporary injunction against further fines pending the outcome of the trial.

Riggs hired former Democratic U.S. Senator from Texas Joseph Bailey as chief counsel and Hogan as assistant counsel. For its part, the Treasury lined up an impressive team led by noted New York trial lawyer Samuel Untermyer, Assistant Attorney General Charles Warren, and Boston progressive Louis D. Brandeis, "the people's lawyer," who had persuaded the Supreme Court (*Muller v. Oregon*) in 1908 to approve lowering the limit on women's work hours to ten per day. Brandeis's approach ushered in a new era of "sociological jurisprudence" in which social science data, health and medical information, and statistics, not just abstract principles, decided cases. The *Evening Star* cast Hogan's fervent opening statement as a "vitriolic excoriation" of Comptroller Williams and Secretary McAdoo, contrasting it with Untermyer's "quiet, wholly unimpassioned manner."[4] But Hogan's passion camouflaged a calculated strategy to lure opposing counsel into a trap.

On Thursday, May 20, the fourth day of the trial, Hogan and Bailey introduced an affidavit written by Hogan in which president Glover, vice president William Flather, and Flather's brother Henry, a cashier at Riggs, swore that Riggs National Bank had never been a party to any of the more than 3,000 stock dealings that were the core of the government's case against the bank. Yet their signatures clearly were on the documents. The Treasury's lawyers argued against the admissibility of this seemingly flagrant falsehood, but Judge McCoy allowed it.

Joseph Bailey also could be impassioned. One morning early in the trial his emotion got the upper hand. Judge McCoy was testily denouncing a newspaper article that described him as having shown bias in the previous day's proceedings by ruling on a matter still under discussion. The judge denied he had made any such ruling and warned reporters in the courtroom against any further distortions. Bailey chose that inopportune moment to rise and present additional arguments he had prepared in support of Hogan's affidavit, whereupon McCoy impatiently told him he didn't have to take up court time because the affidavit already had been admitted. Bailey sarcastically replied, "The court has taken more time in correcting me than I would have taken in argument." The irritated judge commanded the court reporter to repeat Bailey's statement, and then threatened the ex-congressman with removal from the case. Bailey, unabashed, threw his arms up, bowed deep to the bench, and grandly offered to withdraw. Tempers cooled and apologies were exchanged, but the damage had been done. Thirty-eight-year-old Frank Hogan now found himself Riggs's chief attorney in the trial.

Numerous fine points and jurisdictional questions consumed the month of June, so Judge McCoy carried the trial over to October to allow him to catch up on other cases and to take a summer vacation. Meanwhile, the Treasury's attorneys pondered a response to the curious Riggs affidavit Hogan had successfully introduced. On October 1 they stopped nibbling and seized the bait, obtaining grand jury indictments for perjury against Charles Glover and the two Flather brothers. Judge McCoy placed the conspiracy case on hold so the perjury trial could proceed. That trial opened in May 1916 in D.C. Criminal Court Number 1 before Judge Frederick Siddons, a former D.C. commissioner. Frank Hogan was pleased to have the assistance of his mentor, J. J. Darlington, and attorney John B. Stanchfield.

Hogan argued that Riggs Bank had not *itself* been a stock trader nor had it speculated or profited on its own behalf. Instead, it had simply assisted its customers in placing stock orders, a widespread and common bank practice prior to passage of the Federal Reserve Act of 1913. Riggs Bank, said Hogan, had ceased that practice after the act's passage. His affidavit had simply stated this point, which was literally true. Glover and the Flathers had indeed placed stock orders, but since they had done so only as a service to customers, they and Riggs Bank could not be considered parties to the transactions. Opposing counsel probably missed Hogan's hair-splitting logic, but Hogan successfully turned the perjury indictment against the accusers, offering it as yet another example of how the Treasury was going out of its way to put his client out of business.

FORMER PRESIDENT THEODORE ROOSEVELT AND FRANK HOGAN.

Frank Hogan always kept the pictures of two people on his desk — his law mentor, J. J. Darlington, and President Theodore Roosevelt. Darlington was Hogan's model of the successful, civic-minded attorney who, through fairness and quiet generosity, earned the admiration of the entire community. Roosevelt, on the other hand, was an activist who sought publicity and used it masterfully as an instrument for reform. Hogan blended both ideals. In the local Washington community he raised funds for hospitals and charities, donated large sums to a variety of causes, and took on several pro bono cases of poor veterans referred by the War Department. He also was a much sought-after speaker at trade association and Gridiron Club dinners, community center and Boys Club openings, police and fireman award banquets, and Georgetown University gatherings. In bar activities and in the courtroom Hogan was a feisty advocate for his profession and for his clients and used the media skillfully to marshal public support for his viewpoints.

ON MAY 31, 1916, A GROUP OF WELL-WISHERS SENT D.C. DELEGATE FRANK HOGAN (L OF CENTER, HOLDING HAT) TO THE REPUBLICAN NATIONAL CONVENTION IN CHICAGO.

Politically Hogan was a lifelong Republican, as was Theodore Roosevelt, though both broke ranks with the party in 1912 when the former President led a third-party Progressive effort aimed at regaining the White House from William Howard Taft and the Republican establishment. When Roosevelt declared that he felt "as fit as a bull moose" for the campaign, newspapers seized the image as a perfect moniker for the Progressive, now "Bull Moose," party. Roosevelt defeated Taft by a wide margin, but the resulting split in the Republican vote handed the election to the Democratic candidate, Woodrow Wilson. Roosevelt's platform included such reforms as the direct election of United States senators, women's suffrage, and child labor laws. Hogan served as the D.C. head of Roosevelt's campaign, then returned to the Republican fold following Woodrow Wilson's election. He was Washington, D.C.'s, delegate to the Republican National Conventions in 1916 and 1920.

On the morning of May 15 former President William Howard Taft appeared unexpectedly in court as a character witness for the Riggs defendants, testifying that he had known Charles Glover for twenty-six years and regarded his character as excellent. Taft, then a law professor at Yale, rushed off to catch a train back to New Haven, but the trial's biggest surprise was still in the making. Just one week after Taft's appearance, Hogan was seated in the courtroom when a messenger came up to his table and handed him a telegram. It was from former President Theodore Roosevelt. "Yes," said Teddy, he would indeed be able to appear in court as a character witness for the defendants the next morning. Hogan immediately turned around and handed the telegram to the reporters behind him, too late for Darlington to stop him. The senior lawyer's intended strategy had been to use Roosevelt as a surprise witness, but Hogan's idea was to make the most out of the popular ex-President's crowd appeal. The excited cry "Teddy is coming!" flashed like heat lightening over the capital city.

Hogan's public relations gambit worked. Several thousand people, including law students from a class Hogan was teaching at Georgetown, showed up at the courthouse the next day to see Roosevelt, Hogan, and co-counsel John Stanchfield arrive in a car belonging to the Speaker of the House, Roosevelt's son-in-law, Nicholas Longworth. The cheers, Hogan recalled, "could have been heard by the jury even if they were confined in a hermetically sealed room."[5] Roosevelt, the most electrifying public figure of his era, charged into D.C. Criminal Court Number 1 to the acclaim of a handkerchief-waving, standing-room-only crowd whose spontaneous outpouring wilted the trial's formality and joined as one with the jubilant throng on the streets and lawns outside.

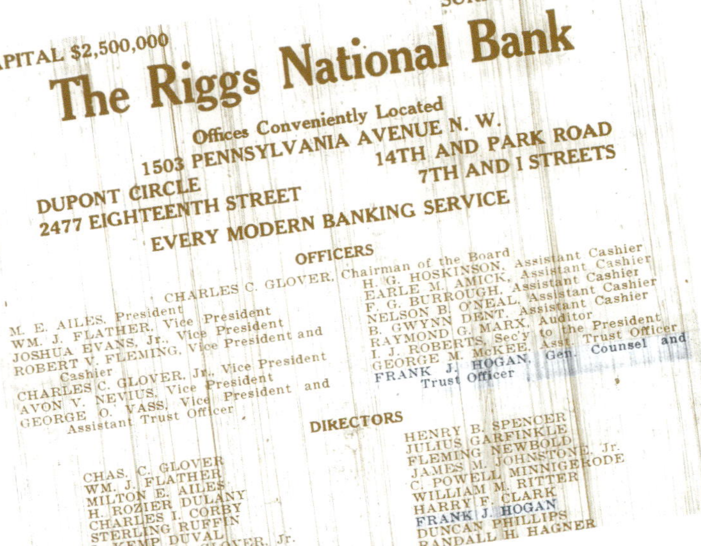

SURPLUS $1,250,000

APITAL $2,500,000

The Riggs National Bank

Offices Conveniently Located

1503 PENNSYLVANIA AVENUE N. W.
14TH AND PARK ROAD
7TH AND I STREETS
DUPONT CIRCLE
2477 EIGHTEENTH STREET

EVERY MODERN BANKING SERVICE

OFFICERS

CHARLES C. GLOVER, Chairman of the Board
M. E. AILES, President
WM. J. FLATHER, Vice President
JOSHUA EVANS, Jr., Vice President
ROBERT V. FLEMING, Vice President and Cashier
CHARLES C. GLOVER, Jr., Vice President
AVON V. NEVIUS, Vice President
GEORGE O. VASS, Vice President and Assistant Trust Officer
H. G. HOSKINSON, Assistant Cashier
EARLE M. AMICK, Assistant Cashier
F. G. BURROUGH, Assistant Cashier
NELSON B. O'NEAL, Assistant Cashier
B. GWYNN DENT, Assistant Cashier
RAYMOND G. MARX, Auditor
I. J. ROBERTS, Sec'y to the President
GEORGE M. McKEE, Asst. Trust Officer
FRANK J. HOGAN, Gen. Counsel and Trust Officer

DIRECTORS

CHAS. C. GLOVER
WM. J. FLATHER
MILTON E. AILES
H. ROZIER DULANY
CHARLES I. CORBY
STERLING RUFFIN
KEMP DUVAL
GLOVER, Jr.
HENRY B. SPENCER
JULIUS GARFINKLE
FLEMING NEWBOLD
JAMES M. JOHNSTONE, Jr.
C. POWELL MINNIGERODE
WILLIAM M. RITTER
HARRY F. CLARK
FRANK J. HOGAN
DUNCAN PHILLIPS
RANDALL H. HAGNER

The former President was "dee-lighted" to testify to the sterling character and philanthropic work of Charles Glover and to the solid standing of the Flather brothers, though he couldn't be so sure of Glover's political views. "I know he was either for Mr. Wilson or Mr. Taft. At any rate I know he was against me," Roosevelt joked about his unsuccessful third-party presidential bid in 1912. "Remember, this is a court," Judge Siddons admonished the amused crowd.[6] Under the rules governing character witness testimony, Roosevelt's remarks were to be limited to general statements only, but he routinely veered into specific examples of Glover's upstanding citizenship. The opposing counsel objected, the judge sustained, the former President apologized, then added that he had intended to speak only in the most general terms and would try to do better, which he then tried to do, but managed to insert still more specifics, with more objections, and more sustaining, until the frustrated district attorney finally turned to Hogan and muttered a resigned, "Oh, hell."

As Roosevelt left the courtroom, he commended the jurors for their public service and told them he was sure they would "do the right thing." Judge Siddons, meanwhile, "was suffering facial and vocal paralysis," Hogan said later. In a further demonstration of the ex-President's appeal, during the noon break one of the jurors exchanged his seat for the one Roosevelt had used. "Thereafter," Hogan noted, "he drew in his inspiration in a way theretofore unthought of by counsel."[7]

Hogan called character witness after witness, until Judge Siddons at last asked when he would be finished. With mock gravity Hogan confessed to the great difficulty in restricting the number of Washingtonians who would be willing to testify to the defendants' high reputation. But with June's heat and humidity approaching, Siddons ordered a halt. The next day the defense rested its case and on May 27 the jury, which had been sequestered during the trial, retired to consider its verdict. Judge Siddons figured he had time for lunch.

He didn't. Nine minutes later the judge had to drop his meal and return to court, for the jury had decided. When all twelve rose together and thundered "Not guilty!" for the three defendants, courtroom decorum dissolved. A tearful Mrs. Hogan added her measure of pride and joy, while Judge Siddons

WILLIAM H. "DONNIE" DONOVAN, CLASS OF 1913, GEORGETOWN LAW SCHOOL.

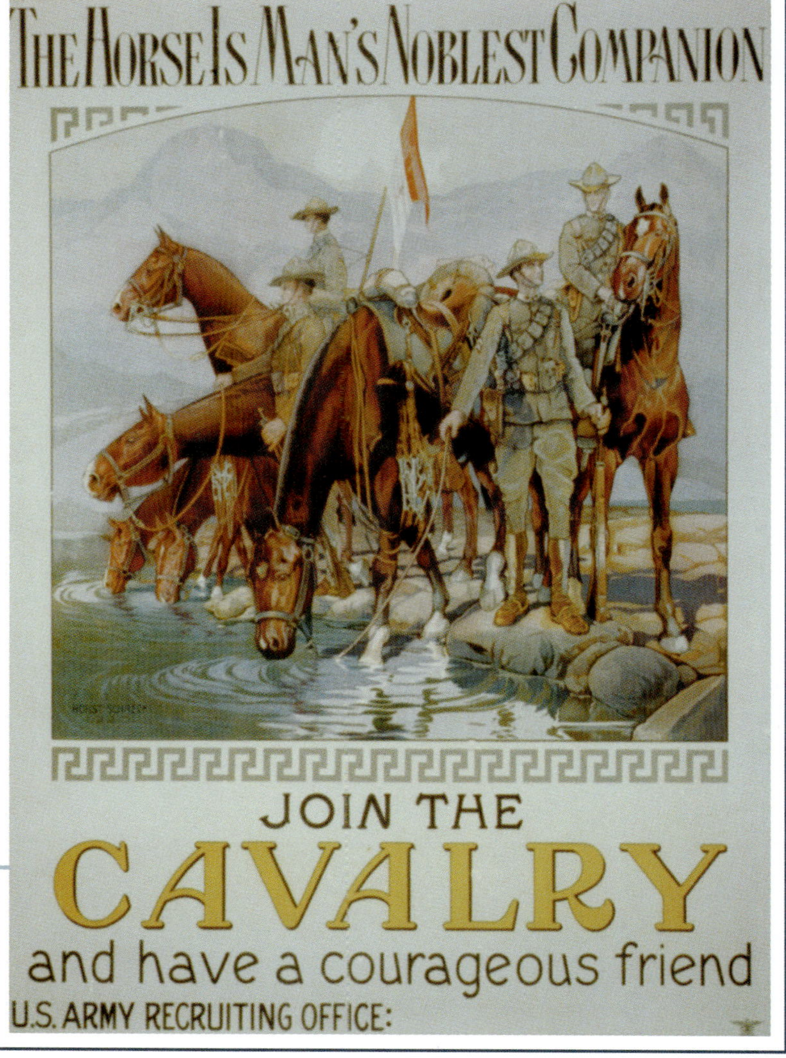

HOGAN'S SUCCESSFUL DEFENSE OF WAR SURPLUS CONTRACTORS SUCH AS THE U.S. HARNESS COMPANY IN THE EARLY 1920S HELPED SPREAD HIS REPUTATION AS AN EXCEPTIONALLY TALENTED LITIGATOR.

Frank Hogan formed his political views during a tumultuous period in U.S. history. When wartime inflation raised the cost of living by more than 70 percent in 1918-1919, workers pushed for higher wages as well as for shorter hours and better working conditions. Twenty percent of American workers participated in 3,300 strikes in 1919 alone. Many Americans thought they saw a connection between labor unrest in the United States and the 1917 Bolshevik Revolution in Russia. Fear of internal subversion created a "Red Scare" that fueled popular support for government surveillance of union leaders and political radicals. When a labor radical blew himself up trying to bomb the Washington, D.C., home of U.S. Attorney General A. Mitchell Palmer in 1919, Palmer appointed a young attorney named J. Edgar Hoover to gather intelligence on socialists and labor unions.

Objectivity and fairness often suffered in an effort to assure domestic stability. In 1921, for instance, proclaimed anarchists Nicola Sacco and Bartolomeo Vanzetti were arrested in Massachusetts and charged with armed robbery and murder. After a trial that many observers thought focused more on the defendants' political beliefs than on the actual evidence of their alleged crimes, the two men were convicted. On August 23, 1927, Sacco and Vanzetti were electrocuted. In 1977 Massachusetts Governor Michael Dukakis proclaimed that day a memorial day in their honor and called on all citizens to guard against prejudice, intolerance, and the "failure to defend the rights of persons who are looked upon as strangers in our midst."

Frank Hogan condemned violence and vehemently disagreed with anarchists' views. At the same time, he warned against what he saw as a pernicious "enemy within" — the government's tendency to run roughshod over citizens' constitutional rights when conducting investigations.

busied himself shuffling papers at the bench in studied ignorance of the outburst he had just warned against. Several jury members sought out Glover and the Flathers to shake their hands. Glover bravely said the outcome had never been in doubt. The Flathers said they were glad it was over. Hogan volunteered fulsomely that "the shafts of malice have failed to reach their targets."[8]

Four days later Judge McCoy rendered an opinion in Riggs Bank's now anticlimactic civil suit against the Treasury officials. Both sides and their lawyers won and lost points. There had been no conspiracy to wreck the bank, said the judge, and the Treasury was free to deposit in whatever bank it chose; but he also voided the financial penalties Comptroller Williams had levied on Riggs and, more importantly, affirmed his court's jurisdiction in the matter, which the Treasury had challenged from the outset. With that assertion of judicial authority, the Riggs-Treasury controversy quietly subsided, having helped nurture the careers of two talented attorneys. Riggs Bank promptly hired Frank Hogan as its new permanent counsel, and Woodrow Wilson soon named Louis D. Brandeis an Associate Justice of the U.S. Supreme Court.

By 1918 Nubby Jones had returned from the war and resumed law school and clerking at the firm. Hogan's secretary, Virginia Warren, had been a great

Collier's, The National Weekly, *for* January 26, 1924

Grown Men Talk While Children Toil

By Harold Cary

It's time to put your foot down on this shameful business of child slavery. You wouldn't let greed squeeze health and happiness out of your own children. The Child Labor Amendment is now in committee. Why is it being held up? Senator McCormick, who introduced it, says no more hearings are necessary. It should be reported on the floor of Congress and voted on without delay. Write your Congressman to-day, or see him or wire him. Tell him to get the Children's Amendment out of committee and on to the floor. Be emphatic. Suppose they were your kids.

63D CONGRESS, 1ST SESSION.

H. R. 6562.

IN THE HOUSE OF REPRESENTATIVES.

JUNE 28, 1913.

Mr. BARNHART introduced the following bill; which was referred to the Committee on the District of Columbia and ordered to be printed.

A BILL

To regulate the employment of minor children in the District of Columbia.

Be it enacted by the Senate and House of Representatives of the United States of America in Congress assembled, That no child under fourteen years of age shall be employed, permitted, or suffered to work in the District of Columbia in, about, or in connection with any mill, factory, workshop, mercantile or mechanical establishment, tenement-house manufactory or workshop, store, office, office building, restaurant, boarding house, bakery, barber shop, hotel, apartment house, bootblack stand or establishment, public stable, garage, laundry, place of amusement, club, or as a driver, help since coming to the office in 1915, but Milton Kaufman had died and the practice needed additional assistance. So Hogan hired a new, full-time attorney, shy and bookish William H. "Donnie" Donovan, a Georgetown Law School graduate, and a part-time legal researcher, Tom Fields. Two years later Hogan moved back to the Colorado Building, where he remained for the rest of his career.

The World War increased the scope and scale of the federal government and had a parallel effect on Hogan's practice, which focused on defending War Department contractors against charges that they had defrauded the government. The U.S. mobilization effort had been a marvel of resourcefulness and organization, turning the tide of battle in an exhausted Europe so quickly that suppliers were left with about $1.5 billion worth of surplus military goods when peace descended on November 11, 1918, just twenty months after the United States' declaration of war. But soon the glow of victory gave way to widespread disillusion over The Great War's destruction, and to suspicions that businessmen had "profiteered" from it. The line between profit-making and profiteering was difficult to draw, however, especially under the widely used "cost plus" contracts that encouraged rapid production at the cost of a certain level of waste. Some postwar profiteering prosecutions were both justified and successful, but many were neither.[9] Frank Hogan shouldered the defense of several executives targeted by the U.S. Department of Justice.

The Riggs Bank case had strengthened Hogan's aversion to the capricious exercise of government authority, but his experience in five separate "war fraud" cases in the early 1920s hardened that aversion into a political conviction. The cases involved former government and military officials as well as private businessmen who had built army barracks; renovated buildings for military use; disposed of surplus lumber after the war; sold off the assets of the massive Old Hickory powder and explosives plant in Jacksonville, Tennessee; and lastly, refurbished for civilian sale a huge surplus of horse harnesses and related leather supplies no longer needed by the Army.

In September 1920 the U.S. War Department hired the U.S. Harness Company, which had been formed by several former War Department officials, to dispose of its surplus leather supplies. The company agreed to buy 120,000 surplus sets of military harness from seventeen separate producers, convert them for civilian use, and sell them to the public on a profit-sharing basis with the government. The endeavor was hardly a windfall for the harness company. Breast collar harnesses with copper-clad cables for pulling artillery pieces, for instance, needed substantial refitting before they were suitable for pulling carts, plows, or other farm equipment. Moreover, many of the harnesses had lain for months in ship holds and warehouses. Damaged by mildew and salt water, they required extensive reconditioning.

The prospect of so many surplus harnesses on the open market irked commercial tanners, who appealed to their representatives in Congress. Six hundred employees of a harness manufacturing facility at Rock Island, Illinois, protested to Congressman William J. Graham when Army Major Joseph C. Byron closed that facility after the war. Months later, Byron, now a civilian and president of the U.S. Harness Company, appeared before a committee chaired by Representative Graham to investigate the war contracts of the Wilson

BUSINESSMAN ERNEST C. MORSE, ONE OF THE MANY FORMER WAR DEPARTMENT OFFICIALS WHOM HOGAN SUCCESSFULLY DEFENDED IN THE "WAR FRAUD" CASES OF 1921-1925.

administration. Surely, thought Graham, Byron's motives in closing Rock Island had been tainted. The U.S. Harness Company looked like a grand scheme by an insiders' group to defraud the government by throwing the Rock Islanders out of work and cornering the surplus harness market. Additionally, a former Army officer, angry because Byron had caused him to lose his commission, told Graham that U.S. Harness had obtained the contract without proper bidding.

When Republican Warren G. Harding succeeded President Woodrow Wilson in 1921, Congressman Graham and Attorney General Harry Daugherty asked War Department Secretary John Weeks to cancel the U.S. Harness Company's contract. Instead, Weeks carried out his own investigation, found Byron's operation to be efficient and fair, and refused to cancel the contract. Graham and Daugherty then went to the White House and convinced President Harding to cancel the contract himself. The trusting president complied.

At that juncture Frank Hogan, who had been retained by the U.S. Harness Company, delivered a brief to the White House arguing that the President did not have the authority to void a valid contract. Only the courts could do that, and as yet there had been no hearing. When the U.S. Harness Company defied the government's order to cease operations and return all surplus material to federal officials, Attorney General Daugherty dispatched a company of seven hundred soldiers with orders to seize the goods "unless opposed by force or legal process."[10] The troops arrived at the harness company's plant in Charles Town, West Virginia, on July 15 and set up camp on the racetrack grounds. Then they marched over to the plant, surrounded it, and sent a contingent inside to seize the goods.

The soldiers had loaded less than a truckload of bridle bits when the bugle sounded for lunch. When they returned the harness plant was locked. Officers went searching for a long-distance phone to consult with Daugherty on whether or not a locked door amounted to being "opposed by force." But in the end it didn't matter, because in the meantime the officers were served with an injunction Hogan had obtained from Judge J. M. Woods of the Circuit Court of Jefferson County, West Virginia, restraining them from any further attempt to enter the property.

Local residents also had time to mull things over. Annoyed by the presence of federal troops whose mission was to close down a principal local employer, they asked their sheriff to take action. The sheriff drove over to the soldiers' camp, a machine gun mounted on his truck "as is customary in that state," noted a *New York Times* reporter, and gave the troops twenty-four hours to get out of town or he would start firing.[11] After a brief huddle the officers promised to be off first thing in the morning. This satisfied the sheriff, who advised that the quickest way out of the state was the way they had come in, through Harpers Ferry.

Meanwhile, Assistant Attorney General Guy Goff went to federal court in Martinsburg, West Virginia, to try to lift Judge Woods' injunction. Hogan met him there and argued before Judge William E. Baker that the federal government had violated the Constitution and the rights of the harness company. Furthermore, said Hogan, President Harding had no right to void the contract without a hearing. Judge Baker agreed but it no longer mattered, for the U.S. Harness Company had taken advantage of the injunction, finished all the work on hand in just a few days, and then shipped it out of town. There was nothing left for the government to seize.

The War Department chose not to deliver any more surplus material to the U.S. Harness Company, which quickly went out of business, having returned to the government a profit share of nearly $1.3 million — double the minimum level called for in the contract. The War Department disposed of its remaining surplus through numerous other contracts, losing what U.S. Harness Company officials later estimated to be millions of taxpayer dollars. Sixteen thousand sets of refurbished harnesses went to the Department of Agriculture in a well-intentioned effort to serve the citizenry, but that department never found any use for them.

The troops may have retreated from West Virginia but the Justice Department did not. Instead, the Attorney General spent two years gathering evidence against former War Department officials and U.S. Harness Company officers and, on July 23, 1923, charged seven of them with conspiracy to defraud the government. The indictments said they had overstated water and mildew damage to the harnesses to make them appear unsaleable; closed the contract in secret and without bidding; conspired to close Rock Island so the government itself could not do the work; undertaken only cursory and sham advertising campaigns to sell the surplus to harness dealers so they could keep the business to themselves; and engaged in bribes and other enticements to War Department officials to close the deal.

[TOP] HOGAN WAS ACTIVE IN REPUBLICAN POLITICS. HERE (SECOND TO THE LEFT OF LIGHT FIXTURE) HE WATCHES PRESIDENT WARREN G. HARDING DELIVER A MEMORIAL DAY SPEECH. [BOTTOM] THE GOVERNMENT OIL LEASING SCANDAL KNOWN AS TEAPOT DOME BECAME THE WATERGATE SCANDAL OF ITS DAY, FILLING YEARS OF HEADLINES AFTER IT BROKE IN 1924. HERE A COLLIERS CARTOON ANNOUNCES THAT "WASHINGTON IS FLOODED WITH GOSSIP OF CORRUPTION, GRAFT, POLITICAL BLACKGUARDISM."

After extensive pre-trial preparation on both sides, the ten-day trial opened on Monday, January 14, 1924, in Parkersburg, West Virginia, before Judge Duncan Lawrence Groner, specially assigned to the case by U.S. Supreme Court Chief Justice and ex-U.S. President William Howard Taft.[12] The government rested its case on Friday, January 18, after calling its last witness, Representative Graham of Illinois. An angry Hogan waved aside the opportunity to cross-examine the congressman, dismissing him with a contemptuous, "You may go back to Washington now, Mr. Graham."[13] The next day, Saturday, Hogan was confident enough to ask Judge Groner for a directed verdict of not guilty for all seven defendants. That was the extent of his defense. Groner agreed to do so for two of them, saying that at the end of the government's case "there was no evidence — not even a scintilla of evidence — against the defendants."[14]

Five days later, on Thursday evening, January 24, Judge Groner summoned the attorneys into his chambers for an hour's conference. Then he returned to the courtroom and, in a lengthy charge, instructed the jury to find the remaining defendants not guilty. He addressed each count in the indictment, then concluded, "I haven't heard any evidence which would justify the conclusion that they had abused their trust."[15] Said a leather industry trade journal, "Seldom have Government lawyers been so openly lashed with the stinging whip of deserved censure."[16] The jury complied, despite its disappointment over missing a good closing fight between Hogan and his opposing counsel. The jurors later visited Hogan, his associate counsel, and the former defendants in the dining room of the Chancellor Hotel to congratulate them and offered backhanded praise for Judge Groner's careful reasoning: "It would have taken us only ten seconds," said one, "to have said in effect what he was so careful to say in several minutes."[17]

DOHENY CASE IS SET FOR OCTOBER 20 IN L. A.

Frank Hogan's charm, intelligence, and accessibility endeared him to most newspaper reporters, though some criticized him for representing oil magnate Edward Doheny, whose wealth alone seemed to them evidence enough of his guilt. Jose Rodriguez, a reporter covering the Doheny pre-trial proceedings in Los Angeles for The Record, took a lighter tone, stressing style over substance in his July 22, 1924, story. Rodriguez described Atlee Pomerene, the government's lead attorney and former U.S. senator from Ohio, as having a "round, placid face, chubby, heavy-lidded." In the courtroom Pomerene stood "in the traditional attitude, one foot forward, two fingers on the table top, the other hand swinging or pointing, perorating in monotonous voice, maddeningly slow. The phrases fall, formal and colorless."

Frank Hogan, on the other hand, impressed viewers with his "impeccable attire, his meticulous manner, his precise phraseology, all blended in a precocious style of oratory." Hogan's voice, Rodriguez observed, "rises to an incredible pitch and volume at times. It is a cold, furious voice." Hogan indeed was an angry man on Edward Doheny's behalf. Long discussions with Doheny had convinced Hogan that his client was neither a robber baron nor an arrogant plutocrat but another victim of runaway prosecutorial zeal.

Before Hogan sat down to dine in the Chancellor, he fired off a telegram to Attorney General Daugherty, making sure that the press got a fresh copy. "My clients were not only acquitted," he proclaimed, "they were vindicated, as any lawyer worthy to hold a certificate of admission to the bar, or as the most incompetent man who ever obtained a position in the Department of Justice at Washington, must have known they would be had he given the slightest honest attention to the case." Hogan castigated the "so-called War Frauds Section" in the Justice Department and demanded that Daugherty investigate this "series of utterly unfounded political indictments" instead of "bending to demagogic political propaganda." Hogan's anger was personal as well as professional. "I am sending this not as the attorney for the United States Harness Company defendants," he wrote, "but as an indignant and outraged American citizen. Personally any reply to this telegram is of no consequence to me. . . . I have an abiding confidence that the outcome of the Harness case today in a United States Court will have its effect on the American people."[18]

Meanwhile, the well-prepared defense team packed fifteen bound volumes of newspapers and trade journals for return to the Library of Congress, as well as ten boxes of harnesses, saddles, reins, bridles, and blankets it had brought as evidence, but which were never used in the trial. In the end, Hogan and his satisfied clients settled with the government to recover half a million dollars in damages they sustained from the illegal voiding of the contract.

The other four "war fraud" cases Hogan defended ended

[L TO R] ALBERT B. FALL, EDWARD L. DOHENY, FRANK J. HOGAN AND MARK B. THOMPSON. DOHENY HIRED ATTORNEY AND AUTHOR THOMPSON TO WRITE A SYMPATHETIC BIOGRAPHY OF HIS FRIEND FALL. THOMPSON FINISHED A DRAFT IN 1925 BUT DOHENY NEVER PUBLISHED IT.

in similar fashion. The previous July, in Washington, D.C.'s, Supreme Court, Judge Jennings Bailey had dismissed an indictment involving construction costs for a building in Boston that had been converted for War Department use. And a week after the U.S. Harness case's conclusion, Judge Adolph Hoehling in Washington, D.C., dismissed indictments in the barracks construction case. Six months later, in July 1924, Washington, D.C.'s, Judge Bailey directed verdicts of not guilty in the surplus lumber case for Hogan's client E. C. Morse, former director of sales for the War Department, who also had been a defendant in the U.S. Harness case.

Two other Hogan clients in the alleged lumber fraud conspiracy were acquitted by a jury two weeks later, including millionaire John L. Philips of the Philips Lumber Company of Georgia. Lastly, in November 1925, the indictments against Hogan's clients for fraud in the sale of the Old Hickory powder plant were dropped, giving the government what the *Washington Daily News* dubbed "a perfect record in war graft prosecutions here, 100 percent of the cases having been lost" to Frank Hogan.

Hogan already had embarked on what became a lifelong crusade against abuses of power by Congress and the executive branch. The law, especially the Bill of Rights, guaranteed every citizen protection from such abuses. When government officials violated rights guaranteed by the Constitution, Hogan felt they were not just being unfair. In addition to violating human rights, they also were dishonoring a sacred and fragile public trust. On April 24, 1924, at a Bar Association dinner in Washington, D.C., Hogan denounced an attempt by friends of Illinois Representative Graham to have the congressman appointed as Chief Justice of the U.S. Court of Appeals, District of Columbia Circuit, to fill the vacancy created by the death of Judge Constantine Smyth. Hogan decried Graham's use of indictments as political weapons, his failure to understand "the simplest rules of evidence," and the "legal fiascoes" engineered by Graham's investigative committee. Hogan's colleagues agreed but balked at passing a formal resolution. In the end, President Calvin Coolidge compromised by appointing Graham to the U.S. Court of Customs Appeals.

The Riggs and war fraud cases established a pattern for Hogan's practice for the rest of his career — complex civil and criminal litigation involving wealthy, high-profile clients in trouble with the federal government.

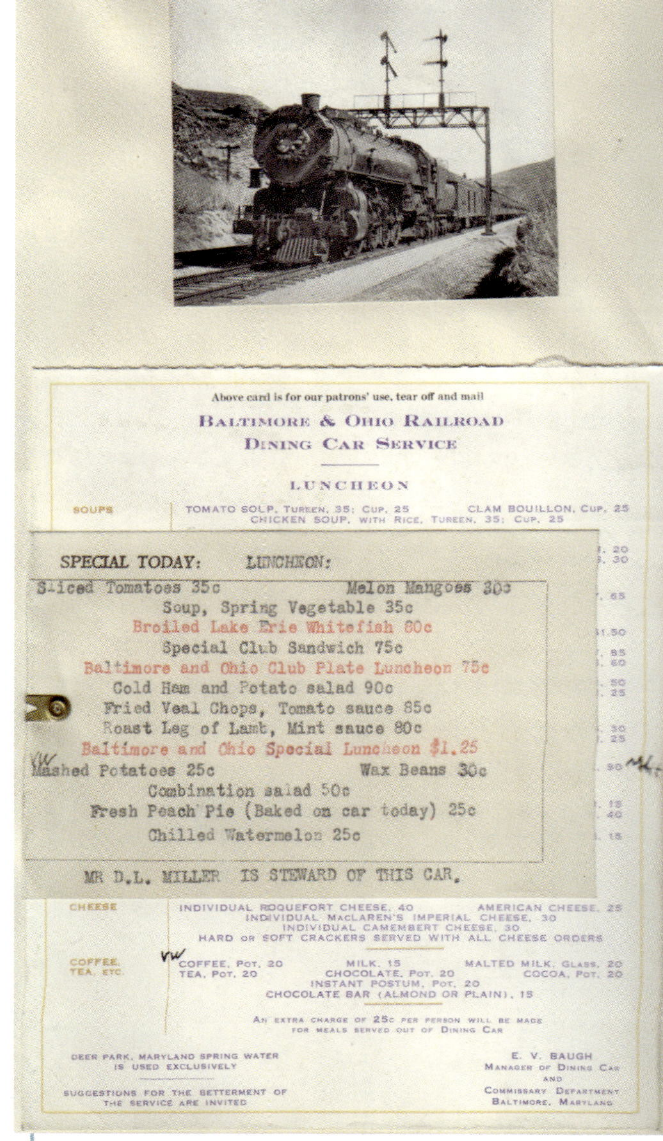

Above card is for our patrons' use, tear off and mail

BALTIMORE & OHIO RAILROAD
DINING CAR SERVICE

LUNCHEON

SOUPS — TOMATO SOUP, TUREEN, 35; CUP, 25 — CLAM BOUILLON, CUP, 25
CHICKEN SOUP, WITH RICE, TUREEN, 35; CUP, 25

SPECIAL TODAY: LUNCHEON:

Sliced Tomatoes 35c — Melon Mangoes 30c
Soup, Spring Vegetable 35c
Broiled Lake Erie Whitefish 80c
Special Club Sandwich 75c
Baltimore and Ohio Club Plate Luncheon 75c
Cold Ham and Potato salad 90c
Fried Veal Chops, Tomato sauce 85c
Roast Leg of Lamb, Mint sauce 80c
Baltimore and Ohio Special Luncheon $1.25
VW Mashed Potatoes 25c — Wax Beans 30c
Combination salad 50c
Fresh Peach Pie (Baked on car today) 25c
Chilled Watermelon 25c

MR D.L. MILLER IS STEWARD OF THIS CAR.

CHEESE — INDIVIDUAL ROQUEFORT CHEESE, 40 — AMERICAN CHEESE, 25
INDIVIDUAL MACLAREN'S IMPERIAL CHEESE, 30
INDIVIDUAL CAMEMBERT CHEESE, 30
HARD OR SOFT CRACKERS SERVED WITH ALL CHEESE ORDERS

COFFEE, TEA, ETC. — VW COFFEE, POT, 20 — MILK, 15 — MALTED MILK, GLASS, 20
TEA, POT, 20 — CHOCOLATE, POT, 20 — COCOA, POT, 20
INSTANT POSTUM, POT, 20
CHOCOLATE BAR (ALMOND OR PLAIN), 15

AN EXTRA CHARGE OF 25c PER PERSON WILL BE MADE FOR MEALS SERVED OUT OF DINING CAR

DEER PARK, MARYLAND SPRING WATER IS USED EXCLUSIVELY

SUGGESTIONS FOR THE BETTERMENT OF THE SERVICE ARE INVITED

E. V. BAUGH
MANAGER OF DINING CAR AND COMMISSARY DEPARTMENT
BALTIMORE, MARYLAND

HOGAN AND HIS STAFF BECAME TRANSCONTINENTAL TRAVELERS WHEN LOS ANGELES OIL MAGNATE EDWARD DOHENY HIRED HIM IN MARCH 1924. HOGAN'S SECRETARY, VIRGINIA WARREN, KEPT TABS ON EXPENSES BY INITIALING HER MENU CHOICES ON THE RAILROAD DINING CAR.

The most notable were the Edward Doheny cases, stretching from 1924 to 1930, that vaulted Hogan from mere professional prominence to national notoriety as America's premier trial attorney. The Doheny cases also made him truly wealthy, not because he charged high fees but, ironically, because he chose the right man with whom not to discuss them.

Edward Doheny had been a schoolteacher, lawman, and prospector in the Southwest but had never struck it rich. In 1892, at age thirty-six, he returned to his sickly wife and daughter in Los Angeles nearly penniless from a failed mining trip. For weeks he wandered the streets in search of work, sinking ever more deeply into gloom and discouragement. Often he just sat brooding on the porch of his run-down boardinghouse at Sixth Street and Figueroa, staring at the street traffic.[19]

One day a wagon rolled by loaded down with a heaping mound of odd-smelling, brown dirt. With a prospector's curiosity he ambled down to the road and asked the driver what he was carrying. "Brea," was the answer, the Spanish word for pitch. "Where'd you get it?" "Over at Westlake Park." Doheny jumped on the next streetcar west. Later he returned with some digging tools and, several months and two hundred feet later, struck liquid gold in what are now Los Angeles's famous La Brea Tar Pits. His seven-year-old daughter died while he was digging, and his wife was beyond despondency. Seven years later she divorced him, and when Doheny soon remarried she committed suicide. But the dig had been the beginning of a great change of fortune. Before long Doheny discovered vast oil fields in California and Mexico that made him one of America's richest men.

Doheny acted much the same as he had years earlier after a lucky day in the southwest hills. He dispensed loans, gifts, and favors to friends, and gave lavishly to hospitals, charities, disaster relief efforts, and churches. His donations to both political parties — although Democratic more than Republican — reflected pragmatism more than any well-honed political viewpoint. But his gifts and loans to friends who also were public officials, such as the president of Mexico or U.S. Secretary of the Interior and former prospecting partner Albert B. Fall, nearly ruined him.

The legal tar pit that snared Doheny had long been bubbling three thousand miles away in Washington, D.C. The ability of private wealth to influence elections and thwart much-needed reforms had dominated national politics for fifty years. Presidents Roosevelt, Taft, and Wilson had tried to pour the cement of integrity on the porous boundaries between private interests and government, with Roosevelt decrying "invisible government" and Wilson flaying "the invisible empire." But scandals in the

[LEFT] HOGAN (CENTER) & COLLEAGUES OUTSIDE THE ENTRANCE TO "HOGAN'S ALLEY" AT THE DOHENY ESTATE IN LOS ANGELES. [MIDDLE] DOHENY'S PRIVATE BOWLING ALLEY WAS REFITTED AS OFFICE SPACE FOR THE HOGAN TEAM DURING THE LOS ANGELES TRIALS. THE NAME "HOGAN'S ALLEY," ALREADY MADE POPULAR IN A COMIC STRIP DATING FROM THE 1890S, WAS IRRESISTIBLE. [RIGHT] OWEN J. ROBERTS (1875-1955) OF PHILADELPHIA WAS HOGAN'S OPPOSING COUNSEL IN THE DOHENY TRIALS. IN 1930 PRESIDENT HOOVER APPOINTED HIM AN ASSOCIATE JUSTICE ON THE U.S. SUPREME COURT, WHERE HE SERVED UNTIL HIS RETIREMENT IN 1945.

The former hard-luck prospector was not stingy in flush times. He built a lavish mansion at Chester Park in west Los Angeles, acquired a splendid yacht, and maintained an apartment in New York City. But when this ritual confirmation of his success was completed,

Harding administration whipped these issues to a new froth in the 1920s. Wisconsin Senator Robert La Follette, a leading voice for reform, was the first to suspect corruption in military oil contracts, but it was Montana Senator Thomas J. Walsh who carried the torch on this issue, persisting almost single-handedly through his investigating committee to dig for evidence of official misconduct.

In late January 1924 Edward Doheny, president of the Pan-American Petroleum Company, made a routine appearance before Walsh's committee. Nothing special was expected from yet another oilman hauled up to Capitol Hill, but when Doheny volunteered that he had hired as consultants four former members of Wilson's cabinet and had loaned $100,000 to Interior Secretary Albert B. Fall in 1921 so that Fall could improve his New Mexico ranch property, senatorial eyebrows arched high on both sides of the aisle.

Every senator recalled that in June 1920 Congress had passed a naval appropriation bill giving the Secretary of the Navy control of oil leasing contracts at the naval oil reserves at Elk Hills, California, and at the Teapot Dome reserves in Wyoming. Yet less than a year later President Harding had signed an executive order transferring authority from the Navy to the Interior Department. Secretary Fall then promptly awarded Doheny's companies contracts to extract the oil at Elk Hills and ship it to new storage tanks at Pearl Harbor, Hawaii, which Doheny had built. Similar loans and gifts to Fall by Harry Sinclair of the Mammoth Oil Company had allegedly won contracts for the naval reserves at Teapot Dome. The scent of bribery and corruption across town in the executive branch awakened the Congress. Could Harding himself have been involved in illicit deals?

By the time Senator Walsh had struck his own version of oil, Doheny had completed about two-thirds of a total $15 million of construction work at Pearl Harbor and President Harding was dead of pneumonia. Harding had planned a trip to Alaska in the summer of

Facsimile of Fall's $100,000 Note to Doheny

A FACSIMILE OF ALBERT B. FALL'S NOTORIOUS $100K PROMISSORY NOTE TO E.L. DOHENY (THE ORIGINAL HAD BEEN TORN.)

Nelson Thomas Hartson, a founding partner of Hogan & Hartson, was born in Spokane, Washington, on November 26, 1887, and started practicing law in Seattle in 1912. After serving as a captain in the U.S. Army in France during World War I, Hartson returned to Seattle and accepted a position as that city's Assistant Corporation Counsel. He relocated to Washington, D.C., in 1922 to become solicitor of the Bureau of Internal Revenue, effective January 1, 1923, then joined Frank Hogan in private law practice in 1925. After forty-seven years with the firm, Hartson retired in May 1972. His skills in tax and other business matters helped Hogan & Hartson earn its reputation as the premier law firm for major Washington, D.C., clients such as Riggs Bank, the Washington Star newspaper, D.C. Transit Company, and the Woodward & Lothrop and Garfinckel's department stores.

Hartson died on November 8, 1976, at age eighty-eight. Senior Partner Seymour Mintz remembered him as "a businessman's lawyer who preferred to give his advice behind the scenes." During the 1930s Hartson had been an Adjunct Professor of Taxation at the Georgetown University Law Center, so Hogan & Hartson established the Nelson T. Hartson Memorial Award there in his honor. The annual $5,000 scholarship is given to a graduating Georgetown University Law Center student for graduate study in a degree program, selected by the recipient, permitting a concentration in taxation. (Jose Valdivia, a partner who joined the firm's Miami office in 2002, is the firm's only lawyer to have received the Hartson Award — in 1984.)

Popular Young Hostess

Mrs. John William Guider, formerly Miss Dorothy Hogan, daughter of Mr. and Mrs. Frank Hogan, who is one of the attractive matrons of the young married set in the Capital.

HOGAN'S DAUGHTER, DOROTHY, WAS A "POPULAR YOUNG HOSTESS" IN WASHINGTON, D.C. IN 1923 SHE MARRIED NAVAL ACADEMY GRADUATE JOHN "DUKE" GUIDER, WHO SUBSEQUENTLY EARNED HIS LAW DEGREE AT GEORGETOWN UNIVERSITY AND JOINED HOGAN'S PRACTICE.

1923 to recoup his spirits and escape the capital's notorious summer heat. In connection with some personal business prior to leaving, he sent for fellow Elk Lodge brother and Republican Frank Hogan. The two commiserated at the White House in shirt sleeves about the weather, and Hogan hoped the President could shed at least some of his cares and have "a bully time" in Alaska. "Thank you very much, Frank," Harding replied, "but I shall never have a bully time again until I am through with this job." The President soon shared a similar confidence with reporter William Allen White: "I have no trouble with my enemies," Harding complained, "but my damn friends, my goddamn friends, White, they're the ones that keep me walking the floor nights."[20] Harding made it to Alaska but died in San Francisco on July 29, on his way back to a job he no longer wanted. Before she died the following year, Harding's wife, Florence, rounded up and burned all his papers and personal correspondence.

The oil lease matter went to court and soon became, in the words of the *Washington Post*, "the greatest legal battle in the country's history."[21] The jurisdictional gray zone of executive versus legislative authority formed the high legal ground — had Harding the authority to transfer contracts from one department to another? But it was the earthier zone of skullduggery and corruption that caught the public's eye. Like President Harding, Doheny had been either crassly manipulative, impulsively generous, or stunningly naive. Or perhaps all three. Certainly he needed a good lawyer, and had read about Hogan's work in the war fraud cases.

In March 1924 Frank Hogan answered Doheny's call and took the train to Los Angeles. Soon afterward the government canceled Doheny's Elk Hills contracts and indicted him and his son, Edward "Ned" Doheny, Jr., Albert Fall, and Harry Sinclair for conspiracy. Additional charges of bribery waited in the wings. "Teapot Dome," like "Watergate" a half-century later, became the catchword for a tortuous excursion of labyrinthine complexity into Washington's netherworld. Though Doheny's trials were subsequently lumped under the "Teapot Dome" umbrella, they concerned only the Elk Hills reserves in California. Teapot Dome, strictly speaking, involved Harry Sinclair and Albert Fall, not Edward Doheny. But it was the same whirlwind that caught them all.

On July 22, 1924, lawyers for both sides met in a Los Angeles courtroom to set the dates for Doheny's civil and criminal trials. The prosecuting attorney was former U.S. Senator from Ohio Atlee Pomerene, but onlookers watched for Hogan, whose fame for oratorical flair preceded him. Among the observers

THE 1925 RULINGS OF U.S. DISTRICT COURT JUDGE PAUL MCCORMICK IN CALIFORNIA *AGAINST* DOHENY, AND OF U.S. DISTRICT COURT JUDGE JOHN T. BLAKE IN WYOMING *FOR* OILMAN HARRY SINCLAIR, IN VIRTUALLY IDENTICAL CASES, PRODUCED A PASSING WONDER IN MANY OBSERVERS.

was another Washington attorney, thirty-seven-year-old Nelson T. Hartson, recently named solicitor of the Bureau of Internal Revenue. Hartson, the son of a Spokane, Washington, lawyer, had earned his law degree at the University of Washington and then joined a Seattle law firm, Donworth & Todd. He served two years with the Army's 91st Division in France during the World War and returned to Seattle

THE END OF PROHIBITION SEEMS HERE TO HERALD AN IRONIC RETURN TO ORDER AND PEACEFULNESS, IN CONTRAST TO THE LAWLESSNESS AND VIOLENCE OF ORGANIZED GANGS POPULARLY ASSOCIATED WITH THE ILLEGAL LIQUOR TRADE THAT FLOURISHED IN DEFIANCE OF THE VOLSTEAD ACT.

as the city's assistant corporation counsel. In 1922 he moved to the nation's capital to be an assistant solicitor for the Bureau of Internal Revenue, later renamed the Internal Revenue Service. He had not yet met Hogan, so in Los Angeles Hartson took the opportunity to get acquainted. They exchanged greetings and Hogan invited Hartson to lunch. Afterwards he suggested they meet again back in Washington.

The civil trial opened in Los Angeles on October 20, 1924. Hogan was flanked by an impressive array of co-counsel, including Henry W. O'Melveny, "the dean of the Los Angeles bar," and his partner, Walter Tuller. Also assisting were Frederick Kellogg of New York, chief counsel for Doheny's Pan-American Petroleum

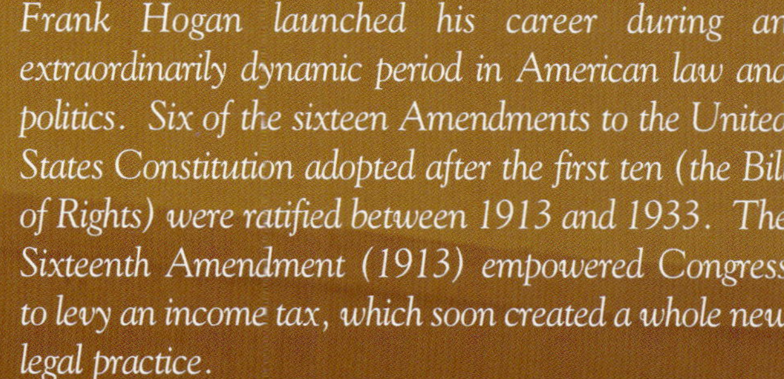

Frank Hogan launched his career during an extraordinarily dynamic period in American law and politics. Six of the sixteen Amendments to the United States Constitution adopted after the first ten (the Bill of Rights) were ratified between 1913 and 1933. The Sixteenth Amendment (1913) empowered Congress to levy an income tax, which soon created a whole new legal practice.

The Seventeenth Amendment (1913) provided for the direct election of United States senators, a change that reformers had been seeking since 1826 in order to make senators more directly answerable to the people. The movement picked up momentum after 1890 from the Progressive movement's "good government," or "goo-goo," anti-corruption campaigns. U.S. senators had been chosen by their state legislatures, not the electorate, a process that occasionally led to irreconcilable conflict and stalemate. Sometimes states sent no senators to Congress, while at other times a decision resulted from bribery and backroom deals. In recent years some states-rights advocates have urged repeal of the Seventeenth Amendment in order to return control of the U.S. senate to state governments.

The Eighteenth Amendment (1919) established Prohibition, or the banning of "intoxicating beverages," and was the ultimate triumph of a century-long temperance movement. Intended to solve serious social problems, Prohibition also carried much wishful thinking about nativist purity, Protestant rectitude, the moral superiority and civilizing influence of women, and nostalgia for vanishing rural communities. Prohibition was a curious and ultimately doomed experiment in enforced sobriety. Though it succeeded in reducing alcohol consumption nationwide, it worsened other problems such as smuggling and organized crime. In 1933, in the trough of the Great Depression, the Twenty-First Amendment repealed it.

The Nineteenth Amendment (1920) granted women the vote, and the Twentieth Amendment (1933) moved the Presidential Inauguration date from March 4 to January 20 in order to reduce the period between the election and the new President's taking office.

Company; Charles and Olin Wellborn, counsel for Pan-American; and Joseph J. Cotter, the company's vice president. The prosecution team split into two groups. Atlee Pomerene and two attorneys from his Cleveland firm handled the civil cases, while Owen J. Roberts, with two attorneys from his own firm in Philadelphia, directed the criminal cases. The U.S. Attorney's office in Los Angeles provided two additional lawyers. There was no jury. U.S. District Court Judge Paul McCormick presided behind a pair of thick, tortoiseshell glasses.

Doheny struck observers as unexpectedly mild and gentle, a quiet man with bright blue eyes and white moustache. Time magazine thought he looked "more like a mediocre dentist than a genius of finance." Time also commented on his counsel, describing Hogan as "a first class fighting court lawyer, clever before judge and jury, capable of profiting enormously by the slower wits of an antagonist."[22]

Hogan's legal team, including Virginia Warren and two male secretaries to Cotter and Kellogg, set up headquarters in a converted bowling alley in the Doheny mansion. They dubbed it "Hogan's Alley." They swam in Doheny's luxurious pool, played tennis, and practiced target shooting to work off the tensions of trial preparation that often kept them working into the early hours of the morning. One day a *Washington Post* reporter showed up to ask Hogan some questions. When Hogan noticed that the reporter was taking notes he pushed a button to summon a stenographer, then dictated a precise account of the major issues in the case and what it all meant to the American people. The appreciative journalist departed with a tidy, readable story for the next day's paper.

Hogan contended that the 1.5 million barrels of oil Doheny planned to transfer to Pearl Harbor would have earned Doheny no undue profit; furthermore, it was a good and strategically important deal for the government. Fall's transfer of leasing authority from the Navy Department to his Interior Department had been approved by President Harding as part of a necessarily secret military plan to defend the Pacific Coast against possible attack by Japan. If the oil were not transferred soon, Hogan's expert witnesses maintained, the reserves would drain into adjacent areas currently being drilled by civilian producers, causing a loss of vital supplies to the military. Hogan told how Rear Admiral John K. Robison had appealed to Doheny, who had agreed on patriotic grounds to submit a bid at virtual cost to undertake the Pearl Harbor work.

Hogan also argued that Doheny's loan of $100,000 to Albert Fall had been just that — a friendly loan dispensed from Doheny's vast wealth with no more fanfare than the average person would give a friend five dollars. It had been entirely coincidental to the oil lease matter. Prosecutors wondered why the $100,000 cash loan had been carried from New York personally by Doheny's son and delivered to Fall in a "little black bag." Was that how honest loans were made? Doheny's answer was that no person other than his son would have been as trustworthy.

But why had Fall's signature on the promissory note been torn off? Where was the bit of paper containing his name? The answer: Doheny had worried that if he and his wife — he had remarried after his first wife died — should be killed in a train wreck and the note were found intact, the executors of his estate might press Fall for payment on the note. Doheny did not want that to happen to his friend, so he tore off Fall's signature from the note and gave it to his wife for safekeeping. But if that were the truth, where was that piece of paper now, three years later? A frantic search located it in a safety deposit box in New York City. Hogan triumphantly displayed the pieces in the courtroom, then brought them slowly together, like pieces of a puzzle, to make a perfect fit.

On November 18, nearly a month after it had started, the civil trial came to a close and Judge McCormick retired to ponder a six-foot-high transcript. A week later Hogan, Mrs. Hogan, and the legal team from Hogan's Alley hauled their own copy of the transcript aboard Doheny's yacht *Casiana* for a trip through the Panama Canal back to Washington, D.C., arriving at Alexandria, Virginia, on December 14. While Judge McCormick wrestled with the trial records, the Navy pleaded to have some oil deposited in the Pearl Harbor tanks to prevent their rusting. But the Navy had to yield to Pomerene's and Roberts's fears that doing so would compromise the government's legal position.

While Doheny's defense increased Hogan's national stature, the local practice back in Washington also was poised to expand in new ways. The Sixteenth Amendment, approved in 1913, had allowed for the collection of federal income taxes, but these remained limited until the costs of World War I placed new demands on the federal treasury. The Wilson administration chose to spread the burden on corporations rather than on wages, and by 1918 corporate "excess profits" taxes accounted for more than half of all federal tax revenues. Anticipating an increase in tax and regulatory practice, Hogan met once more with Nelson Hartson, now the government's chief tax attorney, back in Washington and offered him a position. Hartson accepted and soon took on much of the Riggs Bank work in addition to building the tax practice.

[ABOVE] AN UPBEAT HOGAN, WITH CLIENTS ALBERT FALL (L) AND EDWARD DOHENY (WITH ARM IN SLING), AFTER WINNING THEIR ACQUITTAL FROM BRIBERY CHARGES IN 1926. HOGAN SUSTAINED FALL'S AND DOHENY'S SPIRITS THROUGH MANY YEARS OF LEGAL BATTLE AND DECLINING HEALTH FOR THE TWO MEN. [RIGHT] MEMBERS OF HOGAN'S OFFICE STAFF IN THE 1920S. (L TO R) SWITCHBOARD OPERATOR, MARGARET (LAST NAME UNKNOWN), HOGAN'S SECRETARY, VIRGINIA WARREN, AND NUBBY JONES'S SECRETARY, IRENE BONTZ.

Meanwhile, Hartson had made a happy proposition of his own, and on March 25 he married Vera Bobbitt, with Frank Hogan attending. A few days later Hogan helped him settle into his new office in the Colorado Building. Attorneys John "Duke" Guider, Hogan's son-in-law, and Arthur Phelan, both graduates of Georgetown Law, also joined Hogan's practice. Guider, a 1922 graduate of the U.S. Naval Academy at Annapolis, worked for the Radio Corporation of America (RCA) before entering law school. He married Hogan's daughter, Dorothy, in 1923. His RCA experience, though brief, helped him establish the law office's budding communications practice, for radio licensing was fast becoming a busy legal specialty in Washington.[23]

At last, on May 28, 1925, Judge McCormick handed down his decision in the Doheny civil trial. In a sweeping victory for the government he declared that Harding had exceeded his authority, that Doheny's loan to Fall had been "a colossal infamy regardless of whether it was a bribe, a gift or a loan," and that Doheny's contracts were void. Hogan announced Doheny's plan to appeal to the U.S. Circuit Court of Appeals in San Francisco. When he returned home that evening he met his son-in-law, Duke Guider. "Well, we lost," said Hogan. "Yes," answered Guider, knowing his father-in-law was an ardent baseball fan. "Both games," referring to the Washington Nationals' recent loss on top of Hogan's courtroom defeat.

Perhaps Georgetown University's awarding Hogan an honorary degree on June 8 took some of the sting from McCormick's ruling. But Judge John T. Blake's June 19 ruling from the federal court in Cheyenne, Wyoming, certainly did. In a decision directly opposite that of Judge McCormick and in a virtually identical case, Judge Blake found that President Harding's executive order had been valid. He upheld Harry Sinclair's Mammoth Oil contracts for Teapot Dome. These conflicting opinions heightened the tension when, early in October, Hogan, Kellogg, and Roberts appeared before the U.S. Circuit Court of Appeals in San Francisco. On January 5, 1926, the court handed down its decision, upholding Judge McCormick's decision to void Doheny's Pan-American contracts. That was bad news enough. But then the court rubbed salt in the wound, reversing McCormick's decision to allow Pan-American to be compensated nearly $12 million for work already completed. A month later, his voice intact after a recent tonsillectomy, Hogan filed a petition for certiorari with the U.S. Supreme Court, which agreed to review the case.

Hogan traveled to New York to confer with Joseph Cotter and Frederick Kellogg. The two men wished to send bills to Doheny as well as to his Pan-American Petroleum Company, but they were unsure

REP. RANKIN'S TOSSING AN INKWELL AT FRANK HOGAN IN THE HOUSE OF REPRESENTATIVES ON JUNE 7, 1926, DURING THE FENNING IMPEACHMENT PROCEEDINGS, LEFT ITS MARK ON HOGAN'S PAPERWORK. THE CAPITAL'S CARTOONISTS WIELDED THEIR OWN INK MORE DEFTLY.

about the proper timing. At the time, when professionalism required treating money-making as an incidental by-product rather than a wholly legitimate concern, fees were less of a straightforward matter than they later became. An attorney might simply say, "Pay me what you think the service was worth to you." But such genteel insouciance about money offered scant practical guidance. Cotter and Kellogg decided they would bill Pan-American and also would ask Doheny for a definite retainer for his upcoming criminal representation. Hogan said he too would bill Pan-American, but he had no plans to discuss fees with Doheny for the criminal work. Hogan's instinct about his client's generous spirit proved to be correct, but at the time he did not know for sure how events would unfold.

While Doheny's criminal case inched its way toward a trial in Washington, Hogan once again took on the defense of a District of Columbia official in trouble with Congress. This time it was Commissioner Frederick A. Fenning, an attorney who also maintained a lucrative practice serving as guardian for mentally ill World War I veterans committed to D.C.'s public asylum, St. Elizabeth's. Fenning was permitted fees up to 10 percent of the veterans' assets and monthly compensation payments, but he had never taken less than the maximum amount. His annual earnings from this practice alone were about $15,000, not counting commissions earned by depositing the funds in a bonding company in which he held an interest.

CHARGES OF IMPEACHMENT
AGAINST
FREDERICK A. FENNING
IN THE HOUSE OF REPRESENTATIVES
SIXTY-NINTH CONGRESS
FIRST SESSION
ON
HOUSE RESOLUTION 228

APRIL 19, 1926

CHARGES MADE BY HON. THOMAS L. BLANTON
A MEMBER OF CONGRESS FROM
THE STATE OF TEXAS

CONGRESSIONAL RECORD, PAGES 7611-7614
PRINTED FOR THE USE OF THE JUDICIARY COMMITTEE

WASHINGTON
GOVERNMENT PRINTING OFFICE
1926

In addition, Congressman Thomas R. Blanton of Texas, the Democratic firebrand leading the investigation, alleged that Fenning and psychiatrist Dr. William Alanson White, director of St. Elizabeth's, had kept veterans in the hospital who were not insane in order to extract fees, and that they had engaged in real estate deals together. "Dr. White loves money, himself," Blanton accused from the House floor. To roars of approval from a packed gallery he shouted, "I voted to send these boys into the trenches and, so help me God, I am going to get them away from Mr. Fenning!"

Fenning's congressional hearing opened on May 20, 1926, before the House Judiciary Committee. Frank Hogan was his chief counsel, assisted by two

in a real court — they would put a necktie on him that would be a yellow one, in the shape of a grass rope."[26] This lynching yelp by the "boor of the Senate" was widely denounced. Still, many who disagreed with the verdict sought compensation for their own view of justice by denouncing the "boy jury."

The storm rumbled on, but Hogan was well sheltered that evening by a warm welcome from the American Bar Association during a dinner meeting at Washington's new Mayflower Hotel on Connecticut Avenue. A few weeks later he received a letter from a former juror, a waiter at Union Station, explaining what had happened upstairs in the jurors' room. Two men had held out for conviction. One, a bank clerk, had changed his mind by midnight and the other, an architect, came around at 9:00 the next morning when "he was given to understand that he might find himself in a very unpleasant position if he hung this jury."[27] Had "Bye Bye Blackbird" been merely a harmless pastime or perhaps a veiled threat to the holdouts on the jury? No one ever knew exactly how the jurors had pulled two of their number, chocks before the wheels of justice, into line.

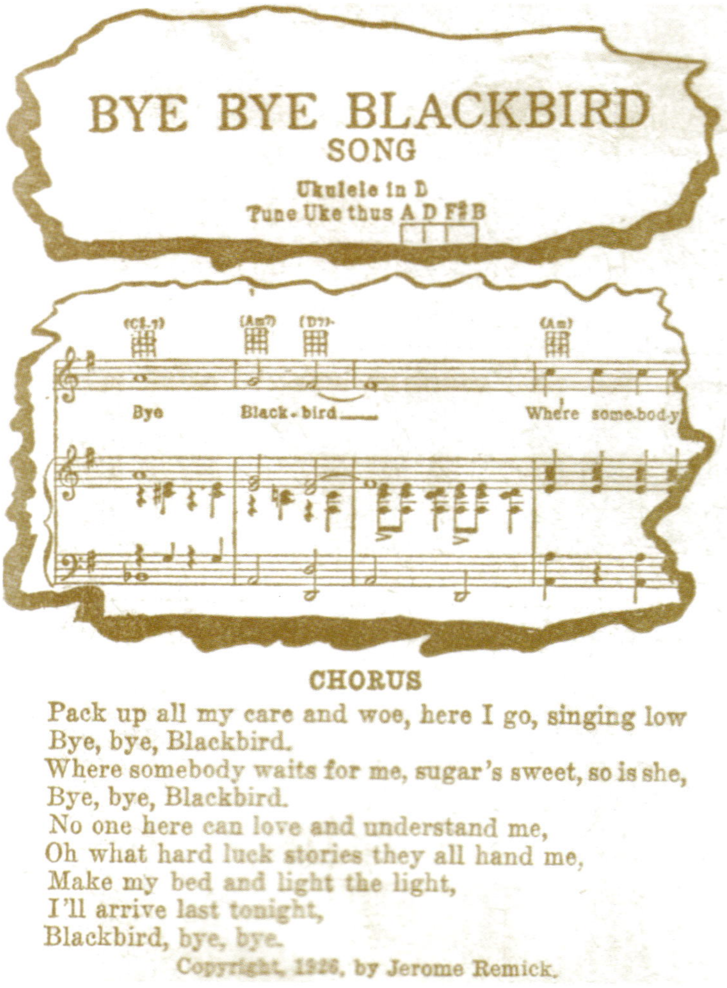

The Dohenys left town for Los Angeles the next day, December 16, but not without leaving Hogan a Christmas gift of a million dollars. Was it a fee or a gift? The ambiguity preserved Doheny's pride while expressing gratitude, as much as obligation, to the man who had crossed the country several times to counsel and console him, who had saved his reputation from the stigma of a criminal conviction, and who had never asked for a penny — not because he didn't want or expect it but because he trusted Doheny to do the right thing. Whether fee, gift, or both, the payment was reported to be the largest ever paid an attorney, surpassing the $750,000 Owen Roberts had collected from Congress in an Indian lands case several years earlier. In the booming atmosphere of the Roaring Twenties, it put a high gloss on "Million Dollar" Hogan's already polished practice.

On February 28, 1927, the Supreme Court delivered its decision in the Pan-American Petroleum Company civil suit. It was another appellate loss for Hogan. Not only did the Court affirm the Circuit Court's denial of payment to Pan-American for work completed, it also required the company to return to the government millions of dollars it had already been paid for Pearl Harbor construction. This was $10.5 million worth of bitter medicine for Doheny but sweet vindication for Senator Walsh, who proclaimed, "Justice travels with leaden heels, but strikes with an iron hand."[28]

Justice's leaden heels shuffled once more toward Ed Doheny and Albert Fall, this time carrying criminal charges of bribery. But first they stopped at the Teapot Dome conspiracy trial of Harry Sinclair and Albert Fall in Washington, where in April 1928, more than a year after the Doheny-Fall acquittals, justice's iron hand descended — but in a velvet glove. The jury took just under two hours to find Sinclair innocent, Fall's trial having been suspended for a time due to his poor health. And when Colonel Robert Stewart of Standard

BYE BYE BLACKBIRD
SONG
Ukulele in D
Tune Uke thus A D F♯ B

Bye Black-bird Where some-bod-y

CHORUS

Pack up all my care and woe, here I go, singing low
Bye, bye, Blackbird.
Where somebody waits for me, sugar's sweet, so is she,
Bye, bye, Blackbird.
No one here can love and understand me,
Oh what hard luck stories they all hand me,
Make my bed and light the light,
I'll arrive last tonight,
Blackbird, bye, bye.
Copyright, 1926, by Jerome Remick.

A GRATEFUL COLONEL ROBERT STEWART (L) OF STANDARD OIL, AFTER HOGAN WON HIS ACQUITTAL FROM CONTEMPT OF COURT AND PERJURY CHARGES IN 1928.

Oil was charged with contempt of the Senate for refusing to answer questions relating to Sinclair and the Teapot Dome reserves, Stewart turned to Hogan, who obtained a not guilty jury verdict on June 14, 1928, in D.C. Supreme Court before Judge Siddons. A grand jury foreshortened Stewart's relief by returning a fresh indictment for perjury. But several months later, on November 21, Hogan won him yet another acquittal.

Hogan's headline-grabbing trial work tended to obscure the fact that, back in the Colorado Building, other parts of his practice were quietly flourishing. Radio had entered American homes faster than telephones after World War I, and the number of broadcasting stations increased nearly twentyfold, from 30 to about 550, between 1922 and 1923. The Radio Act of 1927 revised an earlier, fifteen-year-old law and created the Federal Radio Commission (FRC) to bring order to the airwaves. This, in turn, increased the demand for Washington-based legal services as broadcasters sought to obtain and renew licenses.

Hogan himself handled an important case in which the General Electric Company challenged an FRC ruling restricting the broadcast hours of the company's station, WGY, in Schenectady, New York. The FRC had given a West Coast station permission to operate on the same frequency as WGY, thereby creating a conflict between the two stations. The commission resolved the conflict by restricting WGY's hours. General Electric did not like that solution and in 1928 hired Hogan to challenge it in the D.C. Court of Appeals. Hogan won. The effect of the case was to establish a radio broadcast license as a form of property that could not be removed without due process. That notion survived until 1934, when Congress created the new Federal Communications Commission and decided that the concept of public interest, rather than private property, should guide radio licensing decisions.

During his October trial in Washington Albert Fall's luck gave out with his rapidly failing health, and he was judged guilty of having accepted a $100,000 bribe from Doheny. Fall slumped in his wheelchair, his physician by his side, and was driven back to his room at the Mayflower Hotel. Later Judge William Hitz gave him a relatively light sentence of one year in prison and a $100,000 fine. Doheny wept quietly in the courtroom, still grieving for his only son, Ned, who seven months earlier, at age thirty-five, had been shot to death in Los Angeles by a mentally disturbed friend who then shot himself. Ned's murder devastated his father. And now, in a development that had many scratching their heads, Doheny himself would go on trial before Judge Hitz for having offered the very bribe Fall had just been found guilty of taking.

Chief Justice William Howard Taft's funeral early in March 1930 delayed the opening of Doheny's bribery trial until mid-March. Hogan hammered on the tried-and-true themes about Doheny's generous character, patriotism, and paternal devotion. In one eerie scene Hogan even took the stand to act as Ned, repeating verbatim and without notes the younger Doheny's testimony from a previous trial. After closing arguments Judge Hitz instructed the jury that bribery could be in the mind of the receiver without necessarily being in the intentions of the giver. On March 21 the twelve jurors, including three women and an African-American man, returned a verdict of not guilty. Doheny wished his friend Fall could have enjoyed the same dispensation — and similar instructions from the judge.

In December 1927 Hogan made a statement before the Brooklyn Bar Association in New York that later became famous: "The ideal client is a rich man who is scared." Like most epigrams it contained a certain truth. Hogan wished to make money practicing law, and the wealthy Edward Doheny doubtless had been scared. But the statement's wry intimation of worldly calculation distorted the relationship between the two men while handing critics apparent confirmation of their jaundiced suspicion that justice danced to the jingle of the cash register. Hogan's pithy *bon mot* was endlessly repeated — though never by him.

Fear and riches may have brought Doheny to Hogan's door, but trust and respect for his counsel kept him there. It made the old prospector an ideal client. Hogan took Doheny's measure and found he could return the sentiments. That, no less than his courtroom successes against strong currents of public opinion and an impressive prosecution, confirmed Frank Hogan's renown as the ideal advocate.

EDWARD DOHENY AND FRANK HOGAN, THE IDEAL ADVOCATE, CELEBRATE ANOTHER VICTORY ON THE COURTHOUSE STEPS IN WASHINGTON, D.C., 1930.

CHAPTER 2
PARTNERS
1930-1968

There were no signs of the Depression at Frank Hogan's gracious, limestone house on Sheridan Circle in Washington after Edward L. Doheny left Judge Hitz's courtroom a free man on March 21, 1930. The oil tycoon sent a Rolls Royce town car around, a gift to the Hogans. John "Duke" Guider, Hogan's colleague and son-in-law, and his wife Dorothy found a Lincoln convertible wrapped in a red ribbon outside their home just a half-mile away on Kalorama Circle. Doheny asked Hogan to gather together all the lawyers in his practice, then thanked them for their help. There were only five besides Hogan — Guider, Phelan, Donovan, Hartson, and Jones. It was a tough time. The American economy was in trouble, and Jones later joked that when he received his envelope containing $10,000 he thought himself richer than he ever would be again. But Jones's worry over his ultimate financial future proved unnecessary.[1] Hogan's lucrative trial work, coupled with the office's tax and regulatory practice, helped his colleagues weather the Depression.

HOGAN MOVED INTO THIS NEWLY BUILT HOUSE AT 2320 MASSACHUSETTS AVE., N.W., IN 1920. SINCE HIS DEATH IN 1944 IT HAS BEEN ENLARGED AND SERVES AS THE CONSULAR OFFICE OF THE EMBASSY OF THE REPUBLIC OF KOREA.

Nationally, lawyers' per capita income dropped nearly 40 percent between 1929 and 1932, a rate comparable to that suffered by physicians and engineers.[2] For these professionals, as for most Americans, the early 1930s were years of gnawing worry punctuated all too often by disaster. President Herbert Hoover's programs looked bold to some but did not go far or deep enough to revive the moribund national economy. Shantytowns dubbed "Hoovervilles" sprung up in most major cities, where people slept under discarded newspapers ("Hoover blankets") and hoped for relief from the 25 percent unemployment rate. Riots and protests broke out over authorities' failure to provide adequate relief. What has since become known as the "social safety net" was but a loose collection of voluntary civic and religious charities whose resources were rapidly exhausted by the prolonged national crisis.

ALWAYS ACTIVE AS A FUNDRAISER FOR WASHINGTON, D.C. HOSPITALS AND CHARITIES, HOGAN INCREASED HIS EFFORTS DURING THE DEPRESSION YEARS OF THE 1930S. HE ADVOCATED PRIVATE SOLUTIONS TO THE DEPRESSION'S PROBLEMS AND REGARDED WITH SUSPICION THE NEW DEAL'S LARGE-SCALE, GOVERNMENT-SPONSORED RELIEF PROGRAMS.

EXECUTIVE COMMITTEE SINCE 1959

1959-1962
Nelson T. Hartson
Edmund L Jones
Duke M. Patrick
Seymour S. Mintz

In 1960 the term of office for Executive Committee members was set at three years or until a successor was elected.

1963
Nelson T. Hartson
Edmund L. Jones
Duke M. Patrick
Seymour S. Mintz
Oliver R. McGuire

In 1963 the Executive Committee was increased to five members and it was established that all five members would serve until December 31, 1964, at which time their terms would expire. The fifth member was Oliver R. "Ollie" McGuire.

1964
Nelson T. Hartson
Edmund L. Jones
Paul R. Connolly
Seymour S. Mintz
Oliver R. McGuire

Duke Patrick resigned in May 1964 and was replaced with Paul R. Connolly.

Hoover himself chose the word "depression" to describe the stagnation, not because he believed there was something fundamentally different about it but because he thought that "panic," the usual word used for economic downturns, would sound too pessimistic. But this was not just another cyclical "panic," with investors pulling up stakes for a while until market forces restored balance. This was a disturbing, pervasive breakdown of the entire economic system and no one knew what to do about it, including the unfortunate President.

Hogan had always been careful to balance his growing personal prosperity with a sense of civic obligation, giving both time and money to Georgetown University and to local orphanages, rest homes, and charities without regard to religion. Early in 1927, for instance, he had helped raise money for the Jewish Community Center on 16th Street and had led a citywide fund-raising effort for St. Joseph's orphanage. Later that year he and three other Washingtonians gave $10,000 each to cover a shortfall in funds for the city's foster children when the Senate recessed without passing the required appropriations bill. When the Depression hit, Hogan went on the radio, urging Washingtonians to give generously to the Community Chest. In one such address he described his father's early death in Brooklyn, the hard times his widowed mother had faced, and his own narrow escape from placement in an orphanage.

But for all his heartfelt sympathy for the sick and needy, and for all his efforts to raise money to meet their needs, Hogan's basic political philosophy remained unshaken by the Depression. Like Hoover, Hogan recognized its severity and the necessity of an exceptional government response. But at the same time he shared Hoover's wariness toward bold remedies that only a greatly enhanced federal authority could provide. In 1932, for instance, Hoover established the Reconstruction Finance Corporation (RFC) to provide government loans to businesses in order to "prime the pump" of the economy. Congress approved more than $1 billion for the RFC effort, but conservative RFC officials actually spent only $30 million of it. Additionally, most Republicans, including Hogan, opposed direct relief efforts by the government for the poor and unemployed. They believed that private charities and philanthropies were far less harmful to society than direct government relief, which they thought would undermine the

THIS PORTRAIT OF HOGAN (TOP) WAS DRAWN BY A YOUNG BOY'S CLUB MEMBER, JOHN TRIANTAFFILOS, WHO PRESENTED IT TO HOGAN, THEN GENERAL CHAIRMAN OF THE COMMUNITY CHEST, AT A LUNCHEON AT THE WILLARD HOTEL, SATURDAY, NOVERMBER 25, 1933. (L TO R) MRS. HAROLD ICKES, TRIANTAFFILOS, HOGAN, AND BOY'S CLUB MEMBER BILLY BRAY. TRIANTAFFILOS CAPTURED PERFECTLY THE BALANCE OF SYMPATHY AND TOUGHNESS THAT MADE HOGAN THE NATION'S PREMIER TRIAL ATTORNEY.

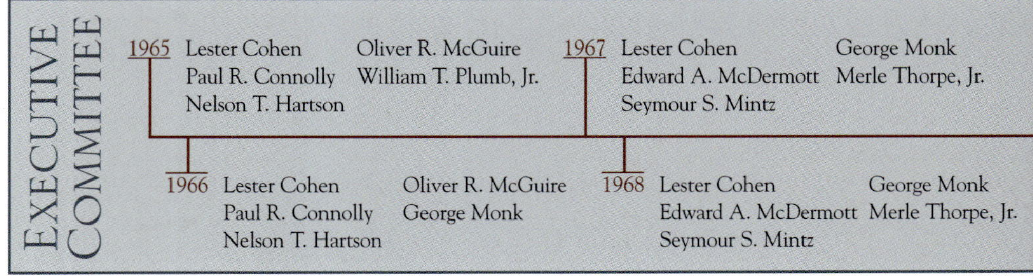

values of self-reliance and individual initiative regarded as central to democracy as well as to capitalism's recovery.

To be sure, Franklin Roosevelt also was uncomfortable with direct relief measures and with the scope of government activity he felt the emergency required. But when all was said and done, it was an emergency and nothing else had worked. Despite the misgivings he shared with many of his critics, Roosevelt was willing to experiment and gave his "brain trust" the go-ahead to draft and implement a "new deal" for Americans. Lawyers like Abe Fortas, Ben Cohen, Tommy Corcoran, Robert Jackson, James Landis, Jerome Frank, and Felix Frankfurter inspired younger attorneys to a new sense of mission in government service. Two-thirds of the *Harvard Law Review's* editors in the classes of 1930-1932 worked for the federal government at some point in the 1930s, prompting the contemporary quip that the most direct route to Washington was to go to Harvard Law and turn left.

Through the New Deal, Congress passed new laws governing banking and securities, agriculture, utilities, communications, conservation, housing, welfare and work relief, and old age pensions. Congress also added four powerful regulatory agencies — the Securities and Exchange Commission (SEC), the National Labor Relations Board (NLRB), the Civil Aeronautics Authority (CAA), and the Federal Communications Commission (FCC) — to existing agencies like the Interstate Commerce Commission (1887) and the Federal Trade Commission (1914). In some ways the Depression was an opportunity for, as much as a cause of, the development of coherent, national regulatory programs, much as economic stringencies in earlier times had given reform-minded politicians like Theodore Roosevelt and Woodrow Wilson a chance to align government authority away from private interests and toward the service of a broad "public interest."

LESTER COHEN, SHOWN HERE IN THE GARDEN AT HOGAN'S HOME ON MASSACHUSETTS AVE., WAS ONE OF THE YOUNG ATTORNEYS WHO JOINED HOGAN'S PRACTICE IN THE 1930S. COHEN SPECIALIZED IN COMMUNICATIONS LAW.

The New Deal did not resolve such tensions, and in time reformers would grapple with the phenomenon of private interests "capturing" the very regulatory agencies that were supposed to control them. The New Deal did not even end the Depression, or convince Roosevelt of the viability of John Maynard Keynes's theories about deficit spending. It took the truly massive challenge of World War II, and its expenditures, to do that. But Roosevelt's "fireside chats," his "alphabet soup" of programs like the National Recovery Administration (NRA), the Works Progress Administration (WPA), the Tennessee Valley Authority (TVA), the Civil Works Administration (CWA), and the Civilian Conservation Corps (CCC) — and his never-give-up experimentalism — kept hope alive for Americans during desperate times.

The Communications Act of 1934 was among the many New Deal laws of interest to attorneys in Frank Hogan's office. It replaced the Federal Radio Commission with a new Federal Communications Commission, removing the Hoover-appointed Republican commissioners as well as the previous notion of broadcast licenses as forms of private property — the argument Hogan had used successfully on behalf of

PARTNERS

1955 AND PRIOR
Howard Boyd
Frederick M. Bradley
John St. Clair Brookes, Jr.
Lester Cohen
William H. Donovan
John W. Guider
Nelson T. Hartson
Frank J. Hogan
George D. Horning, Jr.
Edmund L. Jones
O. R. McGuire, Jr.
Seymour S. Mintz
George E. Monk
Duke M. Patrick
Arthur J. Phelan
James Cunningham Rogers
John J. Sirica
Joseph J. Smith, Jr.
Karl A. Smith

1956
Frank F. Roberson
Merle Thorpe, Jr.

1957 & 58
None

1959
Paul R. Connolly, Jr.
Parker D. Hancock
Corwin R. Lockwood
William T. Plumb, Jr.
C. Frank Reifsnyder

1960 & 61
None

1962
George W. Wise
Robert K. Eifler

The rising popularity of radio in the 1920s and 1930s helped develop a new practice for lawyers in Frank Hogan's office, as broadcast applicants competed for a limited number of licenses. The number of radio sets manufactured in the United States increased twenty-five-fold in the 1920s, in part because of the rapid spread of electrical power to American households. Radio broadcast stations also flourished. In just one year, 1922-1923, the number of radio stations multiplied from 30 to nearly 560. By 1930 there were 641 stations, and 200 more by 1942. The New Deal's Rural Electrification Administration further extended electrical power after 1935, adding rural households to radio's ever-widening national audience.

By 1940 nearly 28 million American homes had radios, double the number at the beginning of the decade. After World War II the radio business soared even higher, with the number of stations nearly tripling between 1945 and 1950. The concurrent growth of Hogan & Hartson's communications practice confirmed Frank Hogan's long-held belief that administrative law would become a major practice area for lawyers, especially in Washington, D.C.

General Electric's WGY six years earlier. The FCC crafted new, complex regulations governing license applications and renewals under the principle that the airwaves were public property and station programming must therefore serve the public interest. Hogan's communications practice grew as the firm's clients adjusted to the new requirements. Duke Moyer Patrick, former general counsel of the Federal Radio Commission, joined Hogan & Hartson to help Hogan's son-in-law, Duke Guider. Karl Smith and Lester Cohen also were hired to handle this burgeoning work in the 1930s.

The growth of the firm's communications practice confirmed Hogan's long-held view that administrative law would provide much new work for attorneys and that they should prepare themselves accordingly. In the mid-1930s Hogan told the New York State Bar Association that the head of a major federal agency had confided to him that few attorneys appearing before that agency had made "the slightest effort to become acquainted with, much less expert in, the substantive law governing their clients' rights or the rules of procedure under which those rights could be enforced." Hogan cited the example of another New Deal regulatory body, the National Labor Relations Board, whose caseload had jumped from 286 in 1936 to 4,400 in 1937, exceeding by 900 the number of cases filed that year in all eleven United States Circuit Courts of Appeals combined.[3]

Notwithstanding such exhortations to attorneys, Hogan continued to sharpen the suspicions about government intrusion and abuse of authority he had formed during his defense of World War I contractors. While the government raised taxes to pay for employment and relief programs that would put money into the pockets of everyday consumers, Roosevelt fought critics on the right such as the Liberty League, whose members, including Hogan, feared the newly empowered federal authorities and resented the increasingly "anti-rich" bias with which the government seemed to pursue tax and antitrust policies.[4]

Bitterly attacked from the political right for the sweeping price controls and minimum wage standards set by the NRA, Roosevelt approached the 1936

PARTNERS

1963	1965	1966	1967
None	None	Howard Roycroft	William O. Bittman

1964

John P. Arness	Stanley S. Harris	J. Bruce Kellison	E. Barrett Prettyman, Jr.
Francis L. Casey, Jr.	Edgar W. Holtz	Edward A. McDermott	John J. Ross
Jeremiah C. Collins	Arnold C. Johnson	Russell B. Pace, Jr.	John Warner

election under mounting pressure from the left, too. Populists like California's Francis Townsend proposed reforms more sweeping than the New Deal, while Louisiana's Huey "Kingfish" Long's motto, "Every Man a King, But No One Wears a Crown," concealed Long's own, far-reaching ambitions. Only his assassination in 1935 stopped Long's serious challenge to Roosevelt's reelection the following year. A Catholic priest in Detroit, Father John Coughlin, took to the radio to push his own melange of anticommunist and anticapitalist themes, woven through with anti-Semitic rant. Roosevelt's response came to be known as the "Second New Deal," notable for the National Labor Relations Act (the "Wagner" Act), guaranteeing workers the right to join unions, and the landmark Social Security Act, both passed in the summer of 1935.

Roosevelt's conservative critics were buoyed in 1935 when the Supreme Court, including Justice Owen J. Roberts, Hogan's former opponent in the Doheny criminal trials whom Hoover had appointed to the Court in 1930, declared the sweeping price-control authority of the National Recovery Administration unconstitutional. But Roosevelt's subsequent effort to change the Court's appointment rules so as to allow him to appoint more justices — the so-called "court-packing plan" — rekindled their anxieties about New Deal plots to "soak the rich." The plan failed, though the controversy it stirred is thought by some to have had a sobering effect on the Justices, who thereafter seemed less critical of New Deal programs.[5] As events would have it, Roosevelt's more than twelve years in office allowed him to appoint nearly an entirely new Court by 1945, including Justices Frankfurter, Black, Reed, Murphy, Jackson, Rutledge, and Douglas — and Hogan's cousin, James Byrnes. But by 1939 Hogan was already calling the New Deal a "bloodless revolution" after which, he warned, businesses could no longer rely on the Supreme Court for the protection of their constitutional rights.

During this period of increased government regulation, Frank Hogan and his colleagues expanded their practice in many areas in which the government was involved. In February 1935 Robert H. Jackson, not yet appointed to the Supreme Court, was in Pittsburgh before the U.S. Board of Tax Appeals as the government's chief counsel prosecuting charges of tax evasion against multimillionaire financier and art

JAMES FRANCIS BYRNES

Like their cousin and childhood companion Frank Hogan, James Francis Byrnes and his sister Lenore both enjoyed successful legal careers. All three studied shorthand as children in Charleston, South Carolina, under the coaching of the Byrnes's widowed mother. Lenore Byrnes later studied law, was admitted to the District of Columbia bar, and served as assistant to the chief counsel at the Department of Agriculture. James Byrnes became court stenographer to Judge James Aldrich in Aiken, South Carolina, who also taught him law. Byrnes passed the bar in that state in 1904. From 1911 to 1925 he served as a representative in the U.S. Congress from South Carolina. He was raised Catholic, then married an Episcopalian and joined that denomination. Despite his conversion, an anti-Catholic campaign by the Ku Klux Klan helped defeat his bid for election to the U.S. Senate in 1924. He won the next election, though, and served until June 1941, when President Franklin Roosevelt appointed him Associate Justice of the U.S. Supreme Court.

When the United States entered World War II, Byrnes resigned from the Supreme Court to take on, at Roosevelt's request, the duties of director of the Office of Economic Stabilization. Byrnes also served as director of the Office of War Mobilization and director of the Office of War Mobilization and Reconversion. He resigned just after the Allied victory in Europe in April 1945 and returned to South Carolina. But just days later Roosevelt died and President Harry Truman summoned Byrnes back to Washington to serve as his Secretary of State. Byrnes headed the State Department until 1947, when he joined Hogan & Hartson as "of counsel" until his election as governor of South Carolina in 1951. Byrnes retired from public life in 1955 and died in April 1972, just shy of his ninetieth birthday.

U.S. SUPREME COURT ROOM IN U.S. CAPITOL, PRE-1937.

"HE PAINTS HIS CLIENTS RED, WHITE & BLUE." TIME MAGAZINE'S MARCH 11, 1935, ARTICLE ON HOGAN POINTED TO HIS DEFENSE OF EDWARD DOHENY AS A PATRIOT.

collector Andrew Mellon. Nearly eighty years old, Mellon had strongly advocated tax reductions for the wealthy during his eleven years as Secretary of the Treasury under Republican Presidents Harding, Coolidge, and Hoover. Now he hired Frank Hogan to defend him against charges that he owed $3,000,000 in taxes and penalties from his 1931 filing.

Hogan countered that Mellon had made millions of dollars' worth of tax-deductible contributions in the form of paintings acquired for a charitable trust designed for ultimate donation to the public. In fact, he claimed, Mellon actually had overpaid his taxes by $139,000 and deserved a refund. Furthermore, Hogan argued, the government's failure to provide Mellon with the customary thirty-day notice of his alleged tax deficiency prior to announcing publicly the charges against him was evidence that the charges were politically based and without merit. Hogan even managed to extract from the prosecution side an internal letter on which had been stamped, "Case has not been considered on its merits."

The elaborate details of Mellon's tax return confused even expert witnesses, but Hogan's recitation of voluminous facts and figures without ever glancing at notes was, as always, a source of constant amazement to reporters, who watched from the empty jury box. (There was no jury in cases brought before the U.S. Board of Tax Appeals.) The reporters also enjoyed the frequent, sharp exchanges between Hogan and Jackson, both described as brilliant, witty, and respectful of each other despite their barbed repartee. One day, after Hogan finished orating before the board, Jackson joked, "I kept asking where the jury was. Then I noticed it over there," and pointed to several reporters sitting in the jury box. On another occasion when Hogan thought Jackson was leading his witness, he asked, "Does the witness desire to be sworn?" "What witness?" Jackson replied. "You!" Hogan shot back.

The March 11, 1935, issue of *Time* magazine featured Hogan on its cover, staring somewhat grimly through his trademark pince-nez glasses, perhaps at a legal opponent, perhaps at the New Deal, perhaps at the future. As it had done before, *Time* flattered Hogan with praise for his skillful courtroom victories while snobbishly insinuating that his command of the law was not very sophisticated. He was a clever trial lawyer, adept at the theatrical manipulation of juries, the piece said, but inadequately schooled in the finer points of legal argument. To support its biased characterization of the Irish Catholic, evening-law-school graduate, *Time*'s writer cited Hogan's 1925 "loss" in the California Cooperative Canneries antitrust case in which, the writer claimed, there had been "little to dramatize." In fact, though, both the account and the characterization were incorrect, as Hogan had won that case for the canneries and for Armour, Swift, and the other members of the "big five" Chicago meat packers. And in December 1937 Hogan also prevailed in the Mellon trial, where a surfeit of fine points and bloodless detail defied sustained interest and offered no opportunity for melodramatic manipulation of a jury.

The Board of Appeals' ruling in Mellon's favor came too late for the former Secretary of the Treasury, though. He had died four months earlier and never experienced the clearing of his reputation. Mellon's paintings formed the nucleus of the National Gallery of Art, which opened in 1941, but the government's ultimately fruitless and seemingly politicized prosecution remained a sore point with the Mellon family for years.[6]

While the Board of Tax Appeals weighed the merits of Mellon's case, Hogan found himself at odds with yet another attorney soon destined for the Supreme Court, Democratic Senator Hugo Black of Alabama. Black headed a committee investigating the lobbying practices of utility companies, particularly in reference to New Deal legislation to restructure the rates those

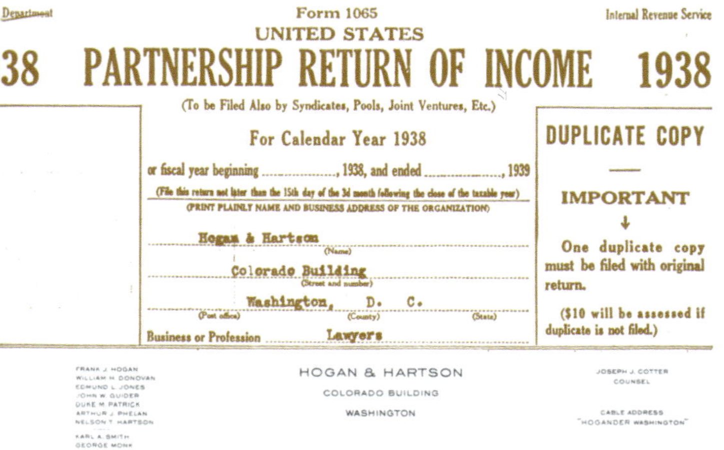

ry Department — Form 1065 — Internal Revenue Service

UNITED STATES

938 PARTNERSHIP RETURN OF INCOME 1938

(To be Filed Also by Syndicates, Pools, Joint Ventures, Etc.)

For Calendar Year 1938

or fiscal year beginning ...., 1938, and ended ...., 1939

(File this return not later than the 15th day of the 3d month following the close of the taxable year)

(PRINT PLAINLY NAME AND BUSINESS ADDRESS OF THE ORGANIZATION)

Hogan & Hartson (Name)

Colorado Building (Street and number)

Washington, D. C. (Post office) (County) (State)

Business or Profession .... Lawyers

DUPLICATE COPY

IMPORTANT

One duplicate copy must be filed with original return.

($10 will be assessed if duplicate is not filed.)

FRANK J. HOGAN
WILLIAM H. DONOVAN
EDMUND L. JONES
JOHN W. GUIDER
DUKE M. PATRICK
ARTHUR J. PHELAN
NELSON T. HARTSON

KARL A. SMITH
GEORGE MONK
LESTER COHEN
O. R. McGUIRE, JR

HOGAN & HARTSON
COLORADO BUILDING
WASHINGTON

JOSEPH J. COTTER
COUNSEL

CABLE ADDRESS
"HOGANDER WASHINGTON"

companies charged customers and to prohibit practices that inflated stock values. With the assistance of personnel from the Federal Communications Commission, Black's committee investigators had visited Western Union offices to round up, without warrant, thousands of telegrams between several utility companies and their lawyers over a period of ten months in 1935. The committee believed that a substantial number of the telegrams had been sent en masse under false signatures, while others, especially those to and from law firms, would reveal the amount of money the companies had spent trying to defeat reform legislation, the Public Utilities Holding Companies Act, which passed in 1935. One of the firms was Chicago's Winston, Strawn and Shaw. Silas Strawn was a prominent Republican, a former president of the U.S. Chamber of Commerce, and ex-president of the American Bar Association, while Ralph Shaw was head of the Liberty League in Chicago.

Strawn called on Hogan, who on March 3, 1936, obtained a temporary injunction from District Supreme

Frank Hogan's diverse legal practice defied a widespread and stubborn stereotype of his day — the silver-tongued courtroom lawyer who could sway juries but was not well schooled in the intellectual intricacies of the law. For example, in April 1925 he successfully concluded an action on behalf of the California Cooperative Canneries, which had suffered great losses under an antitrust consent decree signed in 1920 by the "Big Five" meat packers of Chicago — Armour, Swift, Morris, Cudahy, and Wilson. Fearing that the meat packers, unchecked, would eventually control the entire food supply, the Justice Department had succeeded in obtaining a consent decree that limited the Big Five's businesses to meat — no fruits or vegetables — and included the "meat only" use of railroad refrigerator cars.

The prohibition against using the refrigerator cars, which the meat packers owned, for any other use effectively terminated the Canneries' $4 million annual business with the "Big Five." Without access to the packers' cars, West Coast fruit and vegetable growers could no longer deliver fresh produce to East Coast markets. The canners were then thrown on the mercies of the wholesale grocers, who quickly proved as monopolistic as the government had figured the meat packers would be. Hogan's successful challenging of the five-year-old decree restored the competition between the packers and the wholesale grocers for the canneries' products that the Justice Department's decree had unintentionally quashed.

Court Judge Jesse Corcoran Adkins blocking the Senate's search as a violation of the Fourth Amendment. When it soon came to light that Black's committee had seized or examined millions of telegrams pertaining not only to utility companies but also to other opponents of New Deal policies, such as the Farmers' Independent Council, the National Woman's Party, and the Liberty League, a groundswell of outrage enveloped Capitol Hill and the press. New York Senator Wadsworth called the committee's seizure "New Deal terrorism." The *Chicago Tribune* condemned "Senate black shirts" and "dictatorial autocrats." The respected liberal columnist Walter Lippman asked the question Hogan had been asking for a dozen years: "Against whom and what will this engine be turned next? I do not know," said Lippman, "but I do know that when lawlessness is approved for supposedly good ends, it will be used even more viciously for bad ones."[7]

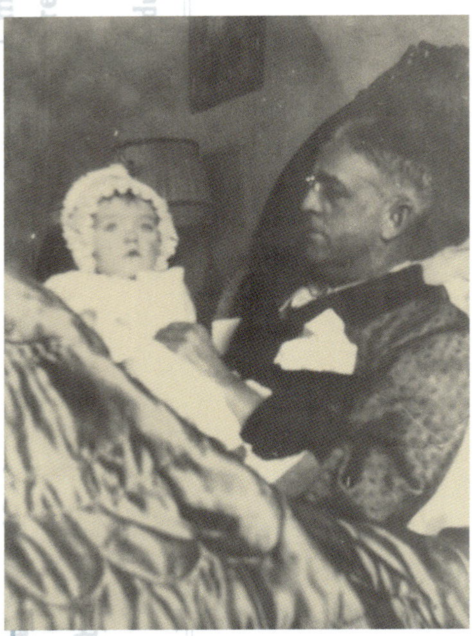

As his health declined in the early 1940s Hogan enjoyed more time at home in his splendid library and with his family. He always was impeccably attired.

On March 11 Hogan argued before the D.C. Supreme Court that there were no exceptions to the protections against unreasonable search and seizure guaranteed by the Fourth Amendment. "The Constitution does not provide that the right shall not be violated except by a committee of the Senate," he declared. But as he prepared to launch further into his speech, Chief Justice Alfred A. Wheat interrupted him. He had heard enough. The judge made the injunction permanent, ruling that the Senate had gone "way beyond any legitimate exercise of the right to subpoena." The next year President Roosevelt appointed Hugo Black to the U.S. Supreme Court, where for nearly a quarter of a century he retained his reservations about the extent of the Fourth Amendment's protections.[8]

In August 1936 Hogan addressed the American Bar Association at Boston's Faneuil Hall, "the cradle of the ideal of liberty under law," and asked his colleagues "to pledge ourselves anew to the maintenance of that constitutional government which is the soul of America."[9] Long active in bar activities and president of the Bar Association of the District of Columbia in 1932, the sixty-one-year-old Hogan was elected president of the 32,000-member American Bar Association in 1938, the first attorney from Washington, D.C., ever to hold that office. Describing his role as "a perambulating Victrola," he traveled extensively to spread the cause of individual rights and the need to protect those rights from public officials more concerned with political ends than Constitutional means.[10]

Hogan's travels and speeches in 1938-1939 took their toll on his health. Never robust, if always spirited, he gradually weakened under the advancing predations of Parkinson's disease. His frequent absences from Washington, as well as his precarious health, alerted him to the prudence of restructuring his law practice. On January 2, 1938, Hogan, Hartson, Donovan, Jones, Guider, Phelan, and Patrick formalized the arrangement, creating a true partnership and a new level of business orderliness. But how would the new partnership be known? Lester Cohen, then an associate with the practice and later a longtime partner, recalled that Hogan's name, of course, had to go first. Adding Donovan, Phelan, or Patrick would make the firm sound too Irish. "Hogan & Jones" sounded too ordinary. "Hogan & Guider" had a nice ring to it but echoed nepotism between Hogan and his son-in-law. Only one option remained — the euphonious and alliterative "Hogan & Hartson." Happily enough, the only option also seemed the best one.

In December 1938, with Nazi racial ideology beginning to spread its infection beyond Germany, Hogan took to the airwaves to blast the bigotry of Father Coughlin, the Detroit priest who had gained notoriety in the 1935 presidential election. Hogan used the same Detroit radio station as "the radio priest" and spoke just after Coughlin had left the air. "My friends," he warned, "the United States will not remain free for any of us unless it remains free for all of us." He pointed to Germany as an example of a nation that had forgotten that truth and was now in the grip of a hate epidemic. Hogan joined notables such as Charles A. Beard, Dorothy Thompson, Alfred E. Smith, and Nicholas Murray Butler in advocating tolerance, declaring "There is no greater curse among any people than intolerance."[11] He was active in the American National Conference Against Racial Persecution in Germany, which encouraged President Roosevelt to use his influence on behalf of Jews in Germany.

Two weeks after Hogan's attack on Coughlin, on Christmas Day 1938, Hogan's mother, Mollie, died in her son's home, which he always had made hers. Hogan and other family members were with her, including her nephew, James Byrnes, who had resigned his Supreme Court position and was now a U.S. Senator from South Carolina. Mollie Hogan had been Frank's great, quiet guiding star, whom he loved to present as a celebrity to the many friends and guests often invited to their handsome Sheridan Circle residence.

After 1939 Hogan spent more time enjoying his family and his collection of carefully — and expensively — acquired books, such as a 1483 edition of *The Canterbury Tales*, an early copy of *Pilgrim's Progress*, and the famous Lord Rosebury First Folio of Shakespeare. Hogan's lessons in the English classics, generously given years ago by the South Carolina Railway clerk John Austin, had taken deep root and now blossomed richly in the attorney's oak-paneled private library.

Hogan did not live to see the end of World War II and the return from military service of several firm attorneys like Duke Patrick, Corwin Lockwood, and Duke Guider. He died on May 15, 1944, at the age of sixty-seven, in his home, surrounded by his family and the books he loved. The Reverend Joseph Moran, who administered the last rites, told a newspaper reporter what Hogan had said to him: "I am grateful beyond words to Almighty God for the blessings He has given me, for the talents He gave me, and for the ability to carry out my work. Now that my usefulness is over, I am resigned." Friendly, democratic, and ever willing to dissolve differences in good humor and fellowship, Hogan had endeared himself to thousands, including his adversaries. Among those attending the funeral in Washington were Robert Fleming, president of Riggs Bank, Major General Patrick A. Hurley, former Secretary of War, and Robert Jackson, his worthy opponent in the Mellon tax case, now a Supreme Court Justice, whom Hogan's colleague Lester Cohen observed "walking slowly down the steps of St. Matthew's cathedral, deep in thought."[12]

"Altogether," a Louisville, Kentucky, *Courier-Journal* reporter had concluded in 1939, "he is a hard man to hate." For his law partners, Hogan also was a hard man to follow, for the national fame that had so brilliantly illumined him had kept them in half-

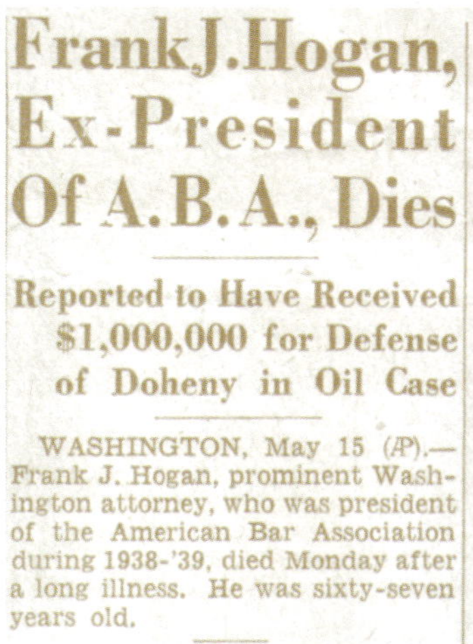

Frank J. Hogan, Ex-President Of A.B.A., Dies

Reported to Have Received $1,000,000 for Defense of Doheny in Oil Case

WASHINGTON, May 15 (AP).—Frank J. Hogan, prominent Washington attorney, who was president of the American Bar Association during 1938-'39, died Monday after a long illness. He was sixty-seven years old.

Won Case for Doheny

FRANCIS J. HOGAN, 1877-1944. HOGAN'S FUNERAL SERVICE WAS CONDUCTED AT ST. MATTHEW'S CATHEDRAL IN WASHINGTON, D.C.

shadow while they serviced local, blue-chip clients like Riggs National Bank, the District of Columbia Bankers' Association, the Capital Transit Company, the *Evening Star* newspaper, the Mayflower Hotel, and the Garfinkel's and Woodward & Lothrop department stores. The firm also represented national clients such as Republic Steel, the Columbia Broadcasting System, Libby-Owens-Ford Glass, Pillsbury Flour, and several broadcast stations, but its image remained primarily that of a local firm. When Frank Hogan died, the national spotlight that had followed his career wandered from his law firm but continued to shine on the city he had chosen for his practice.

Just as Hogan's career formed a legacy for his partners to develop, Roosevelt's long presidency catapulted Washington into new prominence as the center of the nation's political activity and the home of its new regulatory agencies. Roosevelt never wanted a grand memorial erected in his honor.[13] He didn't need one. The city itself had become monument enough to his policies and accomplishments. Before Roosevelt's death on April 12, 1945, the federal city had been transformed by such new structures as the Supreme Court building (1935), the Department of Agriculture (1936), the National Gallery of Art (1941), and the Pentagon (1942), then the largest office building in the world.

The number of federal employees in Washington doubled between 1929 and 1940, contributing to a 36 percent increase in the city's overall population. In 1940 per capita income in D.C. was $1,022 a year, nearly double the national figure of $573.[14] U.S. war preparations — already underway in early 1940 — brought roughly 5,000 new federal workers into Washington every month. After December 7, 1941, the rising tide of newcomers seemed to swamp the city. "Within months after Pearl Harbor," wrote journalist David Brinkley, "the government had spread like a pool of warm axle grease, oozing outward over the city and into 358 buildings that had previously served other purposes." The expansion strained critical services like laundries, buses, and telephones. "All the new agencies," Brinkley said, "talking to each other, so overcrowded the telephones that the Chesapeake and Potomac's system nearly collapsed, causing the company to run ads asking people to use the phones only when necessary."[15] By the end of the war, in 1945, the federal budget reached nearly $93 billion — ten times what it had been in 1939.

[1] [2]

HISTORIANS OFTEN HAVE SAID THAT THE MODERN CITY OF WASHINGTON, D.C., IS VERY MUCH A CREATION OF FRANKLIN ROOSEVELT AND THE NEW DEAL. MANY OF WASHINGTON'S NOTABLE BUILDINGS WERE BUILT DURING ROOSEVELT'S PRESIDENCY.

In the two decades following World War II large law firms in America prospered into a "golden age." The years around 1960, especially, were "a time of prosperity, stable relations with clients, steady but manageable growth, and a comfortable assumption that this kind of law practice was a permanent feature of American life and would go on forever."[16] That sense of permanence, of relatively unhurried ambition, of a career building slowly and without undue anxiety toward the security of partnership, increased proportionately with a firm's distance from Wall Street. But even New York firms tempered their "up or out" promotion systems with outplacements for associates. It was widely believed in New York that "lawyers (especially associates) were not working as hard as they had in earlier times."[17]

There was a stultifying aspect to prosperity in some large firms. Paul Cravath had described to a Harvard Law School class in 1920 the ideal candidate for employment in his firm. The attorney — a Christian white man, he did not have to say — would be efficient rather than charming and not necessarily brilliant. His firm's clients preferred "a man who is primarily honest, safe, sound and steady," who would concentrate dutifully on what counts and "not waste effort and thought on things that are simply interesting."[18] That "ideal" prevailed in many firms through their "golden age."

HOWARD HUGHES (R) WITH ATTORNEY T.A. SLACK.

that their prior success seemed to warrant. Hogan's son-in-law, Duke Guider, was an exception. When he returned from naval service in 1945 he soon left for New Hampshire to set up a broadcasting business. But for those who remained, growth meant hiring an additional attorney every year and minding conscientiously the expanding needs of the firm's clients.

[1] THE NEW AGRICULTURE DEPARTMENT [2] THE NATIONAL GALLERY OF ART [3] THE U.S. SUPREME COURT [4] THE JUSTICE DEPARTMENT [5] THE PENTAGON

Hogan & Hartson's Washington location, its legacy of star litigation under Frank Hogan, its diversified regulatory, commercial, and banking practices, and its penchant for accommodating rather than suppressing individualism helped keep it free from a too-suffocating stuffiness. At the same time, the prosperity that Hogan helped create tempted his partners after 1944 to settle into the comfortable life

Nelson Hartson and his former assistant solicitor at the Internal Revenue Service, James Rogers, had become so busy with the firm's banking, commercial, and estates practice that Hogan's plan for a separate tax department had never fully materialized.

WASHINGTON, D.C. STREET SCENE, C. LATE 1940S, SHOWING CAPITAL TRANSIT STREETCARS AND TRACKS, AND THE CONCRETE "SAFETY ISLANDS" THAT SEPARATED WAITING PASSENGERS FROM AUTOMOBILE TRAFFIC.

JOHN P. "JACK" ARNESS JOINED HOGAN & HARTSON IN SEPTEMBER 1952. DEEPLY COMMITTED TO HIS PROFESSION, ARNESS HAS RECEIVED NUMEROUS AWARDS AND HAS HELD OFFICE IN SEVERAL ORGANIZATIONS, INCLUDING SERVICE AS PRESIDENT OF THE BAR ASSOCIATION OF THE DISTRICT OF COLUMBIA (1977-1978).

So in 1946 the firm hired Seymour Mintz, a talented attorney from the IRS Chief Counsel's office, to create that department. Mintz joined a nineteen-lawyer firm that was, as he later recalled, "still mired in admiration, if not adoration, of Frank Hogan," whom Mintz had never met. A thirty-six-year-old World War II veteran with five years' experience at the Treasury and the IRS, Mintz was not prepared to endure the firm's usual progression through ten or more years as an associate before being considered for partnership. Edward Bennett Williams, a recent Georgetown Law School graduate and husband of Hogan's granddaughter, Dorothy, also grew impatient with the firm's leisurely promotion schedule.

Late in 1948 Mintz asked to be considered for partnership and was accepted, becoming a partner on January 1, 1949. Soon thereafter Ed Williams made the same request but was denied. The committee members "made the mistake of their lives," Mintz observed many years later, "by saying yes to me and no to Edward Bennett Williams." The brilliant and intense Williams left that summer to set up a partnership with veteran Washington attorney Nicholas Chase. At about the same time, a veteran litigator named John Sirica joined Hogan & Hartson. Williams's and Mintz's push for partnership had not worked out well for Williams, but it succeeded in clearing a logjam for associates like Oliver "Ollie" McGuire and George Monk, who had labored dutifully for more than twelve years in hopes of reaching the holy grail of partnership. They, too, soon became partners, but it was Mintz who recognized that initiative, not deferential orbiting, was the most direct path to leadership in the firm.

Mintz's talent and experience justified his rapid advancement and his subsequent election to several terms on the firm's Executive Committee. But in addition, Mintz noted that "the power of the purse is quite tremendous." In 1948 he had netted the tax business of Howard Hughes, one of the world's wealthiest men, while securing Hughes's confidence by understanding, then adjusting to, his idiosyncrasies. Added to his representation of existing firm clients like Republic Steel and Armour & Company, the Hughes work gave Mintz substantial leverage in the firm inconsistent with prolonged associate status. He pressed his advantage before the Executive Committee and won.

The Hughes business came, as is often the case, through the intersection of outreach and accident. Hughes's tax lawyer for 1947 had disappointed his client in a certain transaction and then aggravated the annoyance by forwarding a bill for $75,000. Wishing to avoid a repeat of the unpleasantry that had provoked, the following year Merrill Lynch, with whom Hughes was working on another transaction, looked around for a different tax attorney.

Mintz enjoyed writing about tax law and had recently appeared on a panel with a lawyer who did Merrill Lynch's tax work, so his name went on a short list. Hughes wanted a Washington lawyer. Mintz was closer in age to Hughes than the others, so he got the call from T. A. Slack, Hughes's general counsel: "Mr. Hughes would like to see you in Los Angeles tomorrow morning." "I don't think I can do that," Mintz replied cautiously. It sounded too unusual, too quirky. Slack asked him to think it over. Mintz did and soon called back with a counteroffer to have breakfast instead with Slack in New York that weekend. The proposal was accepted. Shortly after the New York meeting, Mintz made his way to Los Angeles and met Hughes, who became a long-term Hogan & Hartson client.

Hogan & Hartson's hiring decisions in the early 1950s showed little outreach and much accident by comparison to the studied calculations of contemporary law firm recruiting. After service in World War II, young Jack Arness hurried himself through Harvard undergraduate and then Georgetown Law School in a total of four years, using the GI Bill, summer school, and credits earned in Army language training. In 1952 he completed a clerkship with Chief Judge Harold M. Stephens on the D.C. Circuit Court of Appeals, whereupon he received the following advice: "Jack," Judge Stephens declared, "you *read* law well, you *write* law well, you *think* law well, but you don't *speak* law well." The judge had a simple solution for that rather puzzling problem — go work for a law firm with an active trial practice. His secretary had recently done some counting and discovered that Hogan & Hartson was involved in 51 percent of all the cases pending in the U.S. District Court. So Judge Stephens arranged an interview for Arness with Nelson Hartson.

Arness was immediately struck by Hartson's imposing figure — tall, immaculately attired, "the epitome of a gentleman," he recalled. He volunteered that he'd be happy to send in some writing samples, but at the end of the interview Hartson told him there were no openings in the trial department at present. Disappointed, Arness returned to the Court of Appeals to finish out his clerkship. Ten days later Hartson called him: "I thought you were going to send me some samples of your writing." "Well, I was," Arness answered, "but you told me there weren't any openings in your trial department so I decided not to." "Well, send them anyway," said Hartson. In September 1952 Arness signed on as Hogan & Hartson's twenty-second lawyer and joined what he gleefully referred to as a "murderers' row" of seasoned litigators like John Sirica, George Horning, Frank Roberson, and Paul Connolly. Connolly, just a few years older than Arness, made a deep impression. "He was just full of exuberance! Everything was a challenge and everything was wonderful and everything was worth digging into. He was quite a role model for a young, aspiring trial lawyer."

Arness's first office was a chair in the firm's library, but he was in court so much it didn't seem to matter. Roberson accompanied him on his first solo case, a Hogan & Hartson classic "that nobody could possibly have lost," Arness recalled. One Sunday afternoon two elderly sisters, Anna Mae and Zenia Beck, had driven their car into the back of a Capital Transit bus parked at a bus stop. They decided to sue since the public transit system was a notorious target for sympathetic D.C. juries. "I was nervous as a cat," said Arness, representing the bus company, but "it was a case you could afford to make a few mistakes on and still win." He won.

Later the Capital Transit Company asked Arness to take on an important test case. The company and the city of Washington had an ongoing dispute as to which was responsible when pedestrians twisted ankles or

WASHINGTON, D.C., PHASED OUT ITS STREETCARS BY 1962. HERE, VENERABLE CAR #766 STOPS AT THE SUPREME COURT ON ITS LAST DAY OF SERVICE, JANUARY 28, 1962. RAIL BUFFS LINED UP WITH THEIR CAMERAS TO RECORD THE MOMENT.

STANLEY S. HARRIS WAS AN ASSOCIATE AND PARTNER AT HOGAN & HARTSON FROM 1953 TO 1971, WHEN HE WAS APPOINTED JUDGE, SUPERIOR COURT OF THE DISTRICT OF COLUMBIA. SUBSEQUENTLY HE SERVED AS JUDGE, DISTRICT OF COLUMBIA COURT OF APPEALS, THEN AS UNITED STATES DISTRICT COURT JUDGE, DISTRICT OF COLUMBIA. [ABOVE LEFT] THE OLD EBBITT GRILL ON F ST., N.W., WHERE ATTORNEY, LATER JUDGE, STANLEY HARRIS MADE HIS DECISION TO JOIN HOGAN & HARTSON IN 1953. THE STRUCTURE HAS SINCE BEEN DEMOLISHED BUT THE OLD EBBITT CONTINUED IN A NEW LOCATION AROUND THE CORNER ON 15TH. ST.

tripped and injured themselves while walking across the streetcar tracks then imbedded in many of Washington's roads. Often, both the company and the city would be sued and most cases were settled fifty-fifty. But now Capital Transit wanted the matter decided one way or the other. Arness won the case for the company. The city appealed, and the appeals court sustained the ruling. "I *loved* that type of challenge," Arness beamed, his enthusiasm still evident nearly fifty years later. Within five years of joining the firm, Arness had argued forty cases in the D.C. Circuit Court of Appeals. "There," the South Dakotan Arness recalled unabashedly, "was a guy on a horse!"

In 1953, a year after Arness's job interview miscues with Hartson, Stanley Harris, a new University of Virginia Law School graduate, had a similar experience. Harris had written a letter of inquiry and received a reply from "Nubby" Jones that there were no openings at the firm but if Harris were ever in town he was welcome to drop by for a visit. As it turned out, Harris soon was in town interviewing at other law firms. He had finished early and was having a beer at 2:00 p.m. in the Old Ebbitt Grill on F Street while waiting for a friend, Paul McCardle, to finish his day's work as an associate at a D.C. firm.

But that was three hours away, and Harris had more time on his hands than a couple of beers could fill. Suddenly he remembered Jones's invitation and decided to walk the short distance to the Colorado Building. Fortunately, Harris wandered in just as the firm decided it needed help in its radio and television department. After a few impromptu interviews, including one with Jones, who "had sort of a country boy air about him, very likeable, very sharp, very folksy," Harris returned to the Old Ebbitt with a job offer from Hogan & Hartson. Said McCardle when Harris asked his advice, "It's the best firm in town. For heaven's sake, take it!"

Broadcast television had been introduced just after the war, and in the four years between 1949 and 1953, when Harris joined the firm, the number of U.S. households with a TV set had leapt from just under a million to 20 million. The number of stations and license applications before the FCC also increased, as did disputes over the FCC's decisions, role, and jurisdiction. Preparing clients for "comparative hearings" before the commission, which had to decide which of many applicants would get the limited number of licenses, and conducting appeals of commissioners' decisions on behalf of parties who had been refused a broadcast license, became a Hogan & Hartson specialty, keeping about 25 percent of the firm's attorneys busy full time.

When forty-seven-year-old communications lawyer Parker Hancock died unexpectedly in 1960, the firm assigned a new associate, Howard Roycroft, to move into that practice under the tutelage of Lester Cohen. Roycroft had joined the firm in 1958 after declining a prestigious clerkship for Judge E. Barrett Prettyman on the D.C. Circuit Court of Appeals. Later on in his life he thought maybe he had made a mistake in declining such an opportunity, but after three years in the U.S. Marine Corps between college and Georgetown Law School he felt he owed it to his career to make up some lost time.

Roycroft may have lost some time in the Marines but he hadn't left his sense of humor there. During his initial interview at Hogan & Hartson he was struck by the pince-nez eyeglasses worn by both Nelson Hartson and James Cunningham. "They were really an anachronism," he recalled about the Teddy Roosevelt/Frank Hogan-era eyewear, and a bit intimidating as well. Seymour Mintz also had been present, though he wore no pince-nez glasses. Knowing that Roycroft had been offered a clerkship with Judge Prettyman but not knowing whether he intended to take it, Hartson asked him, "If we were to offer you a position, young man, would you accept it?" Roycroft thought about it for a few seconds, then replied, "Well, why don't you try me and see?" No one answered. "I guess they were kind of taken aback that someone would talk to them that way," Roycroft conjectured. "But Mintz laughed quite heartily."

Roycroft, like so many others in the firm, was impressed by Mintz's intellect and was eager to make a good impression. In the months before Hancock's death and Roycroft's reassignment from tax work to communications, Mintz asked him to draft a memo on a very esoteric subject involving the failure of the District National Bank. The issue was "the law of springing and shifting uses in future interests" in real estate law. Mintz thought highly of the memo and, to Roycroft's satisfaction, the case produced a significant fee for the firm.

Shortly afterwards Roycroft produced another memo, this one on oil drilling rights in Alaska. The matter was complicated by Alaska's transition to statehood in 1959, which raised the question of whether the federal authority to grant oil leases had changed as a result of Alaska's new status. "You had to do it right," Roycroft remembered, "because if you filed for the lease in the wrong place, you put your competitor on notice that that's where the oil was and he could file in the right place and trump whatever you did." The memo was so well drawn that Mintz sent it straight out to the client, who called back to say, "For once I got a decision instead of a lot of information."

Having made an excellent debut with Mintz, Roycroft transferred to communications, where he adapted readily to the firm's work with major clients like D.C.'s Evening Star Broadcasting Group (ESBG) and the A. S. Abel Company in Baltimore, publishers of the *Baltimore Sun* newspaper. Roycroft enjoyed the challenges posed by private companies' attempts to purchase FCC-regulated operations like radio and television stations that used public airways. He and Marvin Diamond — "I won't say bright; I would say brilliant," observed Roycroft of his younger colleague — worked out a mechanism for handling that inherent conflict and convinced the FCC to adopt it. Communications, Roycroft recalled, was "an area of practice that I felt I was born to do."

HOWARD ROYCROFT JOINED HOGAN & HARTSON IN 1958 AS THE FIRM'S 33RD LAWYER.

Roycroft's colleague in the practice, Stan Harris, worked next door to the telephone switchboard in the reception area. That strategic location gave him some unexpected insight about the crucial role that the switchboard operator, Kathy Miller, played in Hogan & Hartson's recruitment process. Besides answering the phones and routing all the calls, Ms. Miller received the firm's mail and determined how it should be distributed. All letters came to her, including applicants' letters. Absent any instructions to do otherwise, she parceled them out with benign impartiality to whichever partner seemed not to have received one recently. Of course, the partner who got an applicant's letter on any given day might or might not respond, depending on the needs of his particular department at the moment.

SWITCHBOARD OPERATORS OFTEN WERE THE NERVE CENTERS OF THEIR ORGANIZATIONS IN THE MIDDLE DECADES OF THE TWENTIETH CENTURY.

While clerking for U.S. Supreme Court Justice Robert H. Jackson (above), Barrett Prettyman played a role in the Court's famous decision in Brown v. Board of Education, which consolidated four similar cases and capped a long legal campaign by the National Association for the Advancement of Colored People (NAACP) to end racial segregation in America's schools.

Nearly sixty years earlier the Court's Plessy v. Ferguson (1896) decision had legalized "separate but equal" treatment for racial groups. That ruling, on top of centuries of slavery and segregation in many parts of the United States, posed a formidable challenge and a delicate task for the Court between December 1952, when it heard initial arguments in the case, and May 1954, when Chief Justice Earl Warren delivered a unanimous opinion that racially segregated schools violated the Fourteenth Amendment.

Just as Plessy v. Ferguson's scope had extended far beyond the railroad accommodations case that was its specific focus, Brown v. Board of Education's reasoning also spread beyond schools. In effect, it undid the broad doctrine of "separate but equal" and laid the legal groundwork for a civil rights revolution in America. It is widely regarded as one of the Court's most historic decisions.

During 1953, when Jackson favored ending school segregation but still assumed that other Justices would be writing concurring or dissenting opinions in the Brown case, he asked his law clerk, Barrett Prettyman, to respond to Jackson's own draft opinion, which seemed to Prettyman to be somewhat defensive in tone. Prettyman was direct when he gave his response. "If you are going to reach the decision you do," he wrote Jackson, "you should not write as if you were ashamed to reach it. . . . Some one must make these decisions, and under our system the burden is on the courts. . . . This is a great country, and its people are great, and they will not tolerate lawlessness if they are convinced it is real lawlessness. How can you expect them to be convinced if you are not yourself?"

Twenty-one years later, a major scholar of the Brown v. Board of Education decision wrote, "It is doubtful if any of the many excellent young men who have come fresh out of the law schools or soon thereafter to serve the Justices of the Supreme Court ever served more faithfully or usefully than Barrett Prettyman served Robert Jackson." (Richard Kluger, Simple Justice: The History of Brown v. Board of Education and Black America's Struggle for Equality (New York, Random House, 1975), 691.)

Remembering his own, too-casual experience with Nubby Jones, Harris observed this process painfully for a time, then went to the Executive Committee and complained, "You can't keep doing business this way! You need a system that's consistent." "Fine," said the committee, "you do it." So within a year of his arrival, the firm's newest associate had become its principal point of contact for applicants.

Harris brought an empathic sense of immediacy to the task of addressing young job-seekers' needs. After all, he was closer to that experience than Hartson or Jones, for whom getting a job must have seemed a rather distant worry. For Barrett Prettyman, Jr., Harris's University of Virginia Law School friend and son of Judge Prettyman, job-seeking also appeared a remote problem, though for a different reason: he simply was too busy. In 1955, though nearing the end of a remarkable series of clerkships for Supreme Court Justices Jackson, Frankfurter, and Harlan, Prettyman had not given the matter much thought. Harris called him up and pressed him about his plans. He didn't really have any, now that he thought about it, so Harris asked him to consider coming to Hogan & Hartson, holding forth the enticing opportunity to work directly on a major case, a Pillsbury antitrust matter, with Joseph Judson Smith. Smith was an intense man with "a fire in his belly," Prettyman later said, who had come to Hogan & Hartson in 1945 from a position as assistant chief counsel in charge of the appellate division in the Federal Trade Commission.

Prettyman came in for interviews, but the recruitment nearly derailed over Hartson's objection that the son of E. Barrett Prettyman, a sitting judge on the U.S. Court of Appeals, would be hard to fire if things didn't work out. It was an interesting illustration of how both caution and apparent advantage can backfire. Nevertheless, the firm welcomed Prettyman, who much later quipped that Hartson had been "absolutely right. Here it is some forty years later and they still haven't been able to get rid of me."

IN THE
United States Court of Appeals
FOR THE FIFTH CIRCUIT

No. 18,825

THE PILLSBURY COMPANY, *Petitioner*
v.
FEDERAL TRADE COMMISSION, *Respondent*

BRIEF FOR PETITIONER

PHILIP F. SHERMAN
General Counsel
The Pillsbury Company
Minneapolis, Minnesota
JOSEPH J. SMITH, JR.
800 Colorado Building
Washington 5, D. C.
E. BARRETT PRETTYMAN, JR.
800 Colorado Building
Washington 5, D. C.
Attorneys for Petitioner

HOGAN & HARTSON
800 Colorado Building
Washington 5, D. C.
Of Counsel for Petitioner

PRESS OF BYRON S. ADAMS, WASHINGTON, D.C.

Rev'd, 354 F.2d 952 (5th C. 1966)

E. BARRETT PRETTYMAN, JR. (L, SEATED) AND HIS FATHER, JUDGE PRETTYMAN, ENJOYED A CLOSE, COLLEGIAL RELATIONSHIP. HERE THEY SHARED THE PLEASURE OF TEACHING A CLASS OF HIGH SCHOOL STUDENTS IN WASHINGTON, D.C.

Like most major antitrust cases, the Pillsbury trial was highly charged politically. It involved Pillsbury's acquisition of two relatively small businesses, a matter that would not draw much attention today. But in the 1950s it consumed vast amounts of time and energy because it was the first case prosecuted under the Clayton Antitrust Act's Section 7, which restricted mergers, and the government was eager to see it through to a successful conclusion. Prettyman spent four years taking depositions and researching the case, at times even visiting grocery stores to count the number of various baking products on the shelves. On Christmas Eve 1961, his wife telephoned him in the law library at 11:30 p.m. with an urgent plea of her own to come home. "I had been working so hard as Justice Jackson's only clerk that it was nothing new to me. I assumed everybody did that," Prettyman remembered about the demands of legal work.

In 1962 Prettyman, Joe Smith, and Philip Sherman, Pillsbury's general counsel, filed a 322-page brief, *The Pillsbury Company v. The Federal Trade Commission*, with 369 footnotes and hundreds of case citations, that Prettyman had prepared. The FTC ruled against Pillsbury, but there was a curious possibility for a successful appeal. Much earlier, in the middle of the case, some congressional committee members had grilled FTC Chairman Edward F. Howrey as to why the FTC was taking so long to declare that Pillsbury was in violation of the law. "They had really taken him over the coals," Prettyman recalled. Commissioner Howrey's harsh treatment at the hands of the congressional committee, he reasoned, had made it impossible for the FTC to render an impartial judgment.

In 1966 Prettyman presented his argument before the Fifth Circuit Court of Appeals. "To be quite candid, it was not exactly far-fetched to me, but I didn't hold out a lot of hope for it. Courts don't normally hold that Congress has interfered with the quasi-judicial mind of a commissioner." But to his surprise the Fifth Circuit accepted the argument, reversing the FTC's ruling against Pillsbury. Thereafter, the case frequently was cited as an example of inappropriate congressional intrusion into the decisions of administrative agencies.

ROBERT FLEMING, PRESIDENT OF RIGGS BANK, JANUARY 2, 1953.

Like Howard Roycroft, assistant U.S. Attorney John Warner had served in the Marines prior to starting law school. But Warner had opted for a year's clerkship with Judge Prettyman on the D.C. Circuit Court of Appeals. Warner had made an impression when Judge Prettyman asked him, "You know, I have to tell you, Mr. Warner, that you have a good record, but it's certainly no better than those of easily a dozen other people I've interviewed. Why should you have this job?" Warner leaned over the table, set his jaw, and looked straight at the judge. "I'll tell you why. Because I've read every opinion you've ever written, I've read every article you've ever written, I've read every speech you've ever given. I know you better than anybody but Mrs. Prettyman!"[19] Warner got the job, completed his year, and then in 1956 took a position as an assistant U.S. Attorney in Washington, D.C., fighting his way through an overload of cases in what he recalled as "the rough and tumble" of D.C.'s criminal practice.

Several judges in the District had become concerned about the quality of lawyers appointed to represent indigent cases. There was as yet no public defender system, and the courts relied on volunteers and appointees from the local Bar. Recently the judges had contrived to get the attention of the city's law firms by appointing the firms' senior partners to come down to court to defend the accused poor. One day in 1960 Warner was sitting in his cramped office when a tall, elegantly dressed gentleman knocked at the door. "How do you do?" inquired the visitor. "My name is Nelson T. Hartson and I've been appointed to represent Willy Jones. May I discuss the case with you?"[20]

Hartson calmly told the young prosecutor that he was going to do his absolute best for Mr. Jones, but he had to confess that the last case he had tried had been in 1939, before the Board of Tax Appeals. Warner struggled to conceal his grimace. But the older man quickly added, "I have one of the ablest assortment of partners in trial, and this individual will have $25,000 worth of partners representing him."

Jones had been charged with first-degree murder and multiple counts of assault. It was a death penalty case, and Warner pressed hard against Jones's Hogan & Hartson defense team. In the end, though, both sides worked out a plea bargain that saved the defendant's life. After the sentencing proceeding was finished, Warner remained in the courtroom to complete some paperwork. When he stood up and turned around to leave he saw Hartson, sitting alone. "Mr. Warner, may I visit with you a moment?" The two went back to Warner's office. "Now, this has been a very unusual experience for me," the patrician confided. "And should it happen again, I want to be prepared. Will you come to work for me?" Warner could hardly believe his good fortune, and soon afterwards became the firm's thirty-seventh lawyer.

On his first day at Hogan & Hartson, Warner brought a small bag of personal belongings, ready to organize himself in some tiny office off a back hallway. Hartson greeted him with a smile. "Come in," he said. "Your office is right next to mine and we're sharing a secretary. We'll work on the Riggs Bank." Warner, who had walked in on a cloud, now worried about inciting envy among "the boys down the row." But with privilege came responsibility, and one night Robert Fleming, chairman of the board of Riggs, called him at home. Fleming's voice was strained. "I want to see you right away," he clipped. It was 9:00 p.m. What possibly could it be?

Warner always kept two briefcases at the ready containing the bank codes and other documents he might need at a moment's notice. He changed quickly into his three-piece suit, grabbed the satchels, and hurried over to Fleming's house off Massachusetts Avenue in the Kalorama section of northwest Washington. Fleming answered the door in his bathrobe, looked Warner over, and asked, "What are you doing with all those bags? We don't need to talk law!" Warner respectfully answered, "I didn't know, Mr. Fleming. What is your pleasure?" "My cat's in the tree!" the banker sputtered. "Will you help me get the damn cat out of the tree?"

Warner retrieved the cat, picked up his bags, and went home, mulling over this new branch of his law practice. The next day he and Hartson enjoyed a good laugh over the cat rescue. But Hartson took less lightly his young protégé's budding interest in politics. Not long after joining Hogan & Hartson, Warner took a six-month leave, with Hartson's guarded blessing, to work on Richard Nixon's presidential campaign. When he returned after Nixon's loss to John Kennedy, Hartson said to him, "Okay, you got it out of your system. Keep it out of your system."

The next year Hogan & Hartson faced a new recruitment dilemma. The firm usually hired one new associate each year, but this year the partners could not decide which of two candidates to hire, Robert Elliott or James Hourihan. It was not the first such circumstance for Elliott, who had been born early on New Year's Day in Jersey City but whose family lived in Bayonne. Both cities proudly proclaimed him the first baby born in 1934, triggering a dispute that was never satisfactorily resolved. Jersey City went on the birth certificate, but Bayonne never surrendered its claim.

[1] ROBERT J. ELLIOTT JOINED HOGAN & HARTSON IN 1961 AND RETIRED IN 2000. "A LOT OF ATTITUDES AND CHARACTER THAT HOGAN & HARTSON HAD WHEN I FIRST STARTED HERE HAVE CONTINUED," HE OBSERVED. [2] AT THE F STREET CLUB, C. 1960 (CLOCKWISE, FROM LEFT): PARKER D. HANCOCK, E. BARRETT PRETTYMAN, JR., JOHN P. ARNESS, FRANK ROBERSON, JAMES ROGERS, NELSON HARTSON, SEYMOUR MINTZ, FRANK CASEY, AND ROBERT KAPP. [3] JIM HOURIHAN JOINED HOGAN & HARTSON IN 1961, WHEN, AS HE RECALLED, WASHINGTON, D.C. WAS A "SLEEPY LITTLE SOUTHERN CITY."

In his final year at Georgetown University Law School, editor-in-chief Elliott was sitting with other editors of the *Georgetown Law Review* discussing their upcoming jobs. Elliott stood out from them in two ways: his grades had been exceptionally high, and he didn't have a job. Elliott had delayed for an awkwardly long

GEORGE E. MONK WAS CAREFUL AND SURE IN HIS PRACTICE, AS WELL AS IN HIS MENTORING OF YOUNG LAWYERS.

EDMUND L. "NUBBY" JONES JOINED HOGAN'S PRACTICE IN 1913 AS AN ASSISTANT, THEN AS AN ATTORNEY WHEN HE GRADUATED FROM GEORGETOWN LAW SCHOOL IN 1916. IN 1959 THE BAR ASSOCIATION OF THE DISTRICT OF COLUMBIA NAMED HIM LAWYER OF THE YEAR.

time his expected acceptance of a prestigious D.C. Circuit Court clerkship with Judge Charles Fahy, traditionally reserved for the *Law Review*'s editor-in-chief, because he wished instead to go to Hogan & Hartson. But the law firm had not called, and Judge Fahy could not be put off much longer. It had been a long time since anyone could recall an editor-in-chief of the *Law Review* not going with Judge Fahy, and Elliott had promised the judge an answer by 5:00 p.m. Friday. At 4:55 that afternoon Barrett Prettyman, who had joined Harris to form the firm's recruiting team, called him. "Fine," said Elliott quickly, "I'll accept." "That's it? You don't want to think?" "Barrett, I have about four minutes to phone Judge Fahy and tell him this."

Jim Hourihan's journey to Hogan & Hartson also nearly ran aground on a clerkship offer. The firm had sent Harris and Prettyman to the University of Michigan Law School to scout promising candidates. They had interviewed Hourihan, who had said he was interested. But well into the Christmas holiday break the firm had not yet extended an offer. Meanwhile, Hourihan had put off accepting a clerkship with New Jersey State Supreme Court Justice Haydn Proctor. Hourihan wanted to go to Hogan & Hartson and, hoping he would hear from the firm much earlier, had asked Justice Proctor to extend the offer until the end of the year. Now, with New Year's Day 1961 imminent, Hourihan would feel obligated to accept the clerkship if Proctor called. But at last Prettyman called from Washington. Hourihan accepted, just minutes before Justice Proctor's phone call came through.

So in 1961 Hogan & Hartson hired attorneys #41 and #42, both from New Jersey. It was the first time the firm ever had hired more than one associate at a time. But when the Berlin wall went up that August, an ominous symbol of Cold War conflict, Hourihan went off to fulfill the long-deferred requirements of his college ROTC commission and Bob Elliott claimed the position of attorney #41.

Elliott first reported to Seymour Mintz, who asked him, "Would you like to practice tax?" Well, it wouldn't be his first choice, answered Elliott, but he could try. Maybe he could take a few tax courses to help him prepare. "No, that's okay." So on to Nubby Jones. "How about labor law?" Jones asked. "If I could take some courses I'd be ready," answered the accommodating new associate, but Jones detected no spark of interest. Soon they told him, "We've decided you're going to work with George Monk." "Okay," said Elliott. "What does he do?" "None of us is sure," they answered. There were no courses for that. "We think he does bankruptcy." "All right." So Elliott went to work for George Monk, commercial lawyer.

Some in the firm found Monk a quiet "Mr. Careful," but all attested to his technical competence and thoroughness. Under Monk's direction, an ordinary will signing became a ritual demonstration of sober prudence. Elliott would read some lines out loud for the person whose will had been drafted and for the two witnesses in attendance. Then Monk would take out a bottle of India ink with a dip pen for signing. As each person signed, including initials on every page, Monk stood by with a blotter to dry the ink, waving it in the air between blottings. He then assembled all the pages and asked Elliott to count them out loud — *one, two, three*

— to make sure all would know every page was present and in proper sequence. Then, with a final flourish, Monk produced a rivet machine he kept for the purpose, riveted the pages together, and, like a satisfied clergyman at the close of a service, dismissed the participants.

So serious was this exercise that it took Elliott years to summon the nerve to ask Monk, from curiosity rather than exasperation, "Why do you do this?" Well, Monk explained, in order for a will to be valid, everyone has to be in the same room when it is signed, and how do you prove they were there if the will is contested later on? It turns out that dip pens with nibs are like fingerprints, each leaving its own special mark, and India ink is awfully hard to remove. And the rivets? They are hard to remove too, unlike staples which can be extracted and replaced.

Monk's thoroughness extended to protecting his vacation time at the beach every summer. He refused to have a phone in the house and all calls therefore had to go through his landlord. On more than one occasion he also vacationed in the Soviet Union. A young colleague once asked him why he went there. "Only place you can go where it is safe to walk the streets," he replied.[21] Elliott came to appreciate Monk's time-tested methods and the discipline they imposed. He also warmed to the older man's interest in his career and how Monk sponsored him for membership in the Metropolitan Club and the Rotary. Monk built confidence in a young attorney the way he constructed wills, slowly and unassailably.

JAY RICKS JOINED THE FIRM IN 1962. INTENDING A CAREER IN LITIGATION, RICKS SOON WAS CAUGHT UP IN A COMMUNICATIONS REVOLUTION INVOLVING CABLE TELEVISION AND OTHER NEW TECHNOLOGIES IN WHICH, AS IT TURNED OUT, THERE WAS NO DEARTH OF LITIGATION.

Before heading off for military service, Jim Hourihan spent a few months working with Ollie McGuire, a short, stocky, chain-smoking, corporate lawyer of sparse sentences and gruff words. McGuire handled labor negotiations on behalf of clients like department store Woodward & Lothrop. Hourihan enjoyed watching McGuire dealing with "Woodie's" vice president for personnel, a perfectly coifed and "classy" woman. As ashes dropped from the cigarette always dangling from his lips, McGuire would "curse like a bandit," poles apart from his client in style but a very effective negotiator. But two years trying general court-martials at Fort Knox helped turn Hourihan's already wavering interest in corporate and tax law more firmly toward litigation, and when he returned to Hogan & Hartson in 1963 he joined Jack Arness, Paul Connolly, Frank Roberson, Frank Casey, and others in the trial department.

After a summer clerkship at Hogan & Hartson in 1961, Jay Ricks also was eager to join the firm's trial department when he graduated from the Georgetown Law Center in 1962. But Duke Patrick, head of the communications department, had other plans for him. Described by a younger partner, not fondly, as "an old curmudgeon," Patrick was a powerful figure in the firm because of the large business he managed in the communications department — what one colleague called "the power of the department." He tended to be abrupt with others, which did not help bridge the gap between his generation of founders and the new group of leaders emerging in the firm in the 1960s. One of that group later summoned up an image of Patrick that aptly conveyed the breadth of the generational divide — "right out of the New Yorker, with his straw hat and cane and seersucker suit. He toddled off to their club over there, the Metropolitan, for lunch." The reference to "their" club was entirely unselfconscious.

Ricks asked his friend Howard Roycroft if he could possibly go into litigation instead of communications, but Roycroft told him, "Patrick says you're elected." As it happened, Ricks found plenty of litigation work in the dizzying growth of the communications industry, where established media companies fought at first to restrict, then to absorb, newer technologies. As Ricks summarized the history of the communications business, newspapers had once perceived a threat from radio so

NASA AND THE SPACE PROGRAM CAPTURED MUCH OF THE NEW FRONTIER SPIRIT OF THE KENNEDY PRESIDENCY. HERE ASTRONAUT JOHN GLENN, JR., DESCRIBES TO PRESIDENT KENNEDY THE FRIENDSHIP 7 SPACE CAPSULE THAT CARRIED HIM IN ORBIT AROUND THE EARTH IN FEBRUARY 1962. VICE PRESIDENT LYNDON JOHNSON (R) LOOKS ON ATTENTIVELY.

they bought AM radio stations. Those stations then perceived a threat from FM radio, so they fought for FM licenses. Television was the next technology threat that had to be absorbed, and finally, when Ricks found his feet at Hogan & Hartson in the early 1960s, cable television became the new challenge and opportunity for media entrepreneurs.[22]

Ricks's representation of cable TV clients like Jack Kent Cooke, whose Teleprompter Cable Communications, Inc., became the nation's largest cable provider in the 1970s, at times presented interesting conflicts for the firm's other, more traditional media clients. These were not necessarily conflicts of interest but "philosophical" business conflicts in which traditional television broadcasters, for example, simply didn't like the idea of Hogan & Hartson representing "upstart" cable businesses. In such instances Lester Cohen's deep reservoir of experience and goodwill, and the respect that he elicited from clients, usually succeeded in reassuring long-standing clients that their interests would not be shortchanged by the firm's taking the new work.

John F. Kennedy's narrow victory over Richard Nixon in 1960 brought mixed feelings of regret and relief to Nelson Hartson, who knew he had come close to losing John Warner to politics. But the Kennedys brought a "Camelot" mystique to Washington that even years of hard-boiled fact-finding and revisionism have not successfully expunged from memory or history. The new administration also brought tough new expectations for federal agencies to move quickly and efficiently to achieve their goals. With the glamour and optimism of NASA's space program, the idealism of the Peace Corps, the lean flexibility of the Green Berets, and a charming wife and delightful children, the World War II Navy hero John Kennedy seemed to have it all. Despite the failed Bay of Pigs invasion, the famed Cuban missile crisis just eighteen months later showed his cool courage, belying skeptics who questioned the young President's wisdom and maturity and wondered if he had any substance to back up his style.

The President's brother and U.S. Attorney General, Robert, had known Barrett Prettyman as a fellow law student at the University of Virginia. He called on Prettyman in 1961 to take leave from Hogan & Hartson to help bring 1,113 prisoners home from Cuba after the Bay of Pigs fiasco. Working out of the Justice Department and then in Florida, Prettyman ended up flying to Cuba, negotiating with Fidel Castro inside Ernest Hemingway's abandoned home, and flying out on Christmas Eve with a planeload of Bay of Pigs prisoners. Prettyman subsequently served the Kennedy administration in a number of ad hoc assignments. One November afternoon in 1963, while still on leave from the firm, he returned from a lunch with Stan Harris to his temporary office in the Old Executive Office Building, just west of the White House. He placed a call to Capitol Hill and had just begun to speak when the other person said something rather strange. "No, no, don't worry, we know all about it." Know all about what? "About the President being shot."

Prettyman put the phone down. Here was a crisis like none other. He got up from his desk, went downstairs, and crossed over to the White House. "It was like a death camp," he remembered. "It was just awful. People were sitting and staring, and there was great confusion." Hours later the newly sworn President Lyndon Johnson arrived by helicopter and walked into the Oval Office. The sight of the new President so quickly taking Kennedy's place created a powerful aftershock to the afternoon's trauma. "It brought the whole thing home in a way nothing else could have," said Prettyman.

Prettyman soon returned to Hogan & Hartson, where he promptly received a powerful antidote to the heady atmosphere of the White House. He was appointed by the court to represent a Ms. Jacqueline Johnson, who had been arrested flagging down cars on 14th Street in the early hours of the morning and charged with vagrancy. Among the criteria for vagrancy was "leading a profligate life," a deliciously ambiguous notion that intrigued the former Supreme Court clerk. At Ms. Johnson's trial Prettyman involved the arresting officer in an effort to define the profligate life. "Well," said the officer, "it means doing something partially bad, kind of bad, over a period of time." Like, say, going to the racetrack regularly and betting on horses? "Yeah, that's right." "Well now," Prettyman continued, "I understand that J. Edgar Hoover goes to the track on a pretty regular basis and I assume he bets when he's there. Would you say he's leading a profligate life?" "Yes, sir, I would," answered the officer with admirable consistency, as the courtroom broke out in laughter.

A *Washington Post* reporter who happened to have wandered in caught the exchange and figured he had the makings of an excellent story. The next morning two FBI agents greeted Prettyman when he arrived for work and handed him a scathing letter from Hoover denouncing the use of his name to obtain "cheap publicity." Prettyman wrote back, explaining as best he could that Hoover had missed his point. The reference to the FBI director's racetrack outings had been meant to dismantle, not confirm, the concept of a profligate life, he ventured. In any event, the D.C. Court of Appeals reversed Ms. Johnson's conviction, at Prettyman's behest. That ended the matter, and Ms. Johnson and J. Edgar Hoover went their separate ways.

Inspired partly by John F. Kennedy's call for renewed idealism, by Robert Kennedy's gradual but increasingly clarion call for racial justice, and mostly by the courage of civil rights leaders like Martin Luther King, Jr., and Ralph Abernathy, civil rights workers traveled into the South to confront segregation in its lair. Rosa Parks's refusal to surrender her seat to a white man on a Montgomery, Alabama, bus in 1955 and the "sit-in" conducted at a Greensboro, North Carolina, lunch counter in 1960 by four African-American students were among many acts of bravery that helped embolden demonstrators as they faced the likelihood of arrests, beatings, and possibly death.

In December 1961, at the request of the Kennedy administration, Barrett Prettyman helped manage a herculean effort to exchange goods for the 1,113 prisoners held in Cuba after the failed Bay of Pigs invasion. The task required much diplomacy, as when Prettyman engaged an otherwise antagonistic Fidel Castro in an animated discussion of author Ernest Hemingway, a former resident of Cuba. The operation concluded with the joyous return of the prisoners to the U.S. in time for Christmas.

THE "MARCH FOR JOBS AND FREEDOM" IN WASHINGTON, D.C., ON AUGUST 28, 1963, WAS THE LARGEST GATHERING UP TO THAT TIME. AT THE LINCOLN MEMORIAL ABOUT A QUARTER OF A MILLION PEOPLE HEARD MARTIN LUTHER KING, JR., DELIVER HIS NOW IMMORTAL "I HAVE A DREAM" SPEECH.

The brutality and violence that indeed greeted demonstrators on several occasions galvanized Americans who, for the first time, were able to witness it on national television. Shocked by what the camera revealed, the country moved closer toward fulfillment of its most basic constitutional promises to all its citizens. With help from President Johnson's famously effective jawboning, known by Washington insiders as "the treatment," a strongly Democratic Congress passed the landmark Civil Rights Act in the summer of 1964 and in the following year approved the Voting Rights Act.

But television was equally effective in transmitting scenes of urban rioting, burning, and looting in the summer of 1964 in Harlem and in the Watts section of Los Angeles a year later. Concurrent with the advancement of civil rights was an increasing impatience for justice among African-Americans and a growing belief — fed by frustration — that separation and confrontation, not peaceful integration, were the preferred means of achieving true equality. Not all rioting was ideologically motivated, but it certainly signaled deep and chronic social ills. And at its visible surface it was alarming. Along with a rising crime rate, it heightened many Americans' fears and led to strong calls to restore "law and order." And in the background, the Vietnam War's seemingly endless drain on the Great Society's economic resources sapped Lyndon Johnson's political capital as well. Gambling that the booming economy could support his ambitious domestic agenda as well as a war in the far-off jungles of Indochina, Johnson worriedly burned his presidential candle at both ends.

Hogan & Hartson's offices had been in Washington's central business district for sixty years. Now that district began to suffer as shoppers patronized new, suburban malls and avoided the capital's increasingly crime-ridden downtown streets. The downward slide of D.C.'s urban core was not likely to be reversed anytime soon. Loiterers in the Colorado Building's lobby unnerved tenants and visitors, and the firm's offices had been burglarized twice in the nine months before the summer of 1964, when the firm began looking into an alternate location. A committee reported that the venerable Colorado Building was "62 years old, is dirty inside and out, and generally gives an out-of-date appearance." Associate Charles Halleck, later a D.C. Superior Court Judge, made a report of a different sort by boxing up a dead rat and shipping it off to the landlord.

So in 1965 Hogan & Hartson's forty-three attorneys relocated to the Chanin Building at I Street and Connecticut Avenue, N.W., in the short block of Connecticut Avenue between Farragut Square and Lafayette Park, just north of the White House. The firm had not traveled very far from its former site — both the Colorado and Chanin buildings were only a few blocks from the White House — but now it had a new lease on life in the professional center of town, with fine restaurants and hotel facilities nearby for clients and meetings.

Next year the Executive Committee's "mistake of its life," as Seymour Mintz had called the decision not to make Edward Bennett Williams a partner, came back with an unhappy echo. Since leaving Hogan & Hartson in 1949, Williams had built a thriving criminal practice on his reputation as an inspired and fearsome litigator. But now, in 1967, he needed to hire some help and turned to the experienced litigators at his former firm. Paul Connolly was exuberant, impatient with administrative constraints, and ripe for a change. He had long been at odds with the meticulous head of the firm's trial department, Frank Roberson, whose desk at any hour of the day was a model of cleanliness and order.

Chafing under Roberson's management and temperament, Connolly was restless for both room and recognition. So he took Williams's offer, bringing with him partner Jeremiah Collins and associate David Webster. The new firm of Williams & Connolly was born, vaulting high on the energies and ambitions of its dynamic namesakes. In his day Frank Hogan had been no different. Connolly's leaving re-enacted Williams's earlier departure, reminding Hogan & Hartson of the perennial law firm management challenge of balancing necessary institutional discipline with an appreciation for the equally necessary individualism and entrepreneurship that drive growth.

A few years later Ed Williams, Lester Cohen, and Duke Guider, Williams's father-in-law, were chatting at the Guiders' New Hampshire home, Adair. Williams had remained a close part of the family wing of the firm, and Cohen was a universally loved adoptee. It was an

THE CHANIN BUILDING, 815 CONNECTICUT AVE., N.W., HOME TO HOGAN & HARTSON FROM 1965 TO 1987.

The Colorado Building, at 14th and G Streets, NW, in Washington, D.C., was a prestigious address when Frank Hogan opened his office there in 1907. Built just four years earlier, the Colorado offered tenants proximity to restaurants, shopping, the White House, the Treasury Department, and numerous other government agencies. The building was just one of several constructed by Thomas F. Walsh, an Irish immigrant who struck it rich in a Colorado gold mine in the nineteenth century, then moved to Washington, D.C. Walsh's daughter, Evalyn, became famous as an extravagant hostess and the purchaser of the famous Hope diamond, now in the possession of the Smithsonian Institution.

The Colorado Building suffered a period of decline in the mid-twentieth century as rising crime rates and fear of rioting drove many shops and tenants away from Washington's central business district. In 1965 Hogan & Hartson left the old Colorado's faded glory and moved to the Chanin Building at Connecticut Avenue and 17th Street, NW, where it stayed until relocating to Columbia Square in 1987. Hogan & Hartson's move back to Washington's traditional downtown area corresponded with a general revitalization of the city's center that benefitted the old Colorado Building as well. In 1988 a developer gave the landmark structure a thorough renovation, adding modern conveniences while restoring the Colorado's original grand style.

EDWARD A. MCDERMOTT CAME TO HOGAN & HARTSON IN 1963 AFTER SERVING AS DIRECTOR OF THE OFFICE OF EMERGENCY PREPAREDNESS IN THE KENNEDY WHITE HOUSE. HIS INTERNATIONAL VISION HELPED SHAPE HOGAN & HARTSON'S DEVELOPMENT FROM THE MID 1960S UNTIL HIS RETIREMENT IN 1988.

especially convivial evening at Adair, and the happy trio struck upon the idea that Williams might rejoin his old firm, making it Williams, Hogan & Hartson. That led to further negotiations back in Washington, where it was decided that for trademark preservation reasons the name would have to be Hogan, Hartson & Williams. That suited Williams well enough, recalled Mintz, but Connolly objected to going off the masthead and back into the relative anonymity of mere partnership. His insistence that the name order be Williams, Hogan & Hartson dissolved the reunification move, though it was clearly a proxy for the more important management issue that simply reuniting people under one roof would not resolve. Like a failed marriage, if it hadn't worked before it was not likely to work now.

After Connolly, Collins, and Webster left in 1967, Hogan & Hartson began replenishing its litigator ranks by recruiting assistant U.S. Attorney William O. Bittman. Bittman came to Hogan & Hartson in 1967 with a hard-earned reputation for thoroughness and success in the courtroom. He had won praise from Attorney General Robert Kennedy for his successful prosecution in Chicago, under extraordinary circumstances, of teamster boss Jimmy Hoffa in an extremely complex pension fraud case. Bittman, then just thirty-two years old, had taken on the chief prosecutor's role when the lead attorney became seriously ill just days after the trial had begun. The case could not be postponed or retried. "At that point," explained a former colleague of Bittman, "jeopardy had attached, so if the government walks away from it, that's the end of the case."

Bittman had not been involved in the prosecution up to that point and now had only a few days to master a mountain of complicated evidence involving 120 witnesses. On Monday morning in the courtroom, in his tough, workmanlike way, Bill Bittman set to work as if he'd been on the case for months. Jack Miller, then an assistant U.S. Attorney in Chicago, recalled it as one of the most courageous things he had ever seen on the part of a trial lawyer.[23] Bittman won the case. Three years later he came to Washington, D.C., to prosecute U.S. Senate aide Bobby Baker on tax evasion charges. Baker's attorney was Edward Bennett Williams, who also happened to be Bittman's neighbor in Potomac, Maryland. Bittman could not match Williams for oratory or courtroom flair, but he succeeded in winning Baker's conviction. The emotional Williams did not often lose a case, and the Baker verdict permanently frosted his relationship with the imperturbable prosecutor.

PRESIDENT FRANKLIN D. ROOSEVELT HAD NO GREATER ADMIRER AND EMULATOR THAN U.S. CONGRESSMAN FROM TEXAS, LYNDON BAINES JOHNSON. IN MAY 1937 JOHNSON GREETED FDR IN GALVESTON, TEXAS, AS THE PRESIDENT WAS FINISHING A FISHING TRIP IN THE GULF OF MEXICO.

Edward McDermott was another Kennedy administration official who, like Barrett Prettyman, returned to private practice as the Johnson administration placed its own stamp on official Washington. He had run Kennedy's campaign in Iowa and was rewarded with the directorship of the Office of Emergency Preparedness, a precursor to the present Federal Emergency Management Agency. McDermott also had served as national security advisor to the President and had been present in the White House meetings in October 1962 when Kennedy determined to stare down Nikita Khrushchev as Soviet ships laden with missiles headed for Cuba. He did not forget what he learned there about leadership and judgment.

McDermott, described as "not the kind of lawyer who drafts lengthy, complicated reports," turned his energy and political skill to expanding Hogan & Hartson's practice into new areas when he joined the firm at the end of 1964, and to shaping a new, more ambitious vision for its future. Prettyman used to say that if he knew one or two people on the elevator, McDermott knew them all. Younger attorneys called him "Mandrake," though never to his face, for the seemingly magical things he could accomplish on behalf of clients like Mercedes-Benz of North America, as well as for his sartorial splendor.

McDermott's deft attraction of the Japanese Embassy to the firm was a legendary instance of his Mandrake "magic" at work. While attending a Washington reception with his wife, Naola, he noticed a rather shy-looking couple standing uncomfortably off to the side. He and "Na" went over and struck up a conversation, whereupon they discovered they were speaking with Akitane Kiuchi, a high-ranking Japanese diplomat, and his wife. Mrs. Kiuchi happened to mention that she had been a great admirer of John F. Kennedy, something that McDermott remembered as he later wished the couple a good night.

The new Kennedy half-dollar had just been introduced and was not yet in wide circulation. The next day McDermott found one, slipped it into an envelope with a note of remembrance, and dropped the gift through the mail slot of the Kiuchis's front door. A couple of weeks later Mr. Kiuchi called

HOGAN & HARTSON PARTNERS AT THE F STREET CLUB, 1965.

George U. Carneal joined the firm in 1962. He was instrumental in developing Hogan & Hartson's aviation practice. His eclectic interests include *pro bono* work on behalf of organizations trying to preserve habitat for great apes and other primates.

McDermott and invited him to the embassy to meet the ambassador. The meeting went well, and soon the embassy retained Hogan & Hartson as its legal counsel. A bit of friendliness to strangers, capped by the thoughtfulness of a small memento, had garnered a new client and years of significant legal work for the firm. As McDermott often reminded younger attorneys looking to attract clients, it was quite a return on a fifty-cent investment.

In 1962 another Judge Prettyman clerk, George Carneal, followed John Warner into the firm. Carneal worked with Ollie McGuire on commercial and real estate transactions. McGuire was "not a very loquacious guy," Carneal recalled, echoing Jim Hourihan's experience with the veteran lawyer. Carneal's annual evaluation consisted of McGuire sticking his head in the door and growling, "You're doing fine." But the young lawyer appreciated McGuire's accomplishments, such as his original development of the basic legal infrastructure for regional shopping centers in the 1960s.

Carneal did not always appreciate McGuire's casualness, however. Once McGuire was scheduled to attend a meeting between his client, who owned a tall apartment block across the Potomac in Arlington, Virginia, and a prominent New York buyer, Harry B. Helmsley. At the last minute, though, McGuire could not be found. The Executive Committee called in Carneal and said, "You go do it, kid." So Carneal marched off to face Helmsley and his lawyer, "probably the most experienced real estate lawyer in Manhattan," for his first solo transaction. To make matters worse, Carneal's client, an eccentric man, was nervous and erratic during the negotiations and stayed alone in a separate room while Carneal ran back and forth. At one point Helmsley remarked sympathetically to him, "I really pity you." But Carneal brought the deal off, then went to work with McDermott on a lengthy railroad merger case before the Interstate Commerce Commission.

Jack Arness's practice also had expanded by 1960. The Beck sisters' collision with the back of a D.C. bus had launched his solo trial career years earlier. Now another automobile case, though with more tragic results, led to Arness's winning one of the firm's most loyal clients. A man named Kosberg owned a station wagon and supplemented his income by ferrying children to and from school. It seemed a decent enough way to earn some money. But a torts disaster lay in wait for Kosberg, who had not upgraded his insurance to include livery coverage for this new use of his car. When several children were seriously injured in an accident while riding in Kosberg's wagon, the Hartford Insurance Company brought Arness into the case to establish that there was no applicable insurance. Arness won a declaratory judgment which later was sustained on appeal. He also won Hartford as a regular client. The company thereafter turned to Arness and his team of litigators for help on its toughest cases, including a later avalanche of asbestos cases that continues to the present day.

Stan Harris's practice also broadened, though he shouldered the new work with more grit than zest. He had more than enough work in the communications department, but an emergency cropped up in the firm's energy practice, then known as the power department. One of Hogan & Hartson's senior attorneys, Howard Boyd, had accepted an executive position with a major client, the El Paso Natural Gas Company. George Horning had taken Boyd's place, but Horning's style alienated many of El Paso's mid-level executives. "He recognized only two classes of people, either officers or enlisted men," said a colleague. The client gave Hogan & Hartson a year to put together a new team. Harris was drafted to assist partner C. Frank Reifsnyder. At the same time, the communications department kept handing him assignments, perhaps because it appreciated his diligence. Lester Cohen used to ask, "Has this been Harrisized?" — meaning, had someone gone over the document with a fine-toothed comb?

Harris's solution to these new demands on his time was the only one available to him: "Night work," he said. Night work was not endowed with any special virtue or career advantage at Hogan & Hartson, but everyone knew it was necessary at times. Harris made it his practice to work nearly every night so that he could have the weekends free with his young children. The hard work was eased somewhat by close contact with colleagues who also might be working late. Often they shared supper at a local eatery or at the Hot Shoppes cafeteria downstairs on 14th Street, boosting each other's spirits with coffee refills and commiseration.

In the mid-1960s Hogan & Hartson was already a relatively large law firm. With nearly forty-five attorneys, it just missed ranking among the approximately twenty-five law firms outside New York City with more than fifty lawyers. Unlike most law firms nationally, it had a written partnership agreement and a highly diverse practice intimately connected to the federal government. From the New Deal to the New Frontier to the Great Society, the growing presence and authority of federal agencies seemed an irreversible trend. But Hogan & Hartson also served numerous corporate clients in matters not directly involving federal regulatory disputes. Merle Thorpe, Jr., who had joined the firm in 1941, worked on securities issues, and in 1966 Robert Jeffers joined the firm's corporate practice as its forty-third lawyer.

In 1967 the banking industry was grappling with a flurry of new regulatory and legislative changes. John Warner, who had virtually replaced Nelson Hartson as the firm's principal attorney for Riggs Bank, needed help. Just at that time Dennis Lehr, a former SEC attorney who taught a course on banking law at Georgetown Law School and who now worked at the Treasury Department, took Warner up on a long-standing offer to "give me a call." Lehr had met Warner a couple of years earlier but had not been ready to leave his interesting assignments in the Office of the Comptroller of the Currency at Treasury. Recently, however, his brother had died and thirty-five-year-old Lehr had become the sole support of his mother.

Lehr met with Warner, Hartson, and the Executive Committee and was impressed with their

diversity — the Ivy League Thorpe, living "the Washington bachelor clubby life"; Mintz's intellect and the cachet of representing Howard Hughes; the gregarious McDermott and his political acumen; and Lester Cohen, who "dared to wear a sport coat and would come into anybody's office, put his leg over a chair and ask, 'How ya doin'?'" So on May 1, 1967, Dennis Lehr became the firm's forty-fourth attorney. In eighteen months he was named a partner. He knew through his former Yale Law School classmates of firms where "it was just keep your head down, grind out the hours, and satisfy the partner you're working with." But at Hogan & Hartson, Lehr found that "you could live a likeable, schizophrenic life. I could be second or third lawyer on a project, but also the number one guy on something I brought in. The firm encouraged entrepreneurship, and I found that healthy."

But the diversity only went so far. Hogan & Hartson was an establishment as well as an established firm in the 1960s. When Robert Kapp came to the firm in 1961 from the University of Michigan Law School, he found "a very, very conservative environment that was very imbedded in the local community." With the exception of Mintz, whose reputation as an eminent tax lawyer had drawn Kapp to the firm, the young associate found the old-line clients and the Metropolitan Club connections a bit daunting. This was not the stuff from which social change and reform readily emerged. And yet there was a sometimes surprising streak of affability in the firm that tended to subvert rigidity and give stuffiness an airing out. It was a bit like Frank Hogan, ardent member of the Liberty League, denouncing the New Deal's authority on the one hand while on the other encouraging young attorneys to "enter and graze" on the "greener pastures" that the New Deal's river of administrative law had nurtured.[24]

Early in his career Kapp sought the Executive Committee's approval to take on some pro bono cases for the American Civil Liberties Union. He was surprised to find that Nelson Hartson, who he said "probably was in general disagreement with the agenda of the

American Civil Liberties Union," was very generous in his support. It made a big difference to Kapp that the leadership of the firm let people pursue their own interests and did not try to force its views on others. Persons otherwise inclined, whatever their point of view, usually did not find a permanent home at Hogan & Hartson.

ROBERT H. KAPP JOINED H&H IN 1962 FROM THE TAX DIVISION, U.S. DEPARTMENT OF JUSTICE. RECENTLY HE HAS WORKED WITH FRIENDS AND COLLEAGUES TO ESTABLISH THE INTERNATIONAL SENIOR LAWYERS PROJECT, A *PRO BONO* EFFORT TO UTILIZE THE SKILLS OF RETIRED OR NEARLY RETIRED ATTORNEYS IN A VARIETY OF HUMAN RIGHTS, ECONOMIC DEVELOPMENT AND RULE OF LAW PROJECTS.

Jim Hourihan remembered going before the Executive Committee one year for the annual ritual of setting his salary and awarding his bonus. As Mintz, McDermott, and Roycroft looked on from their seats around the table, George Monk delivered the prefatory incantation, "You've done well," then intoned the young lawyer's accomplishments that year. He announced a bonus of $5,000. Hourihan's face fell; he had expected much more. He looked around the table at the august visages, each partner lowering his head back into his papers as if to say, "That's it, you may go now." But Hourihan hesitated, and Monk asked him, "Is there anything you'd like to tell the committee?" "Yes," came the honest answer, "I'm disappointed." As the heads slowly lowered once more, Hourihan got up to leave. He cast a final, hopeful glance around the table and caught Howard Roycroft winking at him. He later learned that the committee had doubled his bonus. It was, as Dennis Lehr said, a likeable life.

Through the Great Depression, World War II, the assassination of President John F. Kennedy, and the violence attending the advance of civil rights for African-Americans, Hogan & Hartson worked and grew, quietly and respectably, in its Washington, D.C., home. The federal government's role in managing the nation's crises made the city, like a monitoring airplane in the eye of a hurricane, both the center of, and a shelter from, the surrounding social storms of unemployment, war, and civil disturbance. But Washington's relatively sheltered days were soon to end, for it had come to recognize, too late, a storm brewing in its own backyard. In the late 1960s Hogan & Hartson, along with the rest of the nation, encountered the turbulence of changing times.

Chapter 3
Changing Times
1968-1979

On Thursday evening, April 4, 1968, Dennis Lehr was working late in the firm's offices on Connecticut Avenue. The news was still in its first, fresh stage of shock. At 6:00 p.m., James Earl Ray had leveled his rifle across a window ledge in Memphis, Tennessee, and fatally shot Martin Luther King, Jr., in the neck. After three consecutive years of urban rioting across America, King's murder more than extinguished a bright star — it also sparked rioting in more than one hundred cities and eclipsed an era of nonviolent civil rights protest by African-Americans.

Several blocks away from Lehr's office, at the 14th Street headquarters of the local chapter of the Student Nonviolent Coordinating Committee (SNCC), Stokely Carmichael, leader of the Black Power movement, called for a demonstration down the 14th Street commercial corridor to urge stores to close in honor of King. "If Kennedy had died," he exhorted, "all these stores would have closed. Martin Luther King is our leader and we are going to show him some respect."[1] At about 8:00 p.m. dozens of people started moving down 14th Street, gathering more and more until hundreds joined from the surrounding streets.

The crowd was launched. It quickly jettisoned Carmichael, who could not regain control. There was no leader, no purpose, no goal, just an accumulation of anger and the prospect of release. By 11:00 p.m. forty stores had been looted and one car had been set on fire. Lehr had called his wife — yes, he was okay. He'd be home soon. He also had remembered that John Warner and his wife, Cathy, were out of town. So he telephoned Warner's mother in Georgetown to see if she needed anything and to remind her to close the windows and lock the doors. By 2:30 a.m. eighty-five persons had been arrested and D.C. firefighters were dousing several blazes. The violence was starting to spread. By 4:00 a.m. the arrest toll reached two hundred.

Martin Luther King, Jr.'s assassination on April 4, 1968, triggered days of rioting in many American cities, including the Nation's Capital. This scene on 7th St., N.E., shows some of the worst physical damage.

Washingtonians went to work the next morning, most of them unaware of the spreading trouble that King's death had released in their city. After a brief lull at dawn, roving crowds resumed smashing store windows on 7th Street, H Street, lower Georgia Avenue, and

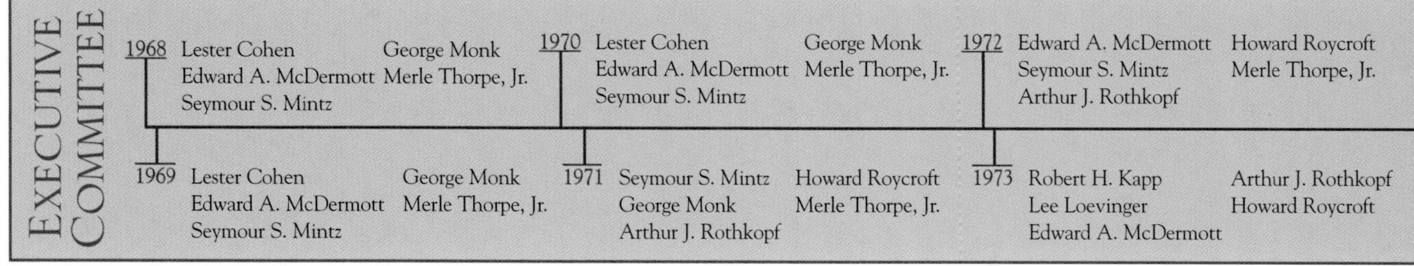

Executive Committee

1968 Lester Cohen, Edward A. McDermott, Seymour S. Mintz, George Monk, Merle Thorpe, Jr.

1969 Lester Cohen, Edward A. McDermott, Seymour S. Mintz, George Monk, Merle Thorpe, Jr.

1970 Lester Cohen, Edward A. McDermott, Seymour S. Mintz, George Monk, Merle Thorpe, Jr.

1971 Seymour S. Mintz, George Monk, Arthur J. Rothkopf, Howard Roycroft, Merle Thorpe, Jr.

1972 Edward A. McDermott, Seymour S. Mintz, Arthur J. Rothkopf, Howard Roycroft, Merle Thorpe, Jr.

1973 Robert H. Kapp, Lee Loevinger, Edward A. McDermott, Arthur J. Rothkopf, Howard Roycroft

PRESIDENT LYNDON JOHNSON AND THE REV. MARTIN LUTHER KING, JR., BOTH WORKED HARD TO ADVANCE THE CAUSE OF CIVIL RIGHTS. BUT AT TIMES THE EFFORT PROVED FRUSTRATING, AS EVIDENCED IN THIS PHOTO OF A MEETING AT THE WHITE HOUSE.

AS ATTORNEY GENERAL, ROBERT KENNEDY PLACED HIS UNIQUE ENERGIES SQUARELY BEHIND THE CAUSE OF EQUAL RIGHTS AND JUSTICE FOR ALL CITIZENS. HIS ASSASSINATION ON JUNE 5, 1968, JUST TWO MONTHS AFTER DR. KING'S MURDER, WAS AN IMMEASURABLE LOSS FOR THE NATION.

across the Anacostia River in Southeast Washington. By mid-afternoon on that clear, sunny Friday, rioters were smashing store windows and looting in the downtown central business district, just next door to Hogan & Hartson's old offices in the Colorado Building. A police captain yelled at a fifteen-year-old carrying an armload of looted clothing, "Why are you taking those things?" "I don't know," the teenager answered.[2]

Visitors on the hilltop of the United States Capitol watched smoke clouds from seventy separate fires drift across the rooftops of Washington's low-lying buildings. The city canceled its annual Cherry Blossom festivities, and Mayor Walter Washington imposed an overnight curfew as federal workers, dismissed early, jammed all roads out of town. Four thousand troops called in to help police were bogged down in traffic and could not reach critical destinations. Telephone service was overwhelmed. "We all bailed out of the office," Stan Harris recalled, "with the fires and the looting and not knowing what in the hell was happening."

The rioting continued through Friday night and Saturday. By Sunday morning 11,500 armed troops and 1,440 police officers patrolled the nation's capital. Four persons had died during the previous day's violence and about 400 were injured. Nearly 2,700 persons were arrested, one-third of them for looting. Tear gas and smoke from 510 fires drifted ominously over the city, and suburban fire departments were called in to help D.C. firefighters. Before the riot was over, nine lives had been lost, along with $15 million worth of real estate and millions more in personal property. A total of 13,600 federal troops and National Guardsmen patrolled the city's streets.[3] When calm returned, Washingtonians, like most Americans, faced an old and vexing problem with a fresh realization: their racially divided house would not stand. Some wished to reinforce it by the vigorous application of "law and order." Others thought a thorough renovation would be a better long-term solution. Hogan & Hartson's leaders were among many in the nation's capital who recognized that the crisis demanded a strong response, but as yet they were not sure what form it should take.

Americans were divided in other ways, too. President Johnson's Great Society had been expensive,

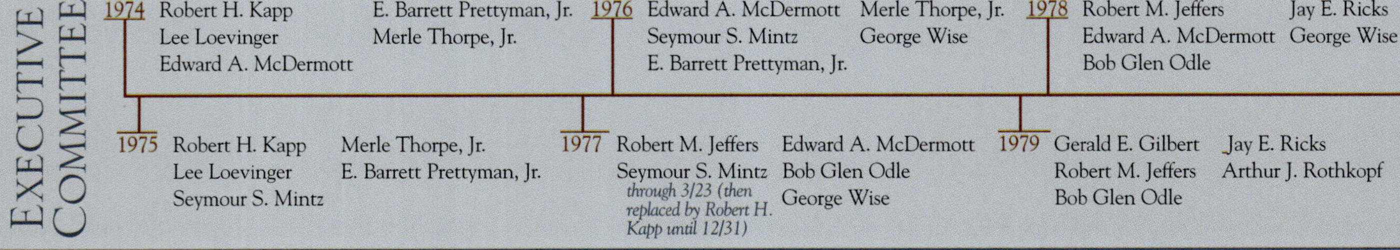

EXECUTIVE COMMITTEE

1974	Robert H. Kapp, Lee Loevinger, Edward A. McDermott, E. Barrett Prettyman, Jr., Merle Thorpe, Jr.
1975	Robert H. Kapp, Lee Loevinger, Seymour S. Mintz, Merle Thorpe, Jr., E. Barrett Prettyman, Jr.
1976	Edward A. McDermott, Seymour S. Mintz, E. Barrett Prettyman, Jr., Merle Thorpe, Jr., George Wise
1977	Robert M. Jeffers, Seymour S. Mintz *through 3/23 (then replaced by Robert H. Kapp until 12/31)*, Edward A. McDermott, Bob Glen Odle, George Wise
1978	Robert M. Jeffers, Edward A. McDermott, Bob Glen Odle, Jay E. Ricks, George Wise
1979	Gerald E. Gilbert, Robert M. Jeffers, Bob Glen Odle, Jay E. Ricks, Arthur J. Rothkopf

but so had the Vietnam War. Fighting communism there cost taxpayers $27 billion in 1967 alone, doubling the federal deficit and triggering an inflation that, boosted by the energy crisis of 1973-1974, lasted through the next decade. Meanwhile, the Cold War rationale for the Vietnam War was losing credibility. Although North Vietnam's Tet Offensive in January 1968 had been turned back by U.S. and South Vietnamese troops, its force and effectiveness, reaching even the U.S. Embassy in Saigon, shocked Americans who had believed government reports that the United States was winning the war.

On March 31, 1968, just five days before Martin Luther King, Jr.'s, murder, President Lyndon Johnson, architect of the most sweeping social change since the New Deal, went on national television to announce he would not seek reelection. It was a stunning moment. Perhaps no President had ever mastered Washington as thoroughly as "LBJ." Still, a rogue conflict on the other side of the world that he did not start — but did not know how to stop — undid him. Johnson was crestfallen on the television screen, his jowly face hanging, as never before, in defeat. Incredibly, the war dragged on for seven more years under a new President, equally determined to master Washington. That determination, rather than Vietnam, would prove Richard Nixon's undoing.

Sirhan Sirhan's assassination of presidential candidate Robert Kennedy in a Los Angeles hotel on June 5, 1968, was an almost unbelievable sequel to Martin Luther King, Jr.'s, murder and a heart-wrenching, haunting reminder of his brother's fate nearly five years earlier. But the traumatic year was not yet finished. The 1968 Democratic National Convention, held in Chicago in August, contrasted old-style politics inside the convention hall with chaotic antiwar protests outside. A nation already reeling from the April riots witnessed assaults on nonviolent protestors by police untrained and unprepared for the task they faced. Television viewers also saw attempts by radicals to provoke police violence as other demonstrators chanted, "The whole world is watching." As the convention hall's air vents sucked in tear gas from the streets, delegates nominated the "happy warrior," Hubert Humphrey, as the party's candidate to face Richard Nixon in the fall.

The fissures created by race and Vietnam were most evident in politics, but they also cut through university campuses, businesses, families, and law firms. In 1969 new associate Sara-Ann ("Sally") Determan unknowingly stumbled on a breach in Hogan & Hartson's usual equanimity when her antiwar activities angered an older partner. Determan had joined the firm's tax and estate practice in September 1968 after a clerkship with noted liberal jurist Henry W. Edgerton on the D.C. Circuit Court of Appeals. Within a year she helped organize a group called Lawyers Against the War and on one occasion circulated to Hogan & Hartson's nearly sixty attorneys a memo announcing an upcoming rally for the group. The next day her telephone rang. "Come to my office," said the partner's stern voice. When she arrived he was livid, grasping her memo in his hand and shaking it as he decried her bad judgment. "You're aiding and abetting the enemy!" he declared, referring to the North Vietnamese. He added that she should resign because he would see to it that she had no future in the firm.

LYNDON JOHNSON'S EFFORT TO CREATE A GREAT SOCIETY EVENTUALLY RAN AGROUND ON THE SHOALS OF VIETNAM. THIS MOVING PHOTO SUGGESTS THE DEPTHS OF THE PRESIDENT'S WEARINESS AND DISAPPOINTMENT.

PARTNERS

1968
John Curtain
Sherwin J. Markman

1969
Kevin P. Charles
Robert J. Elliott
John M. Ferren
Dennis J. Lehr
Jay E. Ricks
Robert M. Jeffers
Arthur J. Rothkopf

1970
John M. Ferren
Gerald E. Gilbert
James A. Hourihan
Lee Loevinger
Charles E. Shreve
Jerome N. Sonosky

1971
Austin S. Mittler
Charles E. Allen

1972
Gary L. Christensen
Vincent H. Cohen, Sr.
Owen M. Johnson, Jr.
Jerris Leonard
Howard R. Moskof

SARA-ANN "SALLY" DETERMAN JOINED HOGAN & HARTSON IN 1968 AND BECAME THE FIRM'S FIRST FEMALE PARTNER IN 1975. DETERMAN HAS HELD OFFICE IN NUMEROUS PROFESSIONAL ASSOCIATIONS, INCLUDING THE PRESIDENCY OF THE DISTRICT OF COLUMBIA BAR (1990-1991), AND HAS BEEN A STRONG ADVOCATE FOR HUMAN RIGHTS AND THE PROTECTION OF CIVIL LIBERTIES THROUGHOUT HER CAREER AS AN ESTATE PLANNING LAWYER.

When attorney Sara-Ann ("Sally") Determan interviewed for positions with law firms in 1967, she stated she had one child already and probably would be having another. She told interviewers that she would be willing to work evenings and weekends at home, but that "except in rare emergencies, I can't work evenings and weekends in the office." A typical response was, "My dear, around here we have rare emergencies three times a week."

However, when Determan presented her situation to Seymour Mintz at Hogan & Hartson, he replied, "Well, none of us likes to work evenings and weekends, if we don't have to." Determan knew then that she had discovered not just a congenial firm but one with a sense of balance. Hogan & Hartson surely had its share of "rare emergencies," but they would be managed with cooperation and understanding. In 1975 Determan became a partner at the firm. Nearly thirty years later, Hogan & Hartson's success in promoting women to partnership topped that of every other large D.C.-based firm.

On her way back to her office Determan passed Bob Kapp. He mentioned some matter they were working on together, but she was still too stunned to concentrate. "What's wrong with you?" he asked. Determan told him what had happened. "You'd better go to your office," he said, which Determan interpreted as not very reassuring. Her spirits sank even lower. If Bob Kapp thought she was in trouble, surely she had gone too far.

THE VIETNAM WAR UNRAVELED THE COLD WAR CONSENSUS AND EXACERBATED GROWING TENSIONS BETWEEN GROUPS OF AMERICANS. PROTESTS AGAINST THE WAR ALARMED MANY WHO SAW IN THEM, AS IN THE URBAN RIOTS OF THE 1960S, A THREAT TO BASIC SOCIAL STABILITY.

That afternoon the firm threw a party at the F Street Club for a departing lawyer. Determan agonized about attending. If her memo had indeed ruined her future with the firm, the party would be an embarrassing ordeal. On the other hand, she had as yet received no formal notice that she was finished. Besides, she believed she had done nothing wrong and should go as a matter of principle. Nevertheless, she circled the block nervously several times before deciding to park her car. When she approached the bottom of the stairs to the club's entrance she looked up and saw Lester Cohen, Seymour Mintz, Ed McDermott, and Merle Thorpe, Jr., the same four members of the Executive Committee who had interviewed her as an applicant. "Oh no," she thought,

PARTNERS

1973
George U. Carneal
Arthur G. Nichols
Bob Glen Odle
Richard J. M. Poulson
Richard S. Rodin
Stuart P. Ross
Alfred T. Spada

1974
Anthony S. Harrington
Peter W. Tredick

1975
Sara-Ann Determan
Joseph M. Hassett
Robert E. Montgomery, Jr.
James J. Rosenhauer
Peter Rousselot

1976
Joseph Chartoff
David J. Hensler
Eric A. Von Salzen

1977
Alphonso A. Christian, II
Alfred F. Dougherty, Jr.
M. Langhorne Keith
Marshall T. Mays
Martin Michaelson
George W. Miller
William R. Schief
David A. Tatel

The incoming president, Richard Nixon, and the outgoing president, Lyndon Johnson, in 1968, separated by much more than a table but united in the weighty responsibilities of office.

climbing the stairs one by one, as if to a hanging. But when she reached the top they all burst out, "*Sally*! We're so glad to *see* you! We're so glad you came." Behind the protective phalanx of the firm's leadership, a much-relieved Determan joined the party.

After advising Determan to return to her office, Kapp raised the issue with Mintz, who then called a meeting of the Executive Committee. The committee quickly summoned the partner who had scolded Determan and sternly reminded him that he had no authority to tell associates to resign. The next day the Lawyers Against the War held their rally. Many in the firm attended, partly to support the cause and partly to support Determan. The Executive Committee stood by its support for the free expression of opinions on the war even when an established client, who had referred much business to the firm, called and threatened never to send another case to Hogan & Hartson again if it did not muzzle its antiwar lawyers. Kapp recalled the committee's response: "Well, that's just the way it will have to go, then."

Americans disagreed on how the country should respond to rising crime, to long hair, rock music, and drug use, and to poverty and racial tension. Determan's nemesis had not been reprimanded for his views on the war or for his feelings about antiwar protestors but for an apparent bullying of a less powerful colleague. It was a difficult, even painful, time, and what later was called the "silent majority" of Americans yearned for order. Presidential candidate Richard Nixon promised to deliver.

With Hartson's approval again, John Warner took six months' leave to help with the 1968 Nixon campaign. After Nixon won, Hartson summoned Warner back into the fold. "You're coming back," he said. "I've given you all the leave you're going to get." Warner returned. But soon Nixon asked for his help on the transition team and Hartson, a Nixon supporter, yielded yet again.

Hogan & Hartson developed a strong aviation practice when George Carneal returned to the firm in 1972 after serving as general counsel to the Federal Aviation Administration in Washington, D.C.

Ed McDermott and partner John Warner (L) at Nelson Hartson's retirement party, January 1968. A year later Warner was confirmed as Undersecretary of the Navy. An intended two-year leave from Hogan & Hartson evolved into a new career for the future U.S. senator from Virginia.

1978	1979	
Marvin J. Diamond	Joseph C. Bell	Allen R. Snyder
David B. Lytle	William A. Bradford, Jr.	Robert J. Waldman
Gail S. Marshall	Philip C. Larson	
William S. Reyner, Jr.	H. Todd Miller	
Curtis E. von Kann	Paul G. Rogers	

AUSTIN S. MITTLER CAME TO HOGAN & HARTSON FROM THE JUSTICE DEPARTMENT IN 1968. IN 1975 HE TOOK ON ADMINISTRATIVE RESPONSIBILITY FOR THE FIRM'S GROWING LITIGATION PRACTICES, EVENTUALLY BECOMING PRACTICE AREA ADMINISTRATOR FOR LITIGATION. SAID BOB ODLE IN 2003, "HOGAN & HARTSON ABHORS HIERARCHY THE WAY NATURE ABHORS A VACUUM, SO YOU HAVE TO FIND SOME OTHER WAY TO DO IT, AND AUSTIN IS ONE OF THEM."

Then, in February 1969, Warner was confirmed as Under Secretary of the Navy. "Two years, that's all, two years," Hartson insisted. But Warner never came back. At a lunch meeting at the Metropolitan Club, the elder partner told Warner the firm could no longer hold a position open for him. Warner understood but would not leave his post in the middle of the Vietnam War.

Vincent H. Cohen joined Hogan & Hartson in 1969 and in 1972 became the firm's first African-American partner. Often listed among the nation's most prominent litigators, Cohen was named a Fellow of the American College of Trial Lawyers and held numerous public service and bar positions. He was chair of the Board of Trustees of the Public Defender Service of the District of Columbia, vice chair of the District of Columbia Commission on Judicial Disabilities and Tenure, and served two terms as a member of the Board of Governors of the District of Columbia Bar. He was a tireless advocate for diversity in the legal profession and at Hogan & Hartson, where he recently became of counsel. In a Hogan & Hartson Lecture Series presentation titled "The Art of Litigation," Cohen summarized some of the lessons distilled from his courtroom experience. Among them was the importance of setting a theme pitched to the jury's experience, then staying on message through the trial. In retrospect, Frank Hogan had done exactly that in the Doheny trials with his theme of Edward Doheny as loving father and unappreciated patriot.

Warner was among several Hogan & Hartson attorneys who took positions with the new administration. George Carneal joined Warner in the Nixon transition office, then went to work in the Department of Transportation as special assistant to Secretary John Volpe. Carneal's initial reception was frosty. "I don't need a spy from the White House looking over my shoulder," growled the former Massachusetts governor. But he warmed to Carneal and a year and a half later asked the thirty-five-year-old if he would like to serve as general counsel for the Federal Aviation Administration. Carneal had done some aviation work before the Civil Aeronautics Board with Ed McDermott and had found it interesting, so he accepted Volpe's offer. Two and one-half years later he returned to the firm and started an aviation practice.

Notwithstanding the inflation that eventually undermined it, the economic boom of the 1960s and the growth of the national government under Lyndon Johnson — through the Great Society as well as military spending for the war — created new opportunities and practice areas for Hogan & Hartson attorneys. Early in 1967 Arthur Rothkopf joined the firm after serving eight years with the Securities and Exchange Commission and the Treasury Department. Eager to put his expertise in international tax law to use and unwilling to move to New York, Rothkopf heeded his friend Bob Kapp's suggestion to give Hogan & Hartson a look. Rothkopf found it "a real quill pen operation" technologically but, unlike other D.C. firms, Hogan & Hartson had a diverse, traditional practice with a large tax and corporate component ripe for further growth. Rothkopf also showed a keen interest in the firm's administration and soon joined the recruitment committee to spread the firm's reputation more widely and broaden the range of applicants.

The firm's litigation department also attracted new talent in the late 1960s. William Bittman encouraged Austin Mittler, a former colleague at the Justice Department, to consider joining, but Mittler was not interested in working for a large law firm. With about fifty-five lawyers, Hogan & Hartson was roughly the same size as D.C.'s Arnold & Porter and only half the size of Covington & Burling, the other "large" firms in town. But Mittler wanted to concentrate on criminal work and had his mind set on a small litigation boutique. Bittman invited him to come over for lunch and meet with Lester Cohen, Ed McDermott, and Seymour Mintz. Mittler visited several times during the next few months. "I really took a liking to the people I met," he said. "I started to get a good feeling about it."

In February 1968 Mittler joined the firm and quickly was engaged in the white-collar defense work he had sought. Hogan & Hartson's ten-attorney litigation practice included high-profile cases defending a U.S. congressman, a U.S. senator, and a corporation connected with a bribery case against a former U.S. senator. Most of Mittler's time in his early years at the firm went into two criminal cases involving a financier and racehorse owner who had been charged with securities violations and obstruction of justice. As a result of that relationship, Mittler was drawn into work involving horse racing and breeding that embraced tax issues, racetrack financing, litigation, licensing, and syndications — work that developed into a long-standing and unusual equine practice for the firm.

Sherwin Markman was another litigator who joined the firm in 1968, coming over to the Chanin Building, across Lafayette Park, from the White House in September. Markman had been active in Iowa Democratic politics after graduating from Yale Law School. Working with Minnesota's attorney general, Walter Mondale, he did yeoman service for Lyndon Johnson at the 1964 Democratic National Convention in Atlantic City, then returned to law practice in Des Moines until 1966, when Johnson called him to the White House to serve as Assistant to the President. But when Johnson announced at the end of March 1968 that he would not run again, Markman had to find another job. Ed McDermott recruited him for Hogan & Hartson. Somewhat to Markman's surprise, given what he regarded as his respectable but not exceptional trial experience in a small firm in Des Moines, he was assigned to handle complex lawsuits for Hogan & Hartson.

It was hard to surprise Vincent Cohen, who joined Hogan & Hartson's litigation team a year after Markman, in October 1969. The son of West Indian immigrants, Cohen was born and raised in the Bedford-Stuyvesant section of Brooklyn, New York. An all-American basketball player, he graduated *cum laude* from Syracuse University in 1957 and stayed on to earn his law degree in 1960. As a member of the academic honor society, *Order of the Coif*, and an editor of the *Syracuse Law Review*, Cohen was ready for Wall Street. But Wall Street wasn't ready for him. "Look, Vince," said the young white partner in a New York firm who interviewed

RICHARD S. RODIN CAME TO HOGAN & HARTSON'S COMMUNICATIONS PRACTICE IN 1969 AND FORMED AN IMMEDIATE IMPRESSION. "THIS IS THE KIND OF PLACE WHERE YOU'VE GOT VERY SMART PEOPLE BUT THEY DON'T TAKE THEMSELVES TOO SERIOUSLY." LATER HE BECAME THE FIRM'S PRACTICE AREA ADMINISTRATOR FOR GOVERNMENT REGULATION.

In late spring 1979 Rich Rodin launched a tradition when he invited the firm's five summer associates, then called "summer clerks," to his home for a cookout. "It was a way of welcoming them to each other," he explained, as well as an opportunity for them to meet some of the attorneys and partners with whom they would be working.

With every succeeding cookout, Rodin's job of grilling steaks expanded. One year, after a torrential rain in which the party moved indoors while Rodin got soaked at the grill, Rodin decided to use a tent and a caterer, prompting inquiries from neighbors wondering who was getting married.

In 2004 Rodin hosted Hogan & Hartson's twenty-fifth annual summer associates party. About 120 persons attended, including 40 summer associates from the Washington, D.C., McLean, Virginia, and Baltimore offices. Since 1979 about 800 summer associates have enjoyed a relaxed exposure to Hogan & Hartson's culture in Rich Rodin's backyard. Many of them are now partners at the firm, with an opportunity every year in late May or early June to re-experience this happy and memorable introduction to the firm.

him, "if it was up to me, I would hire Negroes, but the clients won't accept Negro attorneys working on their matters." So Cohen took a job with the power company Consolidated Edison.

Like other African-Americans, Cohen found employment easier in institutions whose hiring decisions were largely immune from public influence. "If you didn't like the fact that they hired a Negro attorney," Cohen explained, "then don't use their electricity." It was the same with Robert Kennedy's Justice Department, Cohen's next employer. "If you don't like the fact that Bobby Kennedy hired me, leave the country."

GERALD E. GILBERT JOINED HOGAN & HARTSON IN 1968 AND WAS INSTRUMENTAL IN DEVELOPING THE FIRM'S INTERNATIONAL PRACTICE. GILBERT ALSO SERVED IN THE NAVAL RESERVE JUDGE ADVOCATE GENERAL'S CORPS, RETIRING IN 1992 AS THE CORPS' HIGHEST-RANKING OFFICER (TWO STAR REAR ADMIRAL).

From 1962 to 1967 Cohen worked at Justice in the Civil Division's Torts Branch defending the government against medical malpractice claims. He found Washington "the strangest city I'd ever been in." Across the street from the Department of Justice was a sandwich-and-coffee restaurant called "The Four Boys," long since demolished in Pennsylvania Avenue restoration. Cohen walked in one day and began to order his lunch. "We don't serve Negroes here," he was told. The tone wasn't apologetic, it was simply matter-of-fact, a reminder to Cohen of southern-style racial segregation. When he left the restaurant he could see, just blocks away to his left, the United States Capitol. Even closer, across Pennsylvania Avenue in the National Archives, tourists filed past the glass-encased Bill of Rights. "This," he notes, "was Washington, D.C., in the 1960s." After Cohen's wife, Diane, was rebuffed repeatedly in her search for an apartment, she changed her telephone inquiry. "This is Mrs. Cohen," she said. "Do you rent to Negroes?" "Mrs. Cohen," came the reply, "you don't have to worry, we don't rent to no Negroes."

Restless with the pace of advancement in the government, Cohen took an offer to join Ohio Bell in 1967 and moved to Cleveland. His wife rented a place in a neighborhood she liked, but when the family moved in they discovered it was "off-limits" to African-Americans. This was segregation, northern style. "We would go to the pool and everybody would get out," Cohen recalled. As the hostility grew more open and frequent, he purchased a weapon for the first time in his life. "I couldn't retreat past my door. I mean, I had no place to go." He returned to Washington to work for the Equal Employment Opportunity Commission, but as a political employee he had to leave when the Nixon administration came to power in 1969. Cohen decided that the times might be ripe to try something he hadn't much considered before. He knocked on the door of some Washington law firms.

The broad efforts at hiring fairness that would be called "affirmative action" were just beginning. "Oh, Vince," the recruiting law partners would say, competing for an experienced African-American attorney who could not know if he was truly or only nominally desired, or even a bit of both. "Oh, Vince, this is the place to come. There's not a racist bone in anyone's body," Cohen caricatured. Then he met with recruiters at Hogan & Hartson. "Yes, we've got problems," they said, more realistically. "You'll run into some people and some problems, but basically you're going to get a fair shot at this thing." Cohen said later, "That's all I really wanted."

Cohen also was encouraged by young Hogan & Hartson attorneys like former college basketball player Richard Rodin, who had recently joined the firm's communications practice, and litigator Stuart Ross, who had played for George Washington University. In sports, all a true competitor needed was a fair chance to perform. Maybe the same could also prove true for a litigator. "Because they were that honest," said Cohen, "I decided to go with them."

Gerald Gilbert also wanted a fair chance to perform, not in sports or litigation but in a new practice area — food and drugs. Gilbert had worked as an assistant U.S. Attorney in Washington, D.C., after finishing law school in 1962, then as a regulatory attorney in the Department of Commerce. In 1966 he became the first in-house counsel for the Proprietary Association (PA), a trade association now called the Consumer Health Care Products Association. Gilbert was considering a long-term career as an executive in the PA when he ran into Ed Holtz, a partner in the communications practice at Hogan & Hartson, at a college alumni event. Holtz suggested he contact the firm about setting up his desired food and drug practice.

In 1968 Gilbert had a few interviews at the firm but thought that, with about fifty attorneys, Hogan & Hartson was just too big. He backed away, went home, thought about it, and realized he had made a mistake. He didn't really want to be a trade association executive after all. Oh, well — too late now. But soon the firm called and asked if he would reconsider. Gilbert went back to the Chanin Building and spoke with Seymour Mintz and Lester Cohen. "Those gentlemen — and they really were gentlemen — were *very* persuasive," he recalled. George Carneal, a good friend from the University of Virginia Law School, also was encouraging about Gilbert's prospects at the firm. "It didn't take me long to accept," said Gilbert. "I'm glad I did. It's the smartest thing I've ever done."

PA's chairman didn't think so. When Gilbert turned down his counteroffer of a pay increase ("No, no, it has nothing to do with money!"), the chairman, a former college football tackle, pounded his desk top. "If you leave us now," he exclaimed, "I have to tell you we're not going to retain you. Your phone's not going to ring. You're going to get over there and try to start that practice and you're going to be very nervous and sorry you left us." For a month Gilbert's phone at Hogan & Hartson was silent. Perhaps his former boss had been right. He certainly was getting nervous. Maybe he would be sorry, too.

Then one day the phone rang. A friend who also had left the PA and had experienced the same angry reaction from its chairman had just been appointed president of the Direct Selling Association, the trade association for companies like Amway, which sold home cleaning products, Mary Kay and Avon cosmetics, Time-Life Books, and Electrolux vacuum cleaners. "I'd like you to be my outside general counsel," came the welcome words, and from there, says Gilbert, "my career took off." He continued the food and drug practice until Jonathan Kahan, who joined the firm in 1974, gradually took over. That practice burgeoned in 1976 when Congress passed the Medical Device Amendments to the 1938 Food, Drug and Cosmetic Act, greatly increasing that act's scope.

With Gilbert's assistance, the Direct Selling Association wrote an ethics code and worked with federal and state authorities, including the Federal Trade Commission, to distinguish direct selling businesses from exploitative "pyramid schemes." Hogan & Hartson also represented Amway, and by proxy the direct selling industry, in a significant legal battle, a 1975 antitrust prosecution in which the FTC challenged the very foundations of the direct selling industry.

The FTC's case focused on the limitations Amway imposed on its 2,500 distributors — on the prices they could charge for the products, for example, or the ways in which they could advertise and recruit new distributors. Additional charges involved allegedly false claims regarding the potential profits of a distributorship. But

[LEFT] PARTNERS ED MCDERMOTT, GEORGE WISE AND ARTHUR ROTHKOPF. WISE HAD JOINED THE FIRM IN 1955, SPECIALIZING IN ANTITRUST MATTERS. [RIGHT] NELSON HARTSON (L) AND PARTNER JAMES ROGERS, JANUARY 1968. ROGERS HAD JOINED THE FIRM IN 1944.

JAMES J. ROSENHAUER WAS THE FIRM'S 45TH LAWYER WHEN HE JOINED IN 1967 FOR THE PRINCELY ANNUAL SUM OF $9,000. HE NOW PUTS YEARS OF DIVERSE PRACTICE EXPERIENCE TO USE AS HOGAN & HARTSON'S PRACTICE AREA ADMINISTRATOR FOR BUSINESS AND FINANCE, AND FOR INTELLECTUAL PROPERTY.

the major allegation was that Amway was basically an illegitimate business, a pyramid scheme. About 150 witnesses testified at the hearings, held in Washington in the summer of 1977. The transcript weighed in at nearly 7,000 pages with more than 1,000 exhibits. Proceedings after the hearings added 1,600 more pages to the nearly three-foot-high transcript.

An antitrust case is almost always a marathon proposition. Hogan & Hartson's ability to marshal top legal talent was key to its preparation for the Amway case, just as it had been for the Pillsbury case back in the 1950s. In July 1968 the firm recruited Lee Loevinger, former assistant attorney general in charge of the Justice Department's Antitrust Division, then FCC commissioner, during the Kennedy and Johnson administrations. The Kennedys had brought Loevinger to Washington from his position as associate justice on the Minnesota Supreme Court in 1961, but the ascent of the Republicans had left his career hanging — albeit at a high level. Loevinger had promised the Senate during his confirmation hearings in the spring of 1963 that he would see his term as FCC commissioner through to its end. He had kept his word. Now Lester Cohen, whom he had known through the firm's dealings with the FCC, approached him about expanding Hogan & Hartson's antitrust practice. Loevinger agreed, joining Hogan & Hartson partner George Wise and others in that well-established practice.

Within a few years the firm hired new associates like Philip Larson and Robert J. Kenney, Jr., who worked with Loevinger on the Amway case. Patrick Raher, who rotated through the antitrust practice as an associate in the early 1970s, recalled walking into Loevinger's office once with Larson to start drafting a brief. As the two associates reviewed the case, Loevinger tapped away on a portable manual typewriter, citing cases from memory while calling out research tasks for them. "See Honeywell, Ninth Circuit," he called out, or "See Supreme Court," with a specific case that Larson or Raher would look up. Four hours later he handed over a fifteen-page brief for them to fact-check. "And it was just a beautiful piece of writing," said Raher. "It was not an outline."

On May 8, 1979, four years after initial charges were filed, the judge found some problems with Amway's pricing and its promises to distributors but cleared the company of the fatal charge of being an illegal pyramid scheme. It amounted to a major win for Amway as well as for the Direct Selling Association, for it legitimized the industry and established a regulatory framework for further growth. Twenty years later direct selling companies were active around the world, including Amway distributorships in the former Soviet Union and in the People's Republic of China.

Increased antitrust litigation was but one aspect of a more general expansion of business-related practice at Hogan & Hartson in the late 1960s as the firm kept pace with that era's "conglomerate wave." James Rosenhauer came straight to the firm in June 1967, three days after his last exam at Yale Law School. "We were extraordinarily poor," he said of himself and his wife, Vivian, so they hurried down to Washington from New Haven as quickly as possible to begin earning his $9,000 annual salary. While waiting for his diploma to arrive in the mail, he rotated briefly through the tax and litigation departments, then joined Merle Thorpe, Jr., and Bob Jeffers in the firm's corporate securities practice. The following year the New York firms boosted starting salaries for associates from $10,000 to $15,000 — from $49,500 to $74,200 in year 2000 dollars. Hogan & Hartson

SHERWIN MARKMAN JOINED HOGAN & HARTSON IN 1968 AFTER SERVING AS SPECIAL ASSISTANT TO PRESIDENT LYNDON JOHNSON. A SPECIALIST IN COMPLEX LITIGATION, MARKMAN ALSO WAS AN ACCOMPLISHED SAILOR AND NOVELIST.

followed suit with a jump to $13,000, the 2000 equivalent of about $64,000.

Rosenhauer remembers Thorpe as "more of a big-picture type of lawyer than a roll-up-your-sleeves-and-do-the-drafting sort of lawyer." Thorpe was especially good dealing with difficult issues and with persuading clients to go "in the right direction." Jeffers was "very careful, terrific at drafting, and would go over things and really teach someone the skills." Jeffers proved to be a great confidence builder, instilling in young attorneys like Rosenhauer "the mindset that if you really are careful and thoughtful about what you do, you can take on anything and be as effective as anybody, even if you're dealing with somebody who has done it many times more than you have."

Jeffers's "terrific judgment on hard issues" and Thorpe's persuasive powers were tested severely in the late 1960s by client Robert Vesco and his International Controls Corporation (ICC). Conglomerates, formed by merging essentially unrelated businesses, had the attraction of slipping past the radar of antitrust authorities. The Celler-Kefauver Act of 1950, which amended the Clayton Antitrust Act to enable intensified antitrust action against corporations, discouraged the two traditional forms of merger — vertical (product line) and horizontal (purchaser/supplier). But it did not clearly aim at preventing growth through acquiring wholly unrelated businesses.[4] About 60 percent of the 1,517 mergers reported by the Federal Trade Commission in 1966 were of the conglomerate variety.[5]

Through most of the 1960s investor enthusiasm for conglomerates greatly outweighed suspicion of them. Seemingly robust conglomerates acquired poorly performing businesses that they were sure could be turned around or sold off at a profit. The conventional wisdom was that conglomerates' managers did not need to know much about the particular products of the companies they acquired. What mattered were the financing and the stock price. Even the language of conglomerate mergers was specialized. Particular acquisitions that boosted each other's value were said to be "synergistic," their merged assets being "pluralized" in the process.

By 1967 the thirty-one-year-old Vesco had cobbled together enough computer, airplane, and machine parts businesses to qualify as a significant government contractor. He was successful enough for ICC to make a public stock offering. A man of rough manners, Vesco was a daring entrepreneur whose facile mind and determination to succeed attracted an enthusiastic team eager for the next acquisition. Vesco had an instinct for finding weak companies and rapidly expanded the assets controlled by ICC. As his grasp wrestled with his reach for more business plums, he engaged numerous legal advisors, adding Hogan & Hartson in 1968.

HOGAN & HARTSON'S OLD POWER DEPARTMENT EVOLVED INTO A MODERN ENERGY PRACTICE, DEALING WITH NEW CRISES LIKE THE OIL EMBARGO OF 1973-1974. LONG WAITS AT GAS STATIONS LIKE THIS ONE IN OREGON UNDERSCORED AMERICANS' DEPENDENCE ON FOREIGN ENERGY SOURCES.

In 1971 Vesco and the SEC, for different reasons, both homed in on jet-setter Bernard Cornfeld's Investors Overseas Services (IOS), an investment fund based in Switzerland that had weakened under Cornfeld's undisciplined management. Vesco acquired a controlling interest in IOS, which he planned to reorganize. Vesco's plans were by turns brilliant, complicated, ruthless, and, with Vesco pushing relentlessly against the boundaries of conventional business practice, very risky.[6]

Bob Jeffers was heavily involved in work for ICC from 1967 to 1971, including many "cutting edge" transactions. ICC did the second Eurobond offering ever done, and the second hostile (unfriendly) tender offer for a public company. Jeffers later recalled that Vesco was very tough (but brilliant, which made him tougher), and that he had "many knock-down, drag-outs with Vesco" and "never consented to his doing anything illegal (or even immoral)." However, Vesco began to engage in certain activities that the firm was unaware of and deliberately kept ignorant of. The firm resigned from the representation of ICC when certain of these activities came to its attention.

At the time, corporate lawyers frequently served on the boards of directors of their clients. Merle Thorpe's presence on ICC's board perhaps gave Thorpe a better view of, but not much control over, unfolding events, and he resigned after disagreements with Vesco. The temperamental financier sank from daring corporate entrepreneur to rogue client and eventually to fugitive from justice even more quickly than he had risen. When allegations that Vesco had helped himself to some hundreds of millions of dollars of IOS funds intensified the enforcement spotlight on his activities, Vesco's house of cards began tumbling. He was indicted in Switzerland for bank fraud and a warrant was issued there for his arrest. Sherwin Markman was called in to handle the matter.

Vesco's New York lawyer and his Swiss lawyer both advised their client to accept the assurances of a Swiss judge that he could travel to Switzerland, testify in the bank fraud matter, then return to the United States without interference from Swiss law enforcement officers. But Markman told him he should "never, ever, ever do this." Vesco went anyway. Markman, who remained deeply concerned, accompanied him. Then, while Markman helplessly watched from the courtroom, Vesco was arrested and jailed. Complicating his situation was the absence of any *habeus corpus* protection in Switzerland. Vesco could be held indefinitely while Swiss authorities figured out what they wished to do with him. Bob Glen Odle, a young associate at Hogan & Hartson, flew to Geneva to assist Markman.

(L TO R) ED MCDERMOTT, LESTER COHEN, NELSON HARTSON AND SEYMOUR MINTZ, JUNE 1972. THESE PARTNERS WERE AMONG THOSE WHO HELPED HOGAN & HARTSON MEET THE CHALLENGES OF THE 1970S.

Markman retained a Swiss attorney and together they developed the argument that the investigating magistrate had overstepped his authority and made misrepresentations in order to get Vesco into the country, that such judicial impropriety invalidated the arrest, and that the prisoner should therefore be released. An appellate court was convened the very next evening and it accepted the argument. Vesco was immediately released. He and Markman headed straight for the airport, leaving "poor Odle behind," as Markman recalled, "to clean up the mess" of uncompleted paperwork and truncated protocol. Odle did, and before long the judge who had jailed Vesco was himself removed from office.

"From that moment on I just could do no wrong, as far as Vesco was concerned," said Markman. But Vesco could. As the SEC closed in on him in the fall of 1972, he hired Harry Sears, a New Jersey lawyer and state finance chairman for the Nixon campaign, to deliver a supposed campaign contribution of $200,000 to former Attorney General John Mitchell and former Commerce Secretary Maurice Stans. Facing a possible indictment on a charge that the contribution was an improper effort to thwart the SEC investigation, he called Markman in his hotel room in New York. They had to talk, immediately. They did. Despite Markman's advice, Vesco fled the country, and the firm's representation of him came to an end.

By the mid-1970s the firm had developed several promising new practices — appellate, equine, aviation and transportation, food and drug, and trade association representation — and had strengthened its regulatory, corporate, tax, and litigation departments. Additionally, the energy crisis, symbolized by long lines at gas stations during the winter of 1973-1974, created new demands on Hogan & Hartson's energy practice, ably headed by C. Frank Reifsnyder. The firm also grappled with fundamental questions of social responsibility and of the relationship between private practice and the public interest. Hogan & Hartson's attorneys, like many of their colleagues in other firms, had always donated free or reduced-fee services to indigent clients and to worthy but cash-strapped organizations. But it had been a personal prerogative, not a firmwide, formally organized effort. Now, in the wake of 1968's multiple traumas, Hogan & Hartson had to decide whether or not to launch such an effort, and if so, what form it would take.

JOHN M. FERREN CAME TO HOGAN & HARTSON IN 1970 TO HEAD THE FIRM'S NEW COMMUNITY SERVICES DEPARTMENT (CSD). INITIALLY SKEPTICAL ABOUT THE *PRO BONO* EFFORTS OF LARGE LAW FIRMS, FERREN SKILLFULLY NURTURED THE FLEDGLING CSD IN ITS EARLIEST YEARS. HE THEN SERVED AS HOGAN & HARTSON'S FIRST ADMINISTRATIVE PARTNER BEFORE BEING APPOINTED TO A JUDGESHIP ON THE DISTRICT OF COLUMBIA COURT OF APPEALS IN 1977.

As Seymour Mintz noted, opposition to the idea of an organized *pro bono* program in the firm was strong and articulate, not just dissident nay-saying or hand-wringing. After all, what were the main purposes of a law firm? Did they include serving society by giving away legal services for free? Or was society best served by "the market," by organizing lawyers to deliver legal services to paying clients? And if somehow a law firm were to try to accomplish both goals, was it fair to require partners to subsidize, in effect, the delivery of *pro bono* services for persons or causes in which some might have little interest or might even oppose? Who would decide which *pro bono* cases to accept? What were the limits on their costs?

The basic issues were neither easy nor easily resolved, but in 1969 the firm overwhelmingly elected to establish a formal *pro bono* program. The Executive Committee charged a Community Relations Study Committee, chaired by partner Bob Kapp, to investigate options and draft suggestions. Associates Sally Determan, Anthony Harrington, Peter Rousselot, and Carl Taylor served with Kapp on the committee. In September 1969 the five reported back to the Executive Committee, affirming the view that private law firms could not be islands untouched in a sea of social change. In the larger, long-term interests of a stable and secure society, law firms must make an effort to ameliorate problems like poverty, racism, and inequitable access to legal services. In addition to the public interest and the short-term interests of law firms themselves, a strong *pro bono* program would help recruit talented, idealistic law students.

Like many others in the 1960s, John Ferren, later to become the first partner-in-charge of Hogan & Hartson's Community Services Department, was inspired by the courage of four African-American freshmen at North Carolina Agricultural and Technical College in Greensboro, North Carolina. On Monday, February 1, 1960, the students — Franklin McCain, David Richmond, Joseph McNeill, and Ezell Blair, Jr., who later changed his name to Jibreel Khazan — left their rooms and headed for the Woolworth variety store on South Elm Street. They took their seats at the whites-only lunch counter and asked for some coffee. They waited all day, and then all week.

The four students soon were joined by large numbers of sympathizers through the remainder of the week, despite threats and heckling from angry onlookers. Sixteen hundred students attended a Saturday rally in favor of the sit-in, which received national news coverage and inspired sympathy boycotts of Woolworth stores across the nation, including a Woolworth in Cambridge, Massachusetts. Eventually the coffee came, and much more. Five months after the Greensboro Four started their protest Woolworth relented and opened its lunch counter to all customers.

Sit-ins were not a new tactic. In 1936, for example, workers at a General Motors plant in Flint, Michigan, staged a "sit-down" in the facility, occupying it for forty-four straight days before the auto company agreed to recognize their union, the United Automobile Workers. And for years civil rights advocates like Rosa Parks in Birmingham, Alabama, and Mary Church Terrell and Pauli Murray in Washington, D.C., had used sit-ins, pickets, and boycotts to draw public attention to the shame of racial discrimination in public transportation, theaters, and restaurants.

But the Greensboro sit-in by four young men, still teenagers, signaled that a new generation was ready and willing to continue until the battle was won. This time, national television assured a wide and mostly sympathetic audience. In January 1995 a section of the famous Woolworth's lunch counter, with four stools in front of it, went on permanent display in the Smithsonian Institution in Washington, D.C.

The study committee explored numerous options, including neighborhood legal clinics that focused on the needs of local residents; releasing individual attorneys from their usual duties for designated periods of time to take on *pro bono* projects of their choice; and large-scale, national representations of such organizations as the American Civil Liberties Union (ACLU), the National Welfare Rights Organization, or the National Association for the Advancement of Colored People (NAACP).

All these approaches were judged worthy but wanting. The first would be helpful but of limited scope. The second would not be identified much with the firm, and with each attorney "doing his own thing" the program might wander, directionless, into some ill-considered or overlapping projects. The last option — large-scale representations — would put Hogan & Hartson's wide resources to good use but by itself was not "of sufficient breadth."[7]

The final form of the firm's *pro bono* initiative emerged from intense committee discussion about how best to mount an effort that would be durable and that would be taken seriously by all the firm's partners, including those who might hold onto their opposition for a while. Other large firms in D.C. had appointed a partner, rather than an associate, to handle their *pro bono* cases. That seemed like a step in the right direction, but not as large a step as Hogan & Hartson wished to take.

Sally Determan, who became the firm's first female partner in 1975, recalled how the committee hit on a solution. "Let's suppose," ventured Carl Taylor, "that we had been told that the firm decided it wanted to have an admiralty practice and we were given that job. What would we do?" "Well," the rest answered, "we'd go find the best admiralty lawyer we could find, bring him in as a partner, give him the assistance he needs and let it rip." "So," Taylor continued, "why couldn't we do that for our *pro bono* department?" Says Determan, "We just went, '*Yes*!!'" The Executive Committee agreed and set out to find that partner to head Hogan & Hartson's new Community Services Department (CSD).

The study committee was impressed with a California rural legal services program run by Gary Bellow. Hogan & Hartson tried to interest Bellow in heading its new CSD, but he had just taken a position at Harvard Law School. However, there was another attorney at Harvard, John Ferren, who had been hired four years earlier to direct Harvard Law School's neighborhood law office program. Under Ferren's leadership, that program attracted national attention as an example for similar programs springing up in major cities with funding from Lyndon Johnson's "war on poverty" flagship agency, the Office of Economic Opportunity (OEO). Ferren had met Bob Kapp while serving with him on a team that evaluated those legal services programs for the OEO. So in November 1969 Mintz wrote a letter to Ferren, inviting him to come to Washington to discuss heading the CSD.

But Ferren had lost interest in large law firms. After graduation from Harvard Law School in 1962, he was packing up his belongings in Cambridge to head for his new job at a Chicago firm when he walked over to the local Woolworth's to buy some twine. When he arrived, several bearded divinity students were picketing on the sidewalk out front and talking about some lunch counter down in North Carolina. This clarion image of civil rights activism stayed with Ferren as he carried out corporate and banking assignments at the Chicago firm. As months went by Ferren became increasingly bothered by the disparity between his work for firm clients and the civil rights activism he had seen on the sidewalk in front of Woolworth's. "I was particularly struck by the fact that our law firm was pouring massive resources into cases which, on occasion, would impact on the lives of people who couldn't possibly afford to stand up to the firm and its clients," he said later. A number of lawyers were going into the South to help civil rights workers. Perhaps he should join them. He called a high school friend, Coleman Brown, who was a Presbyterian minister in Chicago's inner city and told him what he was thinking. "Hey," said Brown, "the South isn't the only place where there's a *profound* need for legal services. Right here in Chicago I minister to people who have every kind of problem you could imagine — and they're not served."

Ferren and another attorney from the firm recruited twelve more lawyers, enlisted Brown's help in scouting out a couple of suitable locations, and set up a volunteer legal services program in the spring of 1964. Within two years the operation, named Chicago Volunteer Legal Services, had attracted two hundred attorneys, as well as the attention of Dean Erwin Griswold at Harvard Law School. Griswold invited Ferren to return to Harvard and set up a neighborhood legal clinic in Cambridge. Ferren accepted. If he could change the law school experience for students, perhaps he also could influence the way they eventually practiced. Many of Ferren's law firm colleagues in Chicago disparaged his decision to leave, which added to the alienation he had felt earlier. By the time Mintz's letter arrived, said Ferren, "I had become very cynical about major law firms." Ferren called Mintz to thank him for the offer, then threw the letter into the wastebasket.

Ferren's wife, Ann, fished it out, curious about what her husband had tossed out with such feeling. When he explained, she encouraged him to reconsider. "You ought to at least look at opportunities," she said. Ferren decided she was right and called Mintz back. "I think I've been premature," he explained. Soon afterwards he visited Mintz in the Chanin Building. Mintz met him wearing a sport jacket with elbow patches. Ferren remembered his old firm in Chicago, where an associate who once showed up in a sport jacket had been sent home for improper dress. Ferren also remembered a prior visit to Hogan & Hartson to see Kapp. At that time he had noticed an attorney "standing around in a yellow sport jacket, light pants, and white bucks." Later he learned it was Howard Roycroft. "Well, this is unusual," Ferren mused at the time. After meeting several more partners at a dinner at Mintz's house that evening, Ferren agreed to come to Washington.

On July 6, 1970, Hogan & Hartson's CSD opened for business with Ferren and an attorney staff of two associates. Harold Himmelman, from the firm's litigation department, was the CSD's two-year, long-term associate while Langhorne Keith, a veteran naval officer who had left the service to obtain his law degree, became the department's first rotating associate. Ferren was brought in as a partner, not an associate, in order to give the CSD the same standing as the firm's other departments. In the months leading up to the July 6 opening, he canvassed every partner to gather opinions as well as to share his own. Many skeptics, like Lester Cohen, soon were won over, but others were more wary. Ferren did not want the CSD to become a *pro bono* ghetto, the only place in the firm that felt responsible for public interest work. On the contrary, he intended the CSD to have a centrifugal effect, spreading enthusiasm for public interest cases throughout the firm. He knew that in the coming months he would have to be a skillful diplomat and administrator as well as an attorney.

On the CSD's first day, Ralph Temple, head of the local chapter of the ACLU, showed up at Ferren's office with a request. Would Hogan & Hartson bring a lawsuit against the Washington, D.C., police department on behalf of the Black Panther Party? Temple claimed that

©GETTY IMAGES USA

Each new Presidential administration brought both changes and opportunities for attorneys practicing in Washington, D.C. Hogan & Hartson was no exception. John Sirica, for instance, had worked actively for the Eisenhower campaigns in 1952 and 1956 in part because he wished to increase his chances for appointment to a federal judgeship. Eisenhower's success led to the fulfillment of that wish, and in April 1957 Sirica was sworn in as a federal district judge.

From his spacious office in the federal courthouse in Washington, Judge Sirica later wrote, he could survey the famous Fifth Street lawyers' offices below, where he had spent fifteen years living hand-to-mouth — "my starvation period," he called it — before landing a job with Hogan & Hartson in 1949. A former professional boxer and close friend of Jack Dempsey, John Sirica had cut no corners and taken no falls on his journey to the bench. With honesty as well as humility, he later acknowledged that it had been "a big jump from Fifth Street to the bench for a guy like me." Sirica's courage and no-nonsense toughness while presiding over the Watergate trials in the mid-1970s earned him high praise. It also won him a Time magazine cover in 1974 and a place in the history books.

several party members had been brutalized by the police over the July 4th holiday during a raid on Panther headquarters at 17th and U Streets. Ferren's mind scrambled into high gear. This was not an ideal "first case" for a department eager to gain the support of all seventy-four attorneys in the firm. Yet Ferren knew that Temple, like himself until just recently, was "a total skeptic" concerning law firms' *pro bono* commitment. Surely they were just public relations operations, designed to ward off criticism at minimal cost to the firm. Despite Ferren's good intentions, Temple probably figured, this case would flush out Hogan & Hartson's true motives. This old-line Washington law firm, a firm that had looked after the interests of banks, businesses, and the transit company for nearly seventy years, wouldn't dare represent the Black Panthers, especially in a lawsuit against the city's police department.

In accordance with CSD's guidelines, Ferren circulated the case among the partners for five days before accepting it.[8] "Eyebrows were raised to the breaking point," he remembered. It was not the firm's idea of what low-income services would be. But the partners took a collective deep breath and told him to go ahead. Ferren and Himmelman went over to the Panther Party's headquarters, which, Ferren recalled, "had sandbags up to the ceiling, and there were guns. It was amazing." Temple arranged a press conference that evening to make sure it was widely known that Hogan & Hartson was representing the Panthers. When Ferren got home, Ann told him he had been on TV with the words "Panther Attorney" under his name. Suddenly, sport coats, even with elbow patches, looked pretty conservative.

Over the next four months, Ferren, Himmelman, and Keith interviewed nearly twenty prospective plaintiffs and several independent observers of the July 4th police raid. They decided to delay civil suits pending the outcome of disorderly conduct charges filed against many of the Panther Party members. When the government later dropped those charges, the CSD filed two civil suits, one on behalf of the Panthers arrested in the headquarters melee and another on behalf of Paul Pumphrey, who had been assaulted by four police officers when he visited the police station to see about the arrestees' release. The lawsuits took time, however, and by February 1971 only four of the original plaintiffs remained in the Washington, D.C., area. Additional delays discouraged other plaintiffs, but Pumphrey held on, and in 1974 Hogan & Hartson attorney Curtis von Kann won a $5,800 judgment for him in Superior Court, one of the highest ever recovered up to that time in any such case in the District of Columbia.

The CSD created plenty of work for Hogan & Hartson attorneys in the early 1970s. But so did a complex political scandal called Watergate. It started in Washington on June 17, 1972, with a bungled, petty burglary of a Democratic Party campaign office on the sixth floor of the Watergate building. An address book carried by one of the burglars listed E. Howard Hunt, a former CIA employee then working for the White House, and G. Gordon Liddy, a former FBI agent. Both men had helped organize the break-in with the support of highly placed White House officials.[9] Eventually investigators used the White House's own secret tapes to connect President Nixon to an attempted cover-up of campaign "dirty tricks" and crimes. Judge John Sirica, the former Hogan & Hartson partner who presided over the subsequent trials, listened to a taped meeting on March 21, 1973, between Nixon and White House counsel John Dean.

Dean told the President that E. Howard Hunt's wife, who had died in a December 8, 1972, airplane crash, had been carrying $10,000 from a secret White House fund to buy the silence of the arrested burglars. A million dollars might be required to keep the burglars, including Hunt and Liddy, quiet. Dean said that Hunt was threatening to talk to prosecutors and wanted $120,000. "Well," said the President, "your major guy to keep under control is Hunt." "That's right," answered Dean. The President continued, "Don't you, just looking at the immediate problem, don't you have to have — handle Hunt's financial situation?" Dean stammered, unsure what to say. "Damn soon," Nixon ordered, "either that or let it all blow right now." They concluded that Hunt would have to get his $120,000. Sirica had believed in Nixon, campaigned for him in 1952 and 1956, and voted for him in 1968 and 1972. But now, after listening to the tapes, he confessed, "I felt foolish."[10]

Watergate had shattered Judge Sirica's confidence in the President. But it also created problems for one of Hogan & Hartson's best litigators. When E. Howard Hunt hit bottom, he looked around for a top-notch, white-collar criminal defense attorney and on July 2, 1972, retained William O. Bittman at Hogan & Hartson. Bittman, recalled colleague Austin Mittler, didn't move in half-steps. "Everything Bill did throughout his career he would do with both feet and his whole body. When

Charles Alan Wright, Clark Clifford, Thomas D. Finney, Jr., Archibald Cox's brother, Maxwell Cox, and Hughes's longtime personal attorney, Chester Davis, and sought to convince the Supreme Court to reverse a judgment against "Hughes Toolco." Wright presented the oral argument to the Court on October 10, 1972.[14] The winning theory surprised Prettyman, who had helped shape the team's strategy, as he had rated it only fourth in order of importance among the several points Wright stressed before the Justices. Essentially, it was that Hughes Tool Company could not have acquired control of Trans World Airlines without the consent of the Civil Aeronautics Board (CAB), and under section 408 of the Federal Aviation Act, CAB approval immunized the company against antitrust charges.

Since arguing his first case before the Supreme Court in 1963, Prettyman had helped earn Hogan & Hartson a reputation for superb appellate work. The firm had no better example of the maxim that publications help practice. Prettyman's 1961 award-winning account of six death penalty cases, *Death and the Supreme Court*, had helped acquaint the attorney-author with many other writers and had occasioned the referral of numerous First Amendment, as well as death penalty, appellate cases.[15] The book also drew the attention of *In Cold Blood* author Truman Capote, who engaged Prettyman to accompany him as his attorney while making a film documentary for ABC on death row inmates. Though the film was never shown, one of the film's subjects, a Colorado inmate named Garrison, soon became one of Prettyman's clients.

Shortly after a trip to Colorado with Capote, Prettyman received a call from one of Garrison's lawyers. "There's nothing more I can do," he said flatly. "He's about to be executed. If you want to take over, you can, but I'm washing my hands."[16] Prettyman decided to take the case. While driving to the prison with Capote, he had heard that another of Garrison's attorneys, the one who had handled his trial, later had been disbarred. Apparently, after defending his clients during the day, the Jekyll-and-Hyde lawyer would go on nightly thieving sprees, stealing typewriters and other office equipment. It seemed to Prettyman that the lawyer-thief hardly could have been conducting an adequate representation in a first-degree murder case if his life were in such disarray. On May 27, 1968, the Supreme Court agreed and Garrison's life was spared.[17]

ELIMINATION OF DISCRIMINATORY HOUSING PRACTICES WAS A PARTICULAR GOAL OF JOHN FERREN WHEN HE CAME TO HOGAN & HARTSON IN 1970 TO HEAD THE FIRM'S COMMUNITY SERVICES DEPARTMENT.

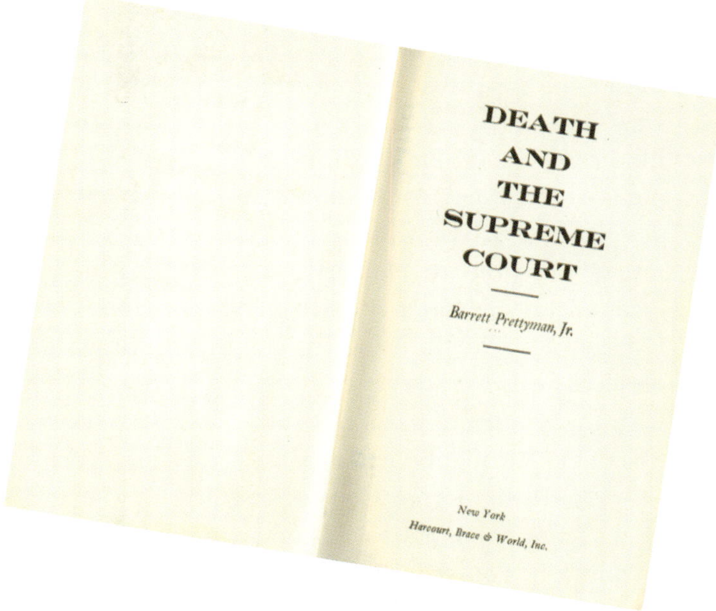

With fewer headlines and less drama, but with no less importance or consequence, Hogan & Hartson attorneys continued to develop their own brands of interesting work in the 1970s. On one occasion Ed McDermott called Bob Elliott to tell him someone from the Japanese embassy might be in touch soon and "perhaps you could help them out." "Yes, sure. Why not?" Elliott answered. Next Saturday he was mowing his lawn when the phone rang. It was an embassy official, wanting some help buying a house in Bethesda, Maryland, for a diplomat. "Sure, I'm happy to do that. When do you want to get together?" "Now." "Okay."

GEORGE P. "SANDY" MAYO, JR. JOINED HOGAN & HARTSON IN 1973 AND NOW IS MANAGING PARTNER OF OPERATIONS. A VIETNAM VETERAN, MAYO WAS INSTRUMENTAL IN ORGANIZING THE EFFORT TO CREATE THE VIETNAM VETERANS MEMORIAL NEAR THE LINCOLN MEMORIAL IN WASHINGTON, D.C.

Elliott left his lawn half done and drove over to Bethesda to look at the house.

"From that little bit of work," says Elliott, "I represented the Japanese embassy for twenty-two years." As it developed, the embassy had very special real estate needs that Elliott learned to fill. He searched out and arranged the purchase of several houses suitable as diplomatic residences, then furnished them so that each rotation of diplomats would not have to start from scratch, worrying about what was or wasn't appropriate for Western guests. Elliott became the embassy's institutional memory, the person newcomers consulted on matters of housing, design, and decor. More than anyone else, he is responsible for the embassy's current, seven-acre location on Nebraska Avenue in Washington, D.C. During construction of the multi-million-dollar project, he would traverse the grounds in hard hat with the architect's plans in hand. "You're not doing this right," he might have to say, or "No, do this over."

In 1974 George Carneal also lost a weekend after answering his phone on a Friday afternoon — not an unusual experience for a lawyer, but not always one so challenging. It was the general counsel at the Detroit Airport. He had met Carneal at an aviation industry meeting and remembered him because at lunchtime he had passed up dessert, a feat Carneal could remember no more than he remembered the man himself. Nevertheless, it had left an impression — another example of the circuitous route of referrals.

The general counsel told Carneal that the airport was about to start construction on another runway but the suburban city of Romulus, next door to the airport, was upset over the prospect of increased air traffic and had filed a request for a temporary restraining order. The hearing was on Tuesday morning. Could Carneal come out and help? The contractor was ready to start pouring concrete and every day of delay cost the airport around $50,000.

On short notice Carneal managed to gather Barrett Prettyman, Jim Hourihan, and Allen Snyder, a young associate and former law clerk to U.S. Supreme Court Justices Harlan and Rehnquist. All four flew out to Detroit, where they spent the weekend preparing for the hearing. "It's hard to believe," says Carneal, looking back on it. "I don't mean to sound conceited, but we had a lot of experience there." During the hearing the city's lawyers argued that the runway construction was in violation of the National Environmental Policy Act of 1969 because the airport had not conducted an adequate assessment of the noise impact on the surrounding area. But the Hogan & Hartson team brought in noise experts who concluded that the runway wouldn't increase noise at all; on the contrary, it would help to disperse it. In about a week the case was won and the team returned to Washington.

The National Environmental Policy Act was a milestone in a new era of regulations aimed at reducing noise, water, and air pollution. In the following year, 1970, 20 million Americans celebrated the first Earth Day on April 22; Congress and the White House inaugurated the Environmental Protection Agency (EPA) in July; and the Clean Air Act set new standards for auto emissions. Two years later two new federal entities, the Occupational Safety and Health Administration and the Consumer Product Safety Commission, were setting and enforcing new standards in their respective domains. Clients like the Chrysler Corporation, which had come to Hogan & Hartson several years earlier for help in product liability cases, now came for assistance in lawsuits over air pollution from its "stationary source" factories as well as its "mobile source" automobiles.

Patrick Raher's career at Hogan & Hartson advanced in the wind stream created by new environmental legislation. After working briefly with Lee Loevinger and Phil Larson on antitrust appeals before the Ninth Circuit, Raher joined Ed McDermott in helping the German automaker Mercedes navigate U.S. safety and pollution laws. McDermott also enlisted Jerome Sonosky, former legislative assistant to Senator Abraham Ribicoff, who had written the National Traffic and Motor Vehicle Safety Act of 1966. The Hogan & Hartson attorneys noticed that Mercedes seemed to take its exceptional safety engineering for granted and suggested that the company highlight it in its marketing. Mercedes' focus on safety made it a hallmark that gave the company a special niche in the U.S. market.

In the mid-1970s the Union Oil Company of California approached Hogan & Hartson for help with the Trans Alaska oil pipeline (TAP), then under construction. Raher had clerked for Roger Robb, the D.C. Circuit Court of Appeals judge who helped send the pipeline project back to the drawing boards in 1970 to fulfill environmental requirements. Now Raher was assigned to help Union Oil, one of the TAP's owners, across the pipeline's regulatory terrain.

One result was the formation of a team of biologists that developed new strains of grass that would thrive in the short, six-to-nine-week growing season in the tundra where pipeline construction had necessarily cleared away trees and shrubs. The service road paralleling the pipeline presented another special challenge because the underlying tundra was too fragile to permit the usual road construction methods. Instead, the pipeline company built the road atop a seven-and-a-half-foot base it constructed on top of the tundra. That brought a new problem, however, as migrating animals needed some way to get through. The answer was one adapted from military pontoon bridges. On the animals' migratory paths, pipeline engineers built bridges that remained in raised positions until a vehicle was ready to come through. Then the bridge was lowered for the vehicle, and raised again when it had passed. Unless a vehicle were on the bridge, the animals enjoyed free passage across the road. The pipeline itself was double-cladded as protection against rupture, though, as Raher points out, nobody foresaw a problem with spills once the oil reached the

FORMER H&H PARTNER, NOW U.S. SENATOR, JOHN WARNER (CENTER, WITH PROGRAM IN POCKET) AND, TO HIS LEFT (FOOT ON SHOVEL), H&H'S SANDY MAYO, AT THE GROUNDBREAKING CEREMONY FOR THE VIETNAM VETERANS MEMORIAL, MARCH 26, 1982. MAYO WAS AMONG THE 100 VIETNAM VETERANS PRESENT WHO HELPED TURN OVER NEW EARTH FOR "THE WALL." TO MAYO'S LEFT IS SENATOR CHUCK HAGEL (R. NEB.), AND SECOND TO SEN. WARNER'S RIGHT IS VIETNAM VETERAN AND ATTORNEY JAN SCRUGGS, WHO INITIATED THE PROJECT AND NOW SERVES AS PRESIDENT OF THE VIETNAM VETERANS MEMORIAL FUND.

ROBERT M. JEFFERS WAS THE FIRM'S 43RD ATTORNEY WHEN HE JOINED HOGAN & HARTSON IN JULY 1966. AS A MEMBER OF THE EXECUTIVE COMMITTEE IN THE EARLY 1970S, JEFFERS HELPED HOGAN & HARTSON'S MANAGEMENT ADAPT TO CHANGING TIMES AND CONDITIONS. HE WAS WIDELY RESPECTED FOR HIS ADVOCACY OF THE HIGHEST ETHICAL STANDARDS IN CORPORATE AND SECURITIES LAW PRACTICE.

A PARTNER AT HOGAN & HARTSON SINCE 1979, ROBERT J. WALDMAN HAS PLAYED A MAJOR ROLE IN BRINGING THE FIRM'S CORPORATE PRACTICE TO NATIONAL PROMINENCE.

bay and was loaded on tankers.

Some cases at Hogan & Hartson in the 1970s approached epic proportions. When the mighty Penn Central, Reading, and Erie Lackawanna railroads went bankrupt in 1970, 1971, and 1972, respectively, Congress stepped in to reorganize the dying rail industry and save what most considered an important component of the nation's transportation system. The government condemned the railroad properties, set up an entity called the United States Railway Association (USRA) to figure out how much to reimburse the former owners, and reorganized the lines' freight businesses as Conrail in 1976. (The passenger lines became Amtrak.) The USRA and its Department of Transportation attorneys were overwhelmed by the size of the task.

Barrett Prettyman's responsibilities as special assistant to Attorney General Robert Kennedy, then to President Kennedy, for transportation matters had helped boost Hogan & Hartson's reputation for railroad expertise, and Ed McDermott's extensive contacts in government and industry also helped garner railroad clients. So when the USRA needed help, Hogan & Hartson readily came to mind. Bob Kapp and Kevin Charles, a commercial attorney at the firm, headed a team that often included twenty attorneys at a time. One of them, George "Sandy" Mayo, recalled that for many years the USRA case was the firm's largest representation. Kevin Charles came to the USRA case in 1973 after winning the largest condemnation award to that date from the federal government, when it condemned O. Roy Chalk's privately owned D.C. Transit Company. Now Charles, who had won $40 million for Chalk, would work for the government side, trying to garner as much value as possible for the taxpayers who were paying for the defunct railroad properties.

Sandy Berger worked long nights on the D.C. Transit Company condemnation when he first arrived at Hogan & Hartson in January 1973. He spent his first "all-nighter" at the firm working on that case during the week his first daughter was born, "which endeared me greatly to my wife, as you can imagine," he recalled later. But instead of migrating to the USRA case, Berger instead moved to the CSD to work with John Ferren and Allen Snyder. Many young attorneys like Berger and Snyder gained invaluable experience in both corporate and litigation work while rotating through the Community Services Department. From its initial baptism with the Black Panthers, the CSD took on several major cases in the 1970s involving housing discrimination, nuclear power generation, defense of the NAACP, and provision of low-cost heating fuel to the poor.

In 1974 Ferren and Snyder won a favorable decision from the U.S. Court of Appeals for the Sixth Circuit in a famous "urban renewal equals Negro removal" case. Lawyers from the University of Detroit law clinic had successfully sued the U.S. Department of Housing and Urban Development and the city fathers of Hamtramck, a Polish enclave within Detroit, over an urban renewal plan that effectively removed Hamtramck's African-American residents. The case now was in its remedy phase — how to fix the problem — and the lead attorney for the legal clinic was moving to Micronesia. Could Hogan & Hartson help? Ferren and Snyder drafted a plan for building new housing and bringing back all the residents who had been displaced. The court accepted

E. TAZEWELL "TED" ELLET, PRESIDENT-ELECT OF THE VIRGINIA BAR, AND JACK KEENEY, JR., PRESIDENT-ELECT OF THE DISTRICT OF COLUMBIA BAR, AT THE ABA CONVENTION, AUGUST 2003.

From Frank Hogan's service as president of the American Bar Association in 1938-1939 to the present, Hogan & Hartson attorneys have been leaders in both local and national bar association activities. In the late 1960s Jim Hourihan and George Carneal, then in the Young Lawyers Section of the voluntary Bar Association of the District of Columbia (BADC), helped rally support for the formation of a mandatory or "unified" bar association which all practicing lawyers in D.C. would be required to join. The purpose of the mandatory bar was reform and professional discipline. Said Hourihan in the D.C. Bar Journal, "Unifying the D.C. Bar would greatly enhance the probability that professional misconduct would not go unpunished."

The 1970 statute authorizing the establishment of a unified D.C. Bar also prescribed a major reorganization of D.C.'s court system, transferring authority over major felonies from federal courts to two newly created local courts, the Superior Court of the District of Columbia and the D.C. Court of Appeals. In 1971 and early 1972 attorney Albert E. Brault of the BADC, working with the D.C. Court of Appeals, chaired the effort to make the unified bar a reality.

In June 1972 Hogan & Hartson's E. Barrett Prettyman, Jr., was elected first president of the unified District of Columbia Bar, which enrolled 15,125 members in its first year.

Prettyman's daunting organizational tasks included everything from the basics of office space and equipment to the formation of a citizens' advisory group and an ethics committee. Nevertheless, a year later Prettyman handed over to successor Charles T. Duncan the presidency of a viable and growing bar association. The BADC continued to function as a voluntary association, and Hogan & Hartson partner Jack Arness served as its president in 1979.

Two Hogan & Hartson partners, Sally Determan and Jack Keeney, later served terms as president of the unified D.C. Bar. In 1990-1991 Determan strengthened the Bar's pro bono activities through a legal clinic program, a telephone information service, and a Family Law Task Force. And in 2004 Keeney succeeded Shirley Ann Higuchi as the Bar's president. Thirty-two years after Barrett Prettyman's presidency, the D.C. Bar boasted over 80,000 members — nearly a fivefold increase. Not to be outdone, Aviation Group partner Ted Ellett, the former chief counsel of the Federal Aviation Administration, began his term as president of the Virginia Bar Association in 2004. He followed in the footsteps of former partner Lang Keith, who served as president of the Virginia Bar Association in 1994.

E. BARRETT PRETTYMAN, JR., FIRST PRESIDENT OF THE D.C. BAR.

HOGAN & HARTSON

FRANK J. HOGAN (1877-1944)
NELSON T. HARTSON (1887-1976)

SEYMOUR S. MINTZ
GEORGE E. MONK
EDWARD A. McDERMOTT
FRANK F. ROBERSON
MERLE THORPE, JR.
LEE LOEVINGER
WILLIAM T. PLUMB, JR.
C. FRANK REIFSNYDER
GEORGE W. WISE
ROBERT K. EIFLER
EDGAR W. HOLTZ
JOHN P. ARNESS
FRANCIS L. CASEY, JR.
E. BARRETT PRETTYMAN, JR.
ARNOLD C. JOHNSON
LINWOOD HOLTON
MARSHALL T. MAYS
JOHN J. ROSS
HOWARD F. ROYCROFT
ROBERT H. KAPP

SHERWIN J. MARKMAN
ROBERT J. ELLIOTT
JAY E. RICKS
ROBERT M. JEFFERS
DENNIS J. LEHR
ARTHUR J. ROTHKOPF
KEVIN P. CHARLES
JEROME N. SONOSKY
JAMES A. HOURIHAN
GERALD E. GILBERT
AUSTIN S. MITTLER
VINCENT H. COHEN
HOWARD R. MOSKOF
GEORGE U. CARNEAL
GARY L. CHRISTENSEN
ALFRED T. SPADA
BOB GLEN ODLE
RICHARD S. RODIN
STUART PHILIP ROSS
RICHARD J. M. POULSON

PETER W. TREDICK
ANTHONY S. HARRINGTON
ALFRED JOHN DOUGHERTY
PETER F. ROUSSELOT
JAMES J. ROSENHAUER
SARA-ANN DETERMAN
JOSEPH M. HASSETT
ROBERT E. MONTGOMERY, JR.
JOE CHARTOFF
DAVID J. HENSLER
ERIC A. VON SALZEN
GEORGE W. MILLER
ALPHONSO A. CHRISTIAN, II
MARTIN MICHAELSON
M. LANGHORNE KEITH
WILLIAM R. SCHIEF
MARVIN J. DIAMOND
GAIL STARLING MARSHALL
CURTIS E. VON KANN
DAVID B. LYTLE
WILLIAM S. REYNER, JR.

J. WILLIAM FULBRIGHT
OF COUNSEL

HOGAN & HARTSON LETTERHEAD, 1978, SHOWS 61 PARTNERS AND 1 OF COUNSEL, J. WILLIAM FULBRIGHT.

the plan, though many of those displaced had made other arrangements during the several years it took to conclude the case and decide the remedy.

In 1975 Bob Jeffers, Patrick Raher, Sandy Mayo, and David Hensler represented the Natural Resources Defense Council (NRDC) in its effort to block construction of the Vermont Nuclear Power Station near Brattleboro. Hensler had joined the firm's litigation department in 1968, working with Jack Arness on "every kind of case, everything you can imagine," he said, echoing Arness's infectious energy. Now Hensler could add a landmark environmental case to his growing litigation repertoire. The CSD team argued that the Atomic Energy Commission (AEC), which had granted a license to Vermont Yankee, had not paid sufficient attention to the power plant's environmental impact. But in the middle of his oral argument, Raher sensed that D.C. Circuit Court of Appeals Judge David Bazelon was more interested in whether or not the AEC had followed proper administrative procedures than in how Vermont Yankee would dispose of spent fuel rods. So, "to the total dismay of our client, who was sitting in the room," Raher recalled, "I completely abandoned my oral argument that we had practiced for months" and instead hammered away on the 1946 Administrative Procedure Act. The tactic worked. The D.C. Circuit decision for the NRDC was so significant, said Hensler, "it shut down the licensing of nuclear power plants in the United States for at least four months."

However, Judge Bazelon's ruling proved to be the straw that broke the camel's back of conservative impatience with "judicial activism," and in 1978 the Supreme Court reversed the D.C. Circuit decision. Justice Rehnquist delivered an especially strong opinion, stating that the lower court had "seriously misread or misapplied" relevant statutes and cautioned courts against "engrafting their own notions of proper procedures upon agencies entrusted with substantive functions by Congress."[18] The firm's CSD had not been involved in the Supreme Court appeal. But the partial meltdown at the Three Mile Island nuclear plant near Harrisburg, Pennsylvania, just a year later, in March 1979, accomplished what the Vermont Yankee suit had not — a prolonged reconsideration of the safety of nuclear power generation.

That year also saw a more successful conclusion in the Fifth Circuit of a Mississippi case that once had threatened the very existence of the NAACP. Fourteen years earlier, in 1965, the NAACP had organized a boycott of Port Gibson, Mississippi, businesses that would not serve African-Americans. The merchants of Port Gibson, a river town in Claiborne County, filed a multimillion-dollar antitrust suit seeking damages for lost business. In August 1976 a Hinds County, Mississippi, judge ruled in favor of the merchants and issued an injunction against continuance of the boycott. He also awarded the merchants $1.25 million in damages.

The NAACP wished to appeal, but under Mississippi law the organization was required to post bond in the amount of 125 percent of the damages in order to stop immediate enforcement of the court's judgment pending appeal. The NAACP did not have

$1.6 million. It asked the Mississippi state court to stay the judgment, but the court refused. So the NAACP called Hogan & Hartson's CSD for help. Attorneys Vincent Cohen, Allen Snyder, Elliot Mincberg, Benton Hammond, Walter Smith, and David Tatel responded.

Tatel had known John Ferren from public interest work in Chicago, where Tatel had attended law school and directed the National Lawyers' Committee for Civil Rights for two years before coming to Hogan & Hartson's CSD in 1974 as the department's Senior Associate. While at the Lawyers' Committee he had noticed something wrong with his eyesight. During his early meetings with Ferren and Bob Kapp at Hogan & Hartson, Tatel thought he should tell them, before they made a commitment, that he was suffering from retinitis pigmentosa and was slowly but surely going blind. "You want to think about it?" he asked. "So," they replied, "what do you need?" It hadn't occurred to them that Tatel was offering the firm a way to back out. Instead, Tatel learned braille and the firm provided him with readers and tape recorders.

In Mississippi the Hogan & Hartson team went to a federal court in the northern part of the state and filed suit to enjoin collection of the $1.25 million judgment from the NAACP. On October 1, 1976, just hours before the deadline for collection, Judge Orma Smith issued a temporary restraining order. The NAACP was not free of the judgment but at least it had been granted time to conduct the lengthy appeals process. In 1979 the Fifth Circuit affirmed Judge Smith's decision. And in 1982, in a related case involving a suit against the NAACP by a Claiborne hardware store, the U.S. Supreme Court ruled that the boycott had not been an exercise in antitrust but an expression of free speech and therefore was protected by the Constitution.[19] Hogan & Hartson was not involved in the Supreme Court case but took satisfaction in having earlier rescued the NAACP from a fate that likely would have rendered the Supreme Court victory pyrrhic.

McDermott's referral of the Citizens Energy Corporation to the CSD was an example of the fulfillment of Ferren's hopes for the department's centrifugal influence on the firm. Founded by Robert Kennedy's son Joseph in 1979, Citizens Energy aimed to take advantage of certain features of the international oil market at the time when market prices were above the official selling price. Prices had soared since the 1973-1974 Organization of Petroleum Exporting Countries (OPEC) oil embargo, peaking again in 1977 in what became known as the "second energy crisis." If Kennedy could use his celebrity and reputation to negotiate contracts at official selling prices with governmental oil companies, he could then capture the difference between the selling price and the market price to subsidize heating fuel for Boston's poor. But he needed expert economic and legal advice. McDermott, whose son had been a close friend of Joe Kennedy, steered him to Joe Bell.

Bell, a new Hogan & Hartson attorney, had learned something about the international oil market while serving as assistant general counsel for international matters at the Federal Energy Administration, just prior to joining the firm, and through his prior work for the Cabinet Task Force on Oil Import Controls. He also had earned a master's degree in economics at Harvard before entering law school. Bell took on the Citizens Energy case through the CSD, accompanying Kennedy on trips to Venezuela, Ecuador, Algeria, and Saudi Arabia and helping the fledgling nonprofit company surmount numerous tax and regulatory hurdles on its way to providing relief to the poor in Kennedy's home state.

As in other departments at Hogan & Hartson, the number and variety of cases handled by the CSD grew dramatically by the end of the decade to include the rescuing of the Office of Economic Opportunity's legal services program for the poor; land rights in Maine for the Passamaquoddy tribe; police brutality in Prince George's County, Maryland; education for children of undocumented aliens in Texas; food stamps for the elderly in Washington, D.C.; rights of the mentally ill; revisions of the federal criminal code; fair wages for sugar cane workers in Louisiana; and services for such organizations as the Legal Services Corporation, the National Hospice Society, and the Vietnam Veterans Memorial Fund.

In 1978 Sandy Mayo had seen a television news report about a Vietnam veteran named Jan Scruggs who was collecting funds to build a memorial but, three months into the project, had only ten dollars to show for his efforts. That bothered Mayo, himself a Vietnam veteran, so he and another veteran, D.C. attorney Jack Wheeler, contacted Scruggs and offered to help get the project moving. Before long the Vietnam Veterans Memorial Fund had raised $9 million, about half of which paid for Maya Lin's remarkable structure, dedicated in 1982 near the Lincoln Memorial. The Vietnam Veterans Memorial has since done much to heal the divisions the war itself created.

In 1977 the Robert Vesco case returned in the form of a multimillion-dollar malpractice suit against Hogan & Hartson brought in the name of ICC, the company previously controlled by Vesco. The suit was initiated and prosecuted by an attorney named David Butowski, who had originally been appointed in 1973 as a special counsel to ICC by the SEC with authority to prepare a report of possible claims by ICC and to hire himself and his law firm to prove them. In September he was prepared to submit his report to the court. But first he offered Hogan & Hartson a choice. He could write the final draft two ways. One, favorable to the firm, hinged on Hogan & Hartson settling the claims. The other, highly critical of the firm, would follow if the firm refused to settle. Hogan & Hartson refused.

Attorneys representing Hogan & Hartson in the suit challenged Butowski's two-report offer, as well as his ongoing representation, citing a conflict of interest between his role as SEC-appointed special counsel and his role as a partner in a law firm that stood to make a considerable profit from the case. But the judge saw nothing untoward in Butowski's offer to settle, and though he recognized that "it would have been preferable for another law firm to represent ICC in this case," he did not think that "the appearance of impropriety alone justifies an order of disqualification."[20] Butowski never had any evidence of malpractice. To the contrary, the ICC-Vesco representation was a classic case of effective, tough-minded lawyering in trying circumstances. Butowski eventually dropped the case in return for a very small payment. Many firm attorneys, including particularly Bob Jeffers, Bob Odle, Joe Hassett, and Sherwin Markman, contributed their efforts to the firm's defense.

Because the ICC malpractice claim originated in the SEC Division of Enforcement, then headed by Stanley Sporkin, it was with much satisfaction that Jeffers received a phone call in June 1997 from partner Patricia Brannan. Brannan had been at a forum on ethics in which Sporkin, then a United States District Judge, cited Jeffers's representation of Vesco as an example of how an ethical lawyer ought to behave with a difficult client.

Jeffers's approach to international corporate practice was an inspiration to young Bob Waldman, who had joined Hogan & Hartson in 1974 after he discovered that two highly respected former law school classmates, Allen Snyder and Sandy Berger, were at the firm. Additionally, Waldman had worked with John Ferren as a member of the board of student advisors when Ferren taught at Harvard Law School. Rounding out his sense that, like his undergraduate education at Duke University, Hogan & Hartson was something of a "well-guarded secret," Waldman discovered that the chair of the firm's recruitment committee was Tony Harrington, whom Waldman had met when Harrington was assistant dean at Duke's law school. Waldman had asked Snyder straightforwardly, "Why are you here?" Snyder had replied, "Because I think young lawyers tend to be happier here."

Several years later, when Waldman himself was recruiting for Hogan & Hartson, he explained what Allen's answer had meant to him: "There's a high degree of talent here, an ability to produce high-quality work, but it's reposed in people who don't have some of the negative characteristics associated with top tier law practice. There are not a lot of egoists here. We have a very low prima donna quotient."

Waldman learned that firsthand under Bob Jeffers's tutelage in the 1970s while working on transactions such as a major investment in some Brazilian subsidiaries of Fried Krupp GMBH by the Imperial Government of Iran. In 1975 Jeffers and Waldman made several trips to Paris and Frankfurt and other cities in Europe, where Jeffers took his younger colleague on extensive tours, sharing his knowledge of neighborhoods, museums, and landmarks, as well as the ways of European business transactions. These included long days and long nights filled with numerous business meetings, receptions, and dinners. As Waldman recalled Jeffers's viewpoint, "How could you be an international lawyer if you didn't appreciate the city and the people and the places and the art and the wine and the culture?"

On one memorable occasion Jeffers and Waldman traveled to Manaus on the Amazon, deep into Brazil's interior, just to explore what was there. Jeffers was experienced at using guides to learn as much as he could in the brief time available. Similarly, on a one-day trip to London — Waldman's first — Jeffers hired a cab to drive him and Waldman throughout the city. "You could not have bargained for a greater experience," said Waldman, recalling his travels and transactions with Jeffers. Later, Jeffers and Waldman found additional use for their international experience when they became the firm's "office experts" on the SEC's "voluntary" disclosure program for questionable foreign payments and later the Foreign Corrupt Practices Act of 1977.

Hogan & Hartson's Executive Committee had long known of Jeffers's conscientiousness and good judgment. In 1970 Jeffers had served on a committee, chaired by Seymour Mintz, to review the firm's governance structure. It was a sensitive task, for it involved changing the way decisions were made at the firm, and who made them. The committee recommended that no member of the Executive Committee be allowed to succeed himself or herself after the three-year term. An individual could be elected again but not without sitting out for at least one year. Wrote Jeffers at the time, the change "not only would give more people a chance to deal with and understand the problems of the firm, but also would discourage vested interest in the Executive Committee."[21] The firm adopted the change, which Jim Rosenhauer credited not only with "enhancing the democracy of the firm, but also with making people feel that the Executive Committee was composed of people who were doing it as a service and not as a power grab."

The newly democratized Executive Committee soon enacted another change in the firm's management by creating an Administrative Partner position in 1973 and appointing John Ferren to fill it. Since 1961 Hogan & Hartson had employed an accountant and controller, Ken Emery, and a personnel and, later, services manager, Natalie Pace. But like many other law firms in the 1970s, Hogan & Hartson had grown beyond the Executive Committee's capacity to manage it effectively on a daily basis. As Administrative Partner, Ferren would have overall administrative responsibility for running the firm, while the Executive Committee continued to make strategic, policy, and compensation decisions. Ferren quipped later that some partners may have thought, "Well, maybe we'll get some work out of Ferren now, because he hasn't brought in a nickel of money." But in truth, as head of the CSD he had demonstrated a talent for administration, and the firm saw use for it on a wider scale. It was under Ferren, for example, and with the prodding of Lee Loevinger, that the firm organized its attorneys' work into specialized practice groups.

Ferren continued to spend a portion of his time in the CSD, but the department was effectively run by its Senior Associate, David Tatel. Ferren returned to the CSD in 1977 but soon was appointed by President Carter to the District of Columbia Court of Appeals. When Tatel, now a partner, also left in 1977 for a two-year stint as director of the Office of Civil Rights at the U.S. Department of Health, Education and Welfare, colleague and partner Sally Determan became head of the CSD.

Jerry Gilbert succeeded Ferren as Administrative Partner and served a year and a half. Labor attorney Peter Tredick took over from Gilbert in 1977, also for a limited time, and turned the job over to Bob Odle in 1979. The Administrative Partner position was deliberately named so as *not* to be confused with the more powerful Managing Partner model that many other large firms had adopted. Hogan & Hartson's Executive Committee had proven a successful management vehicle thus far and was not prepared to dilute its own authority. Additionally, the partners were, as has been said of lawyers generally, notoriously suspicious of any centralized power. As Ferren had said, with self-deprecating perspective, "I was not any czar. Who was I? I was a guy in his thirties who had been doing *pro bono* work." Gilbert had taken the job ("You never said no to Seymour Mintz") on condition he could leave it in a year and a half. Tredick and Odle did likewise, eager to unburden themselves of administrative chores and return to building their practices.

The Administrative Partner job was structured to meet the firm's management needs without arousing anxiety over centralized control and bureaucracy. Odle, who was on the Executive Committee when he also became Administrative Partner, characterized the attitude as, "Mr. Administrative Partner, here's your charter, here are your responsibilities, but be sure that you don't do anything without checking with us first." The position was a compromise between the old Hogan & Hartson and the new, whose outlines were as yet better felt than clearly seen in the turbulence of changing times.

Chapter 4
A Sense of Poise
1979-1989

Between 1979 and 1989 Hogan & Hartson underwent a profound change, partly in its size and in the scope of its practice, but mostly in its sense of its own possibilities. It had prided itself on being a premier Washington, D.C., law firm. But by the end of the 1980s it had opened offices outside the city and was looking overseas for opportunities to serve an expanded corporate and international clientele. The firm's values, its culture, remained remarkably constant throughout this growth, not by accident but by painstaking design. It accommodated both tough-minded competitiveness and patient support for new and untried ideas, both high expectations for performance and a sense of balance and good humor.

In just ten years Hogan & Hartson worked through a certain indefinable hesitation about its own growth. In a word, it achieved a sense of poise. By the end of the 1980s the firm felt sufficiently confident in the strength of its traditions to engage boldly the challenges of continued growth and innovation. The growth wasn't just about geography and offices, but about people and their personal horizons. And the innovation wasn't just about practice areas, but about management and leadership, too. Without exception, and with unreserved gratitude, attorneys in the firm later recalled one of their number as having been the consummate captain and chief navigator during the voyage. And without hesitation Bob Glen Odle returned the thanks and credit. In the late 1970s, though, no one at Hogan & Hartson, Bob Odle included, showed much prescience about, or even interest in, preparing the firm for a wholly new venture.

Jerry Gilbert warned Peter Tredick, his successor as the firm's Administrative Partner in 1977, that he was in for an awkward experience. Anxious about any dilution of its traditional authority, which had served Hogan & Hartson so well for four decades, the Executive Committee had not quite figured out what to do with the new job. More than once Gilbert had found himself in the office of one Executive Committee member who told him, "Do this," then he'd be called into another member's office and told to do the exact opposite. The

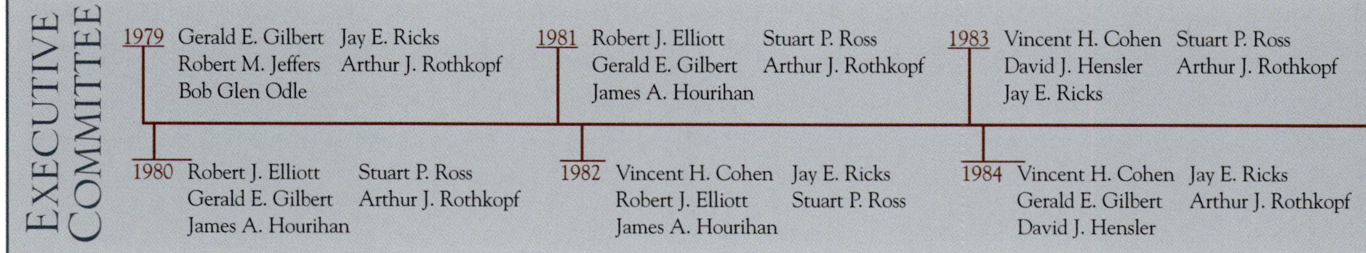

THE COLLIN COUNTY COURTHOUSE IN MCKINNEY TEXAS, HOMETOWN OF HOGAN & HARTSON'S BOB GLEN ODLE.

best Gilbert felt he could do under the circumstances was smooth ruffled feathers and avoid collisions. The Executive Committee, he warned Tredick, was very good at setting policy, "but implementing it was a different story."

Tredick soldiered on for two years, until the end of his term and the need for a replacement forced the issue once again to the attention of the committee. By now the members knew there was a problem and they discussed it openly around the table. "You know," suggested one, "maybe we would feel differently about this job and the responsibilities of the person holding it if that person were a member of the Executive Committee." That seemed like a good idea to all, including the committee's youngest member, Bob Glen Odle, until Odle realized that everyone else on the committee was looking straight at him.

"We're talking about one year, right?" Odle bargained, figuring that his service as Administrative Partner would end along with his term on the Executive Committee. "Yeah, that's what we're talking about," the committee reassured him. "OK," Odle acceded, "I'll do it for a year." When his year was up in 1980 Odle told the committee, "Thank you very much." But the members asked him to continue, reminding him that the job usually had been held for two years. Odle felt he could not refuse. Besides, he and the Executive Committee were forging an excellent working relationship that the committee, at least, did not want to lose. "I knew what the issues were," Odle recalled. "I knew that I could run so far without checking back, and I knew I shouldn't run beyond that point without checking back, and so it just worked really well." The committee saw that Odle possessed an instinct for organizational and human relations, that he was straightforward and focused, and that he inspired trust in others — perhaps in part because he showed only lukewarm ambition for the assignment.

It was not the first time Odle had been a hesitant traveler on the path to his own success. After graduating from the University of Texas in 1960 he and his college roommate, David Kendrick, had entered Army Reserve training. Kendrick had finished before Odle and had gone to Washington to work for his congressman. He wrote Odle, who was still at Fort Ord, California, "What are you going to do when you get out of the Army?" "I don't know," Odle wrote back. "Well, since you don't have anything better to do, why don't you come to Washington? It's a lot of fun!" "Well, maybe," replied Odle, laconically.

Kendrick followed up with a letter telling Odle of a job opening on Capitol Hill, but by the time Odle got around to responding someone else had snapped up the job. Kendrick persisted, inquiring at the office of Odle's congressman, legendary Speaker of the House Sam Rayburn. "Have him write the Speaker a letter and tell him everything good he can say about himself," instructed John Holton, Rayburn's administrative assistant. Odle sent the letter but Rayburn's office never answered. He finished his Army training in March 1961, returned to his hometown, McKinney, and applied to the University of Texas in Austin for a graduate program in city management. "I didn't know what I wanted to do," Odle said later, "and it seemed like something I could do."

EXECUTIVE COMMITTEE

1985 Gerald E. Gilbert, Arthur J. Rothkopf, David J. Hensler, Allen R. Snyder, Robert M. Jeffers

1986 Gerald E. Gilbert, Peter F. Rousselot, Robert M. Jeffers, Allen R. Snyder, Jay E. Ricks

1987 Robert J. Jeffers, Peter F. Rousselot, Jay E. Ricks, Allen R. Snyder, Arthur J. Rothkopf

1988 George U. Carneal, Arthur J. Rothkopf, Anthony S. Harrington, Peter F. Rousselot, Jay E. Ricks

1989 Charles E. Allen, David J. Hensler, George U. Carneal, Arthur J. Rothkopf, Anthony S. Harrington

One day, while waiting to go to Austin, Odle wandered down to the courthouse square in McKinney to "make the rounds," stopping in at stores and businesses to say hello. McKinney had not yet become a bedroom community of sprawling Dallas, thirty miles to the south. One shop was an all-service real estate, notary public, and insurance business owned by the Roberts family. Roy Roberts, grandfather to one of Odle's friends, greeted him warmly. "Come on over, have a seat. Tell me whatcha goin' to do with yourself now that you're out of the army." "Gee, Mr. Roy, I don't know," Odle said hesitantly. "I think I'm going to go back to school."

Bob Odle worked for the storied Speaker of the House Sam Rayburn in 1961. Here Rayburn is ready to go to the Democratic National Convention in Chicago, August 1956.

"The second I said that," Odle later remembered with a laugh, "I knew I'd made a big mistake, because Mr. Roy didn't think a whole lot of education. He thought college was a waste of time; you need to get out there and work." Seeking to smooth things over, Odle recalled that Mr. Roy had been Congressman Rayburn's campaign manager and quickly mentioned his recent effort to get a job in Rayburn's office in Washington. "I wrote Sam Rayburn," he offered in self-defense, "but I never heard from him." "Well, that old sonofabitch," Roberts sputtered, sitting straight up in his chair. "He will too answer your letter!" Odle figured he'd "dodged a bullet" when he managed a clean exit from Roy Roberts's store.

A few weeks later, in April, Odle answered the phone at his new, part-time job in the University of Texas's student center. It was Secretary of the Navy John Connally's assistant, offering a job as a computer programmer. Evidently Rayburn's office was still trying to do right by Mr. Roy. "No, I don't think so. I've decided I'm going to graduate school," answered Odle. About six weeks later he drove home to McKinney to visit before summer classes began. When he arrived late Wednesday night his mother was in a panic. "Where have you been? Sam Rayburn's office is looking for you, and they said if you don't call back by eight o'clock in the morning, forget it, it's too late!"

Odle called Washington first thing in the morning. Rayburn was busy but Holton promised he'd call right back. He did. "Bob, this is Sam Rayburn. You want to work for me?" "Yes, sir, Mr. Rayburn, I do." "Well, good. You be here Monday morning." "Yes, sir." One of Rayburn's employees had quit just when Texas State Senator Ray Roberts, Mr. Roy's son, happened to be in the Speaker's office. Odle's name had come up. Ray had vouched for him, so Rayburn placed the call.

Odle reported for work in Washington early on a Monday in June 1961. He was shown his desk but no one ever told him what his job was. "I just started watching and observing. After a while, you sort of get the hang of it," he recalled. Six months later Speaker Rayburn died of cancer and Ray Roberts won his seat in a special election, with Odle serving as his campaign assistant. Odle returned to Washington to work for now-Congressman Ray Roberts, who began pressing him about going to law school, something Roberts himself regretted he never had done. So Odle enrolled in night classes at George Washington University Law School, rushing from Capitol Hill to

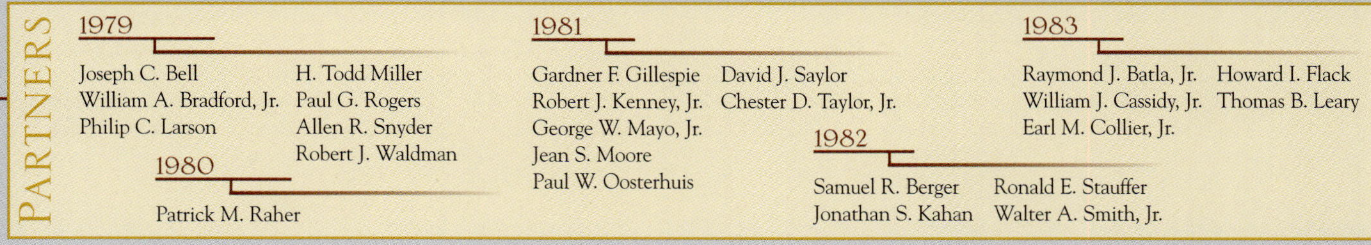

BOB ODLE (L) WITH FELLOW TEXAN, U.S. SUPREME COURT JUSTICE TOM C. CLARK, AT ODLE'S SWEARING-IN AS A MEMBER OF THE TEXAS BAR, 1966.

class at 7:00 p.m., returning home at 10:30 p.m. to fix dinner and study, then showing up for work the next morning in time to have the office running smoothly by 8:00 a.m. when Roberts arrived. It couldn't last and it didn't. If Roberts ever had tried it himself he would have understood.

Still, having to abandon his law classes gnawed at Odle. He had never been ironclad sure about what he wanted to do, but neither had he ever quit something once he had started it. He returned to Austin and enrolled in law school full time in 1963, not because he wanted to practice law necessarily, but because he thought it would prepare him well for whatever else he might do.

Odle did not participate in the annual ritual of job interviews in the fall of 1965, during his final year at the University of Texas Law School. But he had planned a trip to Washington, D.C., during the Christmas break, and some of his law professors, "who, gratefully, were more interested in my career than I seemingly was at the time," he said later, suggested that he interview some law firms while he was there. Odle interviewed at a few firms, including Hogan & Hartson, but still was unsure where he wanted to work. He also interviewed at some Texas firms. Soon he had offers from both locations. Without entirely resolving his uncertainty, he decided to take Hogan & Hartson's offer, and in August 1966 he started with Merle Thorpe, Jr., in the firm's corporate department.

A year-and-a-half later the U.S. Department of Commerce asked Hogan & Hartson to grant a lawyer temporary leave to help out in the Office of Foreign Direct Investments, which was trying to fix the nation's severe balance of payments problem. Odle found the nine-month assignment interesting enough, but as the time approached for returning to Hogan & Hartson in 1969 he simply could not summon any excitement, either for government service or for the work he had been doing at the firm. He met with Lester Cohen, who had interviewed him when he first applied, and told him how he was feeling. He liked the firm and everybody he had met, he told Cohen, but he just wanted to go back to Texas. Cohen didn't want to lose him. "Well, you've got to come back," he cajoled, "we want you to come back." "That makes me feel really good," said Odle, "but I need to try something else, and I think I'm going back to Texas."

Shortly afterwards Cohen invited Odle for another discussion. "Would you come? Ed McDermott and I want to talk with you." They met in the Chanin Building, not around Cohen's desk but in the comfortable chairs that Cohen arranged informally, away from his desk, to help set a relaxed and easygoing mood. Ed McDermott was not a relaxed or easygoing man, often tapping impatiently on his watch during meetings when he thought a speaker was going on too long or wandering

PARTNERS

1984
Benton R. Hammond
John C. Joyce
Janet L. McDavid
Peter J. Romeo
Clifford D. Stromberg

1985
Frank J. Fahrenkopf, Jr.
Prentiss E. Feagles
Richard C. Green
John C. Keeney, Jr.
Neal L. Petersen
Mary Anne Sullivan
Craig H. Ulman
Joel S. Winnik

1986
Patricia R. Ambrose
Steven E. Ballew
Robert B. Cave
Edward B. Crosland, Jr.
J. Warren Gorrell, Jr.
David J. Hayes
Harry T. Jones, Jr.
Andrew J. Kilcarr
Elliot M. Mincberg
Maureen E. O'Bryon
Richard J. Perry, Jr.
Anthony S. Harrington
Peter W. Tredick

Bob Odle (L) and Ed McDermott, January 1988. The opportunity to work with McDermott persuaded Odle to drop his plans to move back to Texas in 1969.

off topic. But for all his hurriedness he was not unpleasant or irascible, and Cohen perhaps sensed that McDermott and Odle would work well together.

When they all were seated and the small talk about Odle's Commerce Department work was over, Cohen asked, "Would it change your mind if you could spend full time working with Ed in his practice?" McDermott's work was wide-ranging, policy-oriented, and client-centered, drawing deeply on the kind of political intuition and personal contact Odle had absorbed, but had never much cared to exploit, while "making the rounds" in McKinney. In the morning McDermott might be on Capitol Hill, gathering information about proposed shipping regulations for a client, the Committee of European National Shipowners Associations, while after lunch he might be looking out for the interests of a hometown Iowa business that was being acquired by a larger New York company. Something clicked for Odle. "Are you kidding?" he exclaimed. "Yes, it would." Characteristically, it had not occurred to him to push for working with McDermott; instead, he seemed to need someone to draw it out of him. The experience was a lesson to Odle about the circuitous ways that human talent often travels on its way to useful expression, and about the importance of discernment, encouragement, and second chances.

While Odle worked mainly with Ed McDermott, his practice also involved a variety of other assignments, including helping Sherwin Markman extract Robert Vesco from a Swedish jail. He described himself as a "utility infielder" attorney, learning about law practice and client development from McDermott, but also, and more important for his future work, about the value of long-range planning and the art of helping people believe in themselves. McDermott himself had learned some things about leadership in the White House while directing the Office of Emergency Preparedness for John F. Kennedy. Once, when he had shared with the President his doubts about his ability to supervise others, Kennedy had reminded him, "I have confidence that you can do the job. That's why I appointed you. I want you to make every decision you can make, and I will support you. If you think it is a decision the President must make, then you come to me and we will make it."[1] These were simple but wise words, respectful of the boundaries separating confidence from bluster, delegation from buck-passing, and leadership from the mere exercise of authority.

Perhaps for this reason as much as any other, Ed McDermott was among the Executive Committee members most dubious about delegating power to the Administrative Partner, but also most likely to acquiesce if it were Bob Odle who would hold the job. By 1980, at the end of his second year as Administrative Partner, Odle's skill at canvassing the partners, conveying their needs to the Executive Committee, and then helping frame and implement solutions that met those needs was obvious to everyone. Odle's two years were up, but as Executive Committee member Arthur Rothkopf said when the committee considered replacing him, "What are we doing this for? We've got the right guy. Let's just leave him there."

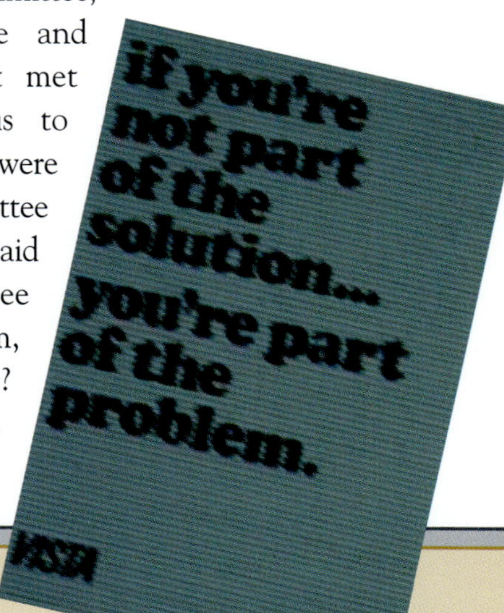

1987

William J. Bowman
Duncan S. Klinedinst
Edward L. Korwek
David B.H. Martin
Peter A. Rohrbach
Helen R. Trilling
Susan Wing

1988

George Beall
Patricia A. Brannan
Ty Cobb
Michael D. Colglazier
Joseph G. Connally, Jr.
Richard E. Dunne, III
E. Tazewell Ellett
Kevin G. Gralley
J. Clinton Kelly
David A. Kikel
Wendy T. Kirby
Lewis E. Leibowitz
Mark S. McConnell
George H. Mernick, III
Dennis K. Moyer
Bruce E. Parmley
John G. Roberts, Jr.
Paul C. Skelly
John S. Stanton
Mark A. Sterling
Ann Morgan Vickery

Frank J. Hogan
(1902-1944) Joseph Sheehy
(1902-1913) D.W. Baker (1910-1913)
Edmund L. Jones (1916-1975) William
H. Donovan (1918-1945) Nelson T. Hartson
(1925-1972) Arthur J. Phelan (1925-1964) John W.
Guider (1926-1946) Duke M. Patrick (1933-1964) Karl
A. Smith (1933-1958) George E. Monk (1934-) Lester Cohen
(1934-1972) O.R. McGuire Jr. (1937-1967) Howard Boyd (1939-1952)
James C. Rogers (1939-1966) Joseph J. Cotter (Of Counsel 1939-1946)
Merle Thorpe, Jr. (1941-) Corwin R. Lockwood, Jr. (1941-1975) Joseph J.
Smith Jr. (1945-1966) John St. Clair Brookes Jr. (1946-1959) Frank R. Roberson
(1946-) George D. Horning, Jr. (1946-1964) Seymour S. Mintz (1946-) Robert
K. Eifler (1947-1979) James F. Byrnes (Of Counsel 1947-1949) Donald S. Russell
(Of Counsel 1947-1949) Paul R. Connolly (1948-1966) John J. Sirica (1949-1957)
Parker D. Hancock (1951-1960) William T. Plumb, Jr. (1951-) C. Frank Reifsnyder
(1951-) John P. Arness (1952-) Francis L. Casey, Jr. (1953-) Stanley S. Harris (1953-1970)
Frederick M. Bradley (1954-1974) Bruce J. Kellison (1954-1973) E. Barrett Prettyman (1955-)
George W. Wise (1955-) John J. Ross (1956-) Jeremiah C. Collins (1956-1966) Howard F.
Roycroft (1958-) Arnold C. Johnson (1959-) Russell B. Pace (1959-1968) Edgar W. Holtz (1960-)
John W. Warner (1960-1968) James A. Belson (1960-1968) James E. Murray (1960-1970) Robert J.
Elliott (1961-) James A. Hourihan (1961-) Robert H. Kapp (1961-) George U. Carneal (1962-)
Jay E. Ricks (1962-) Edward A. McDermott (1965-) Robert M. Jeffers (1966-) Bob G. Odle (1966-)
Peter F. Rousselot (1966-) Alfred T. Spada (1966-1978) Carl L. Taylor (1966-1980) William O. Bitt-
man (1967-1974) Dennis J. Lehr (1967-) Arthur J. Rothkopf (1967-) James J. Rosenhauer (1967-) Stuart
Philip Ross (1967-) Charles Allen (1968-1972) Joe Chartoff (1968-) Sara-Ann Determan (1968-) Marvin
J. Diamond (1968-) Gerald E. Gilbert (1968-) Anthony S. Harrington (1968-) David J. Hensler (1968-)
Lee Loevinger (1968-) Sherwin J. Markman (1968-) Austin J. Mittler (1968-) Jerome N. Sonosky
(1968-) William A. Bradford, Jr. (1969-) Kevin P. Charles (1969-) Vincent H. Cohen (1969-)
Alfred J. Dougherty (1969-) David B. Lytle (1969-) Richard S. Rodin (1969-) Peter W. Tredick
(1969-) Curtis E. von Kann (1969-) Eric A. Von Salzen (1969-) Alfred F. Dougherty, Jr. (1970-
1977) John W. Ferren (1970-1977) Joseph M. Hassett (1970-) M. Langhorne Keith (1970-)
George W. Miller (1970-) Howard R. Moskof (1970-) Richard J.M. Poulson (1970-) William
S. Reyner, Jr. (1970-) Charles E. Shreve (Of Counsel 1970-1972) Philip C. Larson (1971-) Gary L.
Christensen (1972-) Alphonso A. Christian II (1972-) Gail Starling Marshall (1972-)
Allen R. Snyder (1972-) Owen M. Johnson (1972-1975) Martin Michaelson (1973-) H. Todd
Miller (1973-) Patrick M. Raher (1973-) David S. Tatel (1974-) Robert J. Waldman
(1974-) J. William Fulbright (Of Counsel 1975-) Robert E. Montgomery, Jr. (1975-)
Linwood Holton (1975-1978) Joseph C. Bell (1977-) William R. Schief
(1977-) Marshall Mays (1977-1979) Paul G. Rogers
(1979-)

AS OF OCTOBER 1, 1980
PARTNERS AT
HOGAN & HARTSON
(and years with the firm)

HOGAN & HARTSON PARTNERS AT THE F STREET CLUB, OCTOBER, 1980.

The decision seemed made but was nearly upset during the firm's first partners' retreat in 1981 at the Boar's Head Inn in Charlottesville, Virginia. By then both the Executive Committee and the firm's seventy partners had begun to feel comfortable with Odle's handling of the Administrative Partner job, even though it had symbolized for many the unwanted prospect of a more centralized management. But the Boar's Head retreat raised one of the most controversial changes facing Hogan & Hartson, and all mid-size and large firms in the early 1980s — expansion outside its home office.

Many partners felt strongly that the firm's strength and uniqueness came from its reputation as Washington, D.C.'s, premier local firm. To establish offices outside the city, even in its near suburbs, might dilute that reputation and blur the distinction between Hogan & Hartson and other firms. But others saw this as parochialism, a recipe for marginalization in an expanding business world. If Hogan & Hartson did not follow its national and international clients into geographical regions where it could best meet their needs, those clients would look to firms that could. Moreover, Washington, D.C., was getting crowded. In 1970 virtually no large firms outside D.C. had branch offices in the Nation's Capital, but ten years later 178 out-of-town firms had opened D.C. offices, employing about 1,800 lawyers. Seven of those branches were among the 25 largest law offices in the city. And by 1983, just three years later, an additional 79 out-of-town firms had opened D.C. offices.[2] Odle believed that growth was not only desirable but necessary for survival. Others, like Kevin Charles, looked wistfully around the conference room in the Chanin Building and declared, "I don't want to be a part of a firm if we can't all meet in this room."[3]

Hogan & Hartson's future depended on its leaders' ability to discern accurately national trends in the legal profession and to persuade its partners to pull together on their oars, despite their misgivings, to navigate the rapids of change. In the 1980s the legal profession was in the

PARTNERS

1989

Edward C. Dolan	Gary J. Kushner	Edward A. Ryan
Sandra E. Folsom	Robert F. Leibenluft	John T. Schell, III
Howard M. Holstein	Judith G. Muncy	Richard S. Silverman
David W. Hornbeck	Rodney R. Munsey	
Stephen J. Immelt	William D. Nussbaum	

throes of another spasm in its chronic syndrome of episodic self-doubt. The American Bar Association's Commission on Professionalism, known as the Stanley Commission, asked in 1986, "Has our profession abandoned principle for profit, professionalism for commercialism?"[4] This self-flagellation was nothing new. For nearly a century critics had flayed lawyers who chose to serve business clients rather than solve social problems. Theodore Roosevelt and Louis Brandeis had sharpened the Progressive era's social conscience on the whetstone of corporate lawyers and law firms. And Jimmy Carter, Ralph Nader, and Derek Bok had done likewise in the turmoil of the civil rights and consumer movements, the Vietnam War, and Watergate's profusion of grand juries and white-collar indictments. Everywhere they looked, reformers seemed to find lawyers more entangled in problems than engaged in solutions.

But beneath these conspicuous debates about training, values, and responsibilities in the legal profession, an ineluctable reality pushed upward like a tectonic plate, changing the very landscape of legal practice in the 1980s. Law firms, though always part business, were becoming vastly more so.[5] Heightened competition among law firms soon became known in the legal press, with ominous overtones, as "the shakeout." To some it was liberating; to others, threatening. The jeremiads it summoned forth about decline, decay, and capitulation to market forces only underscored the new reality. They did not halt it, for its causes were many and deep, reflecting changes in the business world as well as some pertinent court decisions.[6]

The economics of the energy crisis, inflation, and recession in the 1970s and early 1980s pressured corporate clients to reduce legal costs by using in-house counsel and bidding out specific jobs to different firms. The old days of loyalty to a single firm yielded to a newly competitive market for legal services. Additionally, two U.S. Supreme Court decisions in the mid-1970s furthered the evolution to a more obvious business model for legal practice. *Goldfarb v. Virginia State Bar* (1975) struck down minimum fee schedules, holding them to be in violation of the Sherman Antitrust Act, and *Bates and O'Steen v. State Bar of Arizona* (1977) declared the state bar's ban on lawyer advertising to be a violation of the First Amendment.[7] A later Supreme Court case, *Hishon v. King & Spalding* (1984), ruled that decisions about admission to law firm partnerships are subject to Title VII of the 1964 Civil Rights Act, prohibiting employment discrimination. The evaluation of women for partnership on an equal basis with men became a matter of law, not just fairness and common sense, as expanding firms jostled for the most promising law school graduates.

Competition rendered law firms' fees, management structures, compensation, and hiring practices, as well as their "cultures," more transparent and more intensely interesting to competitors. In 1978 attorney and publisher Steven Brill founded *The American Lawyer* magazine to capitalize on law firms' shift toward open competition. Along with the *Legal Times* newspaper and *The National Law Journal*, *The American Lawyer*, as Odle put it, "just hung everybody's linen out to dry." The new "legal media" increased competition not only by reporting about law firms but by ranking them, repeatedly and relentlessly, in numbing permutations of size, revenues, profitability, and even popularity with summer associates.

The downside of this data glut was an exacerbation of competitive pressure and a frankly Darwinian celebration of "winners," as well as what amounted to a public

U.S. Court of Appeals Judge David S. Tatel (District of Columbia Circuit) was appointed to the bench in October 1994. From 1972 to 1974 Judge Tatel had directed the National Lawyer's Committee for Civil Rights Under Law in Washington, D.C. He then headed Hogan & Hartson's Community Services Department until 1977, while also serving (1975-1976) as General Counsel for the newly created Legal Services Corporation. In 1977 he became Director of the Office for Civil Rights, U.S. Department of Health, Education and Welfare, then returned to Hogan & Hartson and established the firm's education practice. Since 1974 Judge Tatel has successfully overcome gradually declining eyesight due to retinitis pigmentosa.

branding as "losers," those firms that had not read the statistical tea leaves or that had failed to react quickly enough to the new market conditions. But there also was an upside, which Bob Odle keenly grasped: "If you were inclined, and I was, you could learn a lot about what other law firms were doing, and you could test what you were doing versus what they were doing over some period of time."

The number of lawyers in the United States more than doubled between 1963 and 1983, from 296,000 to 612,000.[8] The number of lawyers at Hogan & Hartson in the same period quadrupled from about 40 to 160, reflecting the opportunities Frank Hogan long ago had foreseen in a growing federal government. But success never warranted complacency. In 1979 the *Legal Times* ranked Hogan & Hartson #36 in a nationwide list of the largest 100 law firms. In 1981 the firm's ranking had dropped to #63 among the nation's top 200 firms. The following year it slipped farther, to #72. Only a handful of the top 100 firms had not yet opened out-of-town offices. Hogan & Hartson was in that small group. Admittedly, that was partly because the firm already was located where many large firms were opening offices — in the Nation's Capital. Still, despite Washington's importance, the city would probably never serve successfully as the sole location for a large, diversified firm. Bob Odle saw the tea leaves, but the partnership was not quite ready for the reading.

"Our first partners' retreat was about the worst experience I've ever had at Hogan & Hartson," Odle acknowledged twenty-one years later. "We went down there with the idea that we were going to make some decisions, and it caused people just to be a little aggressive with each other in ways that we weren't accustomed to being." Frustrated and unsure whether he would be able to lead the firm where he believed it needed to go, Odle wondered if he should back out of the job. After all, his effectiveness lay mostly in his skill at building consensus, a slow and painstaking process, rather than in exercising direct executive authority. The Executive Committee still held the firm's reins in its five sets of hands. He chose to stay with the assignment but resolved never again to use a retreat to make decisions. Instead, that rare opportunity to gather together each year would be spent just raising and discussing issues and enjoying each other's company.

[LEFT] ALLEN R. SNYDER JOINED HOGAN & HARTSON IN 1972 AFTER CLERKING FOR U.S. SUPREME COURT JUSTICES JOHN HARLAN AND WILLIAM REHNQUIST. SNYDER CONDUCTED A VARIED, HIGHLY SUCCESSFUL LITIGATION AND APPELLATE PRACTICE WHILE SERVING THE D.C. BAR IN NUMEROUS CAPACITIES, INCLUDING CHAIR OF THE BAR'S DISCIPLINARY BOARD FOR THE D.C. COURT OF APPEALS. [RIGHT] MUCH OF HOGAN & HARTSON'S EDUCATION PRACTICE CONCERNED EFFORTS TO REALIZE THE IDEAL OF RACIAL INTEGRATION AND EQUALITY ARTICULATED IN THE U.S. SUPREME COURT'S HISTORIC 1954 *BROWN V. BOARD OF EDUCATION* DECISION.

Despite Hogan & Hartson's ambivalence about expansion beyond Washington, D.C., the firm supported the development of several new practice areas in the late 1970s and early 1980s. When David Tatel returned to Hogan & Hartson in 1979 after two

U.S. Representative Paul G. Rogers joined Hogan & Hartson in 1979 after an extraordinarily productive quarter-century in Congress.

years directing the Office of Civil Rights at the U.S. Department of Health, Education and Welfare (HEW), he brought with him a barely hatched idea for a new kind of practice. His HEW assignment had given him wide exposure to school boards and university presidents, and he thought there might be a market there for private legal services. Perhaps he could start an education practice.

While helping out in the firm's Community Services Department, then headed by Sally Determan, Tatel spoke with everyone he could about the mechanics and politics of setting up a new practice. He spent two hours with Executive Committee member Jerry Gilbert, asking "How do you do this? How do you do that?" Privately, Gilbert thought, "Sure, David, good luck." But years later Gilbert cheerily withdrew his doubts, gratified that "David went out and built arguably the best education practice in the country."

Tatel enlisted Allen Snyder to help with the practice's first major case, a desegregation matter in 1980 resulting from "white flight" from St. Louis. The case eventually was settled when suburban school districts agreed to accept minority students from the city, while the city established magnet schools to draw suburban students back to St. Louis. In 1985 Missouri's Kansas City Metropolitan School District hired Tatel and Snyder to handle a similar problem. The two picked up the seven-year-old case in midstream, when the school district was struggling to find a remedy for a long-standing pattern of segregation for which it earlier had been found liable. Patricia Brannan, an associate who

Before joining Hogan & Hartson, Paul G. Rogers was known as "Mr. Health" for his well-earned reputation in Congress as the U.S. House of Representatives' leading architect of major health and environmental legislation. He was born in Georgia but at the age of four moved to Florida, where he attended public schools and graduated from the University of Florida at Gainesville in 1942. After service in the U.S. Army in Europe during World War II, he returned to Florida and obtained his law degree at the University of Florida in 1948.

His father's death from a heart attack in 1954 changed Rogers's career. Dwight Rogers had been a U.S. representative from Florida, and in January 1955 Paul won a special election to fill his father's seat in Washington, D.C. The new Representative Rogers won reelection for eleven succeeding terms until retiring from Congress in 1979 to become a partner at Hogan & Hartson.

Rogers's achievements have won him numerous honors over the years. Among them have been the 1978 dedication of the Paul G. Rogers Federal Courthouse in West Palm Beach, Florida; election to the Institute of Medicine in 1980; the National Academy of Sciences Public Welfare Medal in 1982; the National Health Lawyers Association Health Policy Award in 1991; the Albert Lasker Award for Public Service in 1993; and the American Cancer Society's Medal of Honor Award in 2003.

By an Act of Congress on December 21, 2000, the National Institute of Health's main plaza was dedicated in Paul Rogers's name. At the dedication ceremony on June 12, 2001, NIH acting director Ruth L. Kirschstein, M.D., said that "Mr. Rogers knows how to get things done." Former Congressman James Symington added that Rogers had proved that "public service does not need to end when a person leaves public office." Rogers responded, "In all my years, nothing has given me more pride than participating in the success of research, because without research, there is no hope."

ANN MORGAN VICKERY JOINED HOGAN & HARTSON IN 1978 AFTER EXTENSIVE EXPERIENCE AT THE WHITE HOUSE AND THE TREASURY DEPARTMENT. SHE HELPED BUILD HOGAN & HARTSON'S HEALTH PRACTICE, AND NOW IS MANAGING PARTNER OF THE FIRM'S WASHINGTON, D.C., OFFICE.

had clerked for Judge John Ferren on the District of Columbia Court of Appeals before joining the firm in 1980, joined Snyder on the case when Tatel undertook a desegregation case in Milwaukee.[9]

The Kansas City case dragged on for several years over the issue of payment for the proposed remedy, which included $260 million in capital improvements and a $200 million magnet school plan. In September 1987 Snyder won a ruling from U.S. District Court Judge Russell Clark, who ordered an income tax surcharge and a property tax increase to pay for the desegregation remedy. But Missouri law required two-thirds voter approval for any tax increase. The state could not get that approval, leaving it suspended between Judge Clark's ruling and its own law. So Missouri appealed to the Eighth Circuit, which upheld the property tax increase while disallowing the income tax surcharge. Missouri was still caught, if only half-caught now, and proceeded with an appeal to the U.S. Supreme Court, as Snyder had figured it would. On October 30, 1989, Snyder presented his argument to the Justices in Washington, and six months later they agreed by a 5-4 majority to uphold the Eighth Circuit's opinion. Kansas City now hoped it could put its school desegregation legal issues to rest.[10]

Hogan & Hartson's education practice flourished alongside another new practice in health care, which gained momentum when U.S. Congressman Paul Rogers of Florida retired in 1979 after twenty-four years on the Hill and joined Hogan & Hartson to resume his law practice. Rogers had filled the House of Representatives vacancy left when his father, Dwight L. Rogers, died suddenly of a heart attack in 1955. His father's illness had given Rogers a special interest in health issues, and over the years he played a key role in passing many major health-related laws, including the National Cancer Acts of 1971 and 1977, the Medical Device Amendments Act of 1976, the Medicare-Medicaid Anti-Fraud and Abuse Amendments of 1977, and the House Clean Air and Safe Drinking Water Acts. Such successes earned him the title "Mr. Health" among colleagues in Congress.

When David Tatel learned that Paul Rogers was coming to the firm he called Earl Collier, an attorney he had known at HEW, and arranged a lunch meeting. Collier had spent two years with New York State's health planning system before joining the Carter administration to work in the Health Care Financing Administration, the agency that ran Medicare. He knew Rogers and was excited when Tatel mentioned the possibility of teaming up with the former congressman to

IN 1982 ANN MORGAN VICKERY (5TH FROM LEFT ON U.S. CAPITOL STEPS), EARL COLLIER AND PAUL ROGERS HELPED THE NATIONAL HOSPICE AND PALLIATIVE CARE ORGANIZATION WIN MEDICARE COVERAGE FOR HOSPICE SERVICES.

start a new practice. So Collier also came to the firm, where he and Rogers were joined in the health practice by associate Ann Morgan Vickery. Vickery had joined Hogan & Hartson in 1978 after graduating from Georgetown Law School and had been working on the firm's large United States Railway Association case. She brought to her new health practice assignment eight years of pre-law experience in the federal government — five as a researcher and staff assistant at the White House and three in the Treasury Department.

Hogan & Hartson's health practice was young but rich in its knowledge of Congress and the workings of the federal government. The practice well illustrated the close relationship between laws and lawmaking, between regulations and the officials who draft and administer them. One day early in 1981 a group of hospice leaders visited Rogers in his new office in the Chanin Building. Hospital services were covered under Medicare, they explained, and so were nursing homes. But so far, hospice services for persons with life-limiting illnesses had been excluded. Could Rogers help them bring those services under Medicare? Rogers was genial and encouraging with his visitors, assuring them that "If there's anything we can do, we'll help." But he also knew there was trouble ahead. Ronald Reagan had just been elected President on a platform of reducing the federal government and the taxes that supported it. Any growth in programs like Medicare was nigh unthinkable in the new political atmosphere of rebellion against government spending and "entitlement" programs. After the hospice owners left, Rogers called in Collier and Vickery and asked their advice. Vickery recalls what they both recommended: "Pray."

Like the proverbial knight on a white charger, President Ronald Reagan came to Washington, D.C. in 1981 promising a new "Morning in America."

But they did more, realizing the odds were almost completely against them. For the next year and a half, Vickery said, she, Rogers, and Collier became "zealots" on behalf of their hospice clients, who also worked vigorously for their cause. At last, in 1982 Congress surprised everyone by passing legislation allowing Medicare benefits for hospice care. It was the only expansion of Medicare benefits of any kind passed by Congress that year and it was the turning point in Vickery's career. "I've been a health lawyer ever since," she says. "That was my introduction, and it stuck." The National Hospice and Palliative Care Association stuck with Hogan & Hartson, too, and has remained a client ever since.

The nation's air traffic controllers were not as fortunate as the hospice owners in their confrontation with the new Reagan administration. When the controllers' union, the Professional Air Traffic Controllers' Association (PATCO), called a strike in August 1981 to protest poor working conditions, the government declared it an illegal action and fired the nearly 13,000 of 17,500 PATCO members who participated in the strike. The controllers were stunned. PATCO had been one of the few unions supporting Reagan in the presidential election, and during his campaign he had promised to address their concerns. Many controllers were military veterans, unused to the idea of being at odds with their government. Besides, there had been many other unauthorized strikes by federal workers in recent years, including a major, disruptive strike by postal employees who subsequently had retained their jobs.

The controllers gambled their collective importance in the national transportation network against the likelihood of being dismissed, and lost. Few

AMERICANS GAVE A "WELCOME HOME" TO 52 HOSTAGES WHEN THEY RETURNED TO THE UNITED STATES IN JANUARY 1981 AFTER 444 DAYS OF CAPTIVITY IN IRAN. THE CELEBRATION INCLUDED A PARADE IN WASHINGTON, D.C., THAT PASSED THE TREASURY BUILDING ON 15TH STREET ON ITS WAY TO THE WHITE HOUSE.

anticipated the wreckage of mortgages and marriages that the unsuccessful strike left in its wake. Publicly, however, PATCO maintained a stiff, defiant posture, and when at last it fell, it went down hard, taking with it not only its member controllers but much of the already waning power of unions in the United States.

PATCO timed the strike to coincide with the peak vacation travel season, a move designed to create maximum pressure on the airlines but which also proved a public relations disaster for the controllers. Their portrayal of the strike as concerning mostly safety and job stress issues evaporated in the flying public's resentment over interrupted vacations, and over the controllers' somewhat mystifying complaints in the light of what seemed to many to be handsome salaries. George Carneal, former general counsel at the Federal Aviation Agency and founder of Hogan & Hartson's aviation practice, was just settling into his vacation house in Nantucket with his family in August 1981 when the phone rang. It was Jim Landry, general counsel for the Air Transport Association (ATA), a longtime client of the firm. The air traffic controllers had gone out on strike, Landry informed him, and the ATA was going to need some extra help. "You'd be perfect for this," he told Carneal, who gave up his vacation and returned to Washington.

The ATA represented the major airlines, which were losing about $30 million a day during the strike. The ATA soon filed a successful suit against PATCO for damages, but collecting the award proved a challenge because the union had concealed its funds. Carneal asked Allen Snyder of the firm's litigation department to join him in the search. "We had the sense that they were hiding their money but we weren't sure where and how," Snyder recalled, "and so we basically decided to serve liens against union funds and just go into every bank in the city, which you can do. We filed about fifty liens against union money and we learned later, in fact, they were in the process of trying to move the money out of the city. We had just caught it." When PATCO claimed that it wasn't really union money but a separate benefits fund, Snyder and Carneal went back to court, ultimately winning another judgment for the ATA nearly two years after the strike.

Not all cases unfolded so satisfactorily, at least from Carneal's viewpoint. Carneal recalled representing the developers of a coal slurry pipeline project, designed to transport coal from mines in Wyoming to destinations in Texas and Arkansas by flushing it with water ("slurry") through a large pipeline. The problem was not in the technology but in the pipeline's threat to the railroads, a major competitor for coal traffic. When the railroads declined to grant right-of-way to the pipeline to cross under their tracks, the pipeline developers asked for Hogan & Hartson's help in bringing an antitrust suit against the railroads.

But a Hogan & Hartson client, the El Paso Natural Gas Company, held part ownership in the Burlington Northern Railroad, one of the defendants. That created a conflict for the firm, so Carneal went to the firm partner who did El Paso's work. "Would you ask them if they would grant a waiver?" "Forget it," was the summary answer. So the pipeline developers went to a Houston, Texas, firm instead. Carneal participated in the trial as a witness for the plaintiffs. The railroads' lawyers deposed him for five straight days, and he proved to be a star witness. But he would have preferred to be the star attorney. In the end, the pipeline project won an award well in excess of a billion dollars. The Houston firm had taken the case on a contingency basis and earned about $400 million from it. "They were giving secretaries $10,000 bonuses," Carneal said. "I remember that case. You always remember the ones that get away."[11]

Coal and cash flowed into Texas in the early 1980s, and so did silver. Herbert and Nelson Hunt, two of the fourteen children of Texas oil magnate Haroldson Lafayette ("H. L.") Hunt, Jr., decided that silver would be an excellent hedge against inflation in the 1970s and against the general uncertainties of the times. In the Hunts' case the uncertainties sometimes had not been so general, as when Nelson Hunt had lost his rights to the largest oil field in Libya after Mohammar Qaddafi nationalized that country's oil industry in 1973. But the late 1970s seemed especially bleak, as President Jimmy Carter noted in a July 15, 1979, speech to the nation.

"The erosion of our confidence in the future is threatening to destroy the social and the political fabric of America," President Carter warned. Just a few months later, the Iranian Revolution culminated in a demoralizing seizure of the American embassy in Tehran and the holding of fifty-two hostages. This event helped trigger a "second energy crisis" and long lines at gas stations in the United States when Iran and other nations in the OPEC cartel raised oil prices sharply. The Soviet Union invaded Afghanistan in December 1979, which compounded international tensions by triggering a U.S. suspension of grain exports and a boycott of the 1980 Summer Olympics in Moscow. But perhaps, the Hunts figured, these clouds might have some silver linings.

After more than six years of trading, in March 1980 Nelson Hunt alone held contracts representing 60.9 million troy ounces of silver worth $673 million and had become the world's largest private silver investor. Silver's price rise had been steep. Just nine months earlier, in the summer of 1979, it had traded for about $8 an ounce. In September the price doubled, and late in January 1980 it peaked at an unheard-of $50. Then it started sliding. By the end of March it had dropped to $10, then settled into a stable and lower pattern of about $4 to $6 that lasted through the end of the 1980s. Between August 1979 and late March 1980, though, about $400 billion of wealth was made and lost, a large portion of it belonging to the Hunts. They spent much of their $5 billion silver profit in January 1980, at the peak of the silver bubble, taking delivery of silver in coins and bullion to use as collateral against huge loans — to buy more bullion. Then, when prices began to tumble, the brothers found themselves short of cash and holding a cache of precious metal worth only one-fifth of the value it had held when they had converted it, just weeks earlier.

Having lost, at minimum, hundreds of millions of dollars, Herbert and Nelson Hunt were in financial trouble. They also were in legal trouble, charged with cornering the silver market as well as with racketeering and fraud. Congress called on them to testify at hearings, and the Commodity Futures Trading Commission (CFTC), the IRS, and the SEC began investigations.[12] Each brother retained several attorneys. Nelson Hunt asked Barrett Prettyman and Joseph Hassett to help represent him in the CFTC and SEC investigations.

Joseph Hassett was Hogan & Hartson's 62nd lawyer when he joined the firm in 1970. His interest in Irish literature and William Butler Yeats led to a Ph.D. in 1985 (The University of Dublin) and a publication (*Yeats and the Poetics of Hate*, 1986).

Philip Larson came to H&H in 1971. An early rotation in the Community Services Department convinced him that "I really loved complex, protracted litigation." Later he served as Practice Area Administrator for Government Regulation and Practice Group Director for the Antitrust Group.

When Hassett left on sabbatical for Dublin, Ireland, in 1981 to write his Ph.D. thesis on William Butler Yeats, Phil Larson replaced him on the case. While his colleagues argued about the firm's expansion at the Boar's Head Inn, Larson was in his room, mining the labyrinthian veins of the Hunts' silver dealings. He and Prettyman left Charlottesville and the partners' retreat early on a Sunday morning to catch a plane to Dallas. It was a very complicated case. Larson recalled, with quiet understatement, "There was a lot of discovery and we spent a lot of time producing paper and analyzing issues."

Their analysis concluded that the SEC investigation likely had violated Nelson Hunt's rights under the 1978 Right to Financial Privacy Act. That act extended Fourth Amendment protections against unlawful searches and seizures to bank accounts and required investigating agencies to give notice, as well as an opportunity to object, prior to a bank's disclosure of account information. After lengthy hearings in Dallas, Prettyman and Larson obtained a preliminary injunction against the SEC to stop its violation of Hunt's privacy rights.

BUSINESSMAN AND YACHT RACER TED TURNER SET THE TONE FOR THE ENTREPRENEURIAL 1980S WITH HIS BRASH, COMPETITIVE STYLE.

Having achieved what would prove to be a rare victory in Nelson Hunt's long legal struggle, the Hogan & Hartson attorneys returned to Washington, leaving it to other firms to carry on the remainder of the Hunt brothers' defense. Years later, in August 1988, a jury found the brothers guilty of virtually all charges against them and awarded the plaintiff, a Peruvian metals and minerals trading company named Minpeco SA, $65.7 million in damages. The racketeering statute trebled the award to nearly $200 million. When the IRS placed a lien on the Hunts' assets to secure payment of about $600 million in taxes it claimed they owed, Herbert and Nelson declared bankruptcy.

The Hunts' high-wire performance in the silver market exemplified the speculative, no-holds-barred, entrepreneurial daring that came to characterize the 1980s, with its fallout of white-collar crime cases. But few personified its rough and raw edges better than yachtsman and Cable News Network (CNN) founder Ted Turner, whose drive earned him the America's Cup in 1977 as skipper of the Courageous, and whose antics earned him a less flattering companion title, "Captain Outrageous." Both ventures, the America's Cup and CNN, featured bravura performances by Turner, and in 1980 Hogan & Hartson's Jay Ricks had a supporting part in the CNN portion of the show.

Turner had entered the television business ten years earlier when he purchased an independent Atlanta, Georgia, station, WTCG. The station proved a poor competitor to the area's stronger network affiliates, and Turner pondered how he might reach a wider audience with his station fare of sitcom reruns and direct advertising. He hit on a solution — using a "common carrier" of telephone land lines and relay towers spaced about twenty miles apart to send his signal in microwave form into neighboring states.

FCC regulations banned station owners from owning common carrier systems, which were defined as transmission systems having no control over the content of what they sent. In other words, the creator and the sender could not be the same person. So Turner found an intermediary owner for his land line common carrier. Several years later, when he heard about Satcom, the RCA Corporation's satellite system, it occurred to him that he might be able to use it, as he had used the microwave relays, to reach a national, perhaps even a worldwide, audience.

Turner signed up with RCA for a "transponder" slot on Satcom I, then raised funds to establish a satellite "uplink," a powerful transmitter that he named Southern Satellite Systems (SSS), to send the television signals to Satcom. Now he needed a way around the

FCC prohibition on owning both the broadcast station (content) and the SSS common carrier (transmission). He sold SSS for one dollar to an acquaintance, Ed Taylor, who quit his job as a marketing executive with Western Union to manage the thousands of per-household fees he would collect from subscribers. For his own part, Turner counted on reaping a harvest of new advertising revenues resulting from a vastly increased audience.

Competitors complained to the FCC, but an appeals court ultimately validated Turner's deal with Taylor. Then, in 1979, Turner prepared to launch his most daring venture, a twenty-four-hour all-news channel called Cable News Network, or CNN. It would be carried by RCA's new satellite, Satcom III, which was scheduled for launch at the end of the year.

Delta rockets, first launched in 1960, were powerful enough to carry communications satellites like SATCOM into geostationary orbit. Such satellites, in turn, launched communications law into new territory.

As a guest of his client, RCA, Ricks watched Satcom III take off atop a Delta rocket from Cape Kennedy, Florida, on the evening of December 6, 1979. "It was spectacular," he said later, "only after an apparently successful launch the satellite was never heard from again."[13] It is likely that a small booster engine designed to thrust Satcom III into its final, "geosynchronous" orbit 22,300 feet above the earth had failed.[14] RCA would launch a backup satellite in time for CNN's scheduled inauguration on June 1, 1980, but first Turner had a major hurdle to cross. There were six applicants for the four transponders available on the backup satellite, and he had no special edge over the other applicants. "Everything was up in the air except the RCA satellite," said Reese Schonfeld, an attorney and industry executive who worked with Turner on the CNN venture.[15]

Disregarding RCA's neutrality as a common carrier, Turner and Schonfeld stormed company headquarters high in New York's Rockefeller Center to demand a place on the next satellite. Ricks was there representing RCA and reminded Turner and Schonfeld that RCA could not play favorites in assigning the transponder slots. Of course, Ricks thought, RCA would not mind at all if CNN somehow managed to secure a place on Satcom III, for if RCA did not carry the channel a Hughes satellite scheduled for launching several months later would, and Turner's highly publicized, all-news gamble promised to be a big success.

Turner then went to the federal district court in Atlanta seeking an order requiring RCA to reserve a slot for CNN, based on the slim argument that in RCA's original sales agreement with him, the one governing his Atlanta TV station and the still-functioning Satcom, RCA had granted him "right of first refusal" on two additional transponder slots. The slots had been filled by other customers — Turner had needed only one — but RCA had neglected to offer him the chance to refuse their use before it sold them. The matter had been completely forgotten, until now, when it promised Turner a narrow edge on his competitors. It was all the edge the intense yacht skipper needed. Ricks recalled Turner's behavior during a deposition. "He bounced around the

[1] SENATOR J. WILLIAM FULBRIGHT. [2] THE FULBRIGHT TABLE IN THE CHEZ HOGAN CAFETERIA OFFERS A RELAXED LUNCH TIME FORUM WHOSE ONLY RULE IS, "DON'T TALK ABOUT ANYTHING YOU KNOW A LOT ABOUT." [3] SENATOR FULBRIGHT (4TH FROM L) LOOKS ON AS PRESIDENT JOHN F. KENNEDY SIGNS THE NUCLEAR TEST BAN TREATY AT THE WHITE HOUSE, OCTOBER 7, 1963.

J. William Fulbright joined Hogan & Hartson in 1975 after a long and distinguished career in public service. Born in Missouri in 1905, Fulbright earned a bachelor's degree in political science at the University of Arkansas, then studied at Oxford University as a Rhodes Scholar. He obtained his law degree at George Washington University in 1934, then returned to Arkansas, where in just five years he was named president of the University of Arkansas. At age thirty-four he was the youngest university president in the country.

In 1942 Fulbright was elected to the U.S. House of Representatives, where he played a key role in garnering support for what soon would become the United Nations. In 1944 he was elected to the U.S. Senate. He became a member of the Senate Foreign Relations Committee and from 1959-1974 chaired that committee, the longest tenure achieved by any chair in the committee's history.

Fulbright's chairmanship included several acts of political courage. In 1954 he became the only senator who refused to vote for continued funding of Senator Joseph McCarthy's anticommunist investigations. In the 1960s he led his peers in an early questioning of several aspects of the Vietnam War. Senator Fulbright's insights about the uses of power, and his vision of international peace, found expression in his six published books as well as in the famous Fulbright Program for international exchange scholars. In 1993 President Clinton awarded him the Presidential Medal of Freedom.

Shortly after coming to Hogan & Hartson, Fulbright and partner Merle Thorpe visited the Middle East together. "He became my mentor," Thorpe said later. Thorpe schooled himself in the complex affairs of the Middle East and in 1979 founded the Foundation for Middle East Peace. Thorpe died in February 1994 at age seventy-six. J. William Fulbright, age eighty-nine, died in February the following year.

Hogan & Hartson dedicated its 13th Floor conference facility, The Fulbright Center, in his honor. Less formally, Fulbright's colleagues named a lunch table in Chez Hogan, the D.C. office cafeteria, the J. William Fulbright Table. Hogan & Hartson attorneys of all political persuasions gather there daily to carry on Fulbright's passion for good-humored discussion of issues of the day. A regular participant revealed the Fulbright Table's only rule: "You're not allowed to talk about anything you know a lot about."

conference room constantly and answered questions on the run. The stenographer appeared to be in shock. At one point he launched into a rambling soliloquy about the importance of keeping promises and how all of his life he had kept his promises. And then as an afterthought he said, 'except when I promised to honor and obey my first wife, Jane.'"[16]

The Georgia federal court ruled for Turner and CNN, and RCA informed the FCC that it intended to comply with that court's decision unless it ruled otherwise. Meanwhile, Turner's competitors took their objections straight to the FCC. Turner traveled to Washington, too, to press his case. This included dropping to the floor in an FCC commissioner's office and kicking his legs in the air, said Ricks, "to demonstrate how dead he would be if the FCC prevented RCA from distributing CNN." Whether the demonstration helped or not, the FCC did not contradict the federal court ruling in favor of Turner and CNN, and on June 1, 1980, RCA's Satcom III beamed out CNN's first broadcast. Technically, RCA had lost the lawsuit. But, as Ricks said many years later, "It was probably one of the few times that Hogan & Hartson lost and that was the best result for the client."[17]

Turner's demonstrations aside, CNN ably demonstrated technology's capacity to shrink global distances and accelerate the clash and communion of cultures. The same held for commerce, which rapidly acquired new international dimensions in the 1980s. The Trade Act of 1974 had stimulated international trade by reducing import barriers and enlarging foreign markets for U.S. products. "Up until then," said Jerry Gilbert, "there was no single body of law. The Trade Act created a basis for international trade law practice."

Senator J. William Fulbright had played a key role in passing the Trade Act, and when he retired from the Senate in 1975 after thirty years of service, Merle Thorpe, Jr., persuaded him to join Hogan & Hartson. A widely regarded expert on international affairs, Fulbright had chaired the Senate Foreign Relations Committee for fifteen years, the longest tenure in that position in the Senate's history. Hogan & Hartson hoped that Fulbright's experience, especially his knowledge of Middle East issues, would nurture the firm's sprouting international trade practice, which at the time centered mostly on its client, Toyota Motor Sales, USA.

Toyota had become a Hogan & Hartson client initially through Jerry Gilbert's trade association work. But when Sandy Berger joined Gilbert in 1981, they began laying the foundation for Hogan & Hartson's new international trade practice. After four years with the firm, including eighteen months as Senior Associate in the Community Services Department, Berger had taken leave to work in the State Department, first as a speechwriter for Secretary Cyrus Vance, then as deputy director of the department's policy and planning staff. Berger's exposure to international issues there proved to be the "pivot point" in his career, he said later, giving him perspective that he brought back to Hogan & Hartson when he left the State Department following Ronald Reagan's election in 1980.

But Berger was not yet sure how he would use his new insights, and the firm was not sure what it would do with him either. "Everybody respected Sandy and knew how bright he was," said Gilbert, "but he was quite a young man still." Gilbert was on the Executive Committee at the time. "I can remember one of the members saying, 'What are we going to do with Berger?' I said, 'I'll take him!' Not a bad decision on my part," Gilbert reflected years later.

Peter Rohrbach came to Hogan & Hartson in 1979 and has been a key partner in the firm's historically renowned and still thriving communications practice.

It took a while to get the international trade practice started, and for a long time Toyota was its only client. Partner Mark McConnell, then an associate, walked into Berger's office one day and complained, "We don't have a trade practice; we have a trade client." "Mark," Berger reassured him, "that's how it begins, you start with one." It was a big one, though. The three attorneys wrestled almost full-time against proposed protectionist legislation, including "countervailing import duties" and "domestic content laws." The latter effectively would have blocked the importation of foreign-made vehicles by requiring that a high

LESTER AND LYDIA COHEN WERE REGARDED FONDLY BY ALL MEMBERS OF THE FIRM'S EXTENDED FAMILY. THE COUPLE EXEMPLIFIED THE FIRM'S TRADITIONAL IDEAL OF COMBINING PERSONAL CARING WITH A COMMITMENT TO PROFESSIONAL EXCELLENCE.

LESTER COHEN'S 1985 BOOK, *FRANK HOGAN REMEMBERED*, CHRONICLED THE FIRM'S HISTORY THROUGH THE MID-1960S AND INCLUDED MUCH INTERESTING PERSONAL AND ANECDOTAL MATERIAL ABOUT HOGAN, HIS COLLEAGUES AND HIS MOST FAMOUS CASES.

percentage of their parts be manufactured in the United States.

"We normally didn't do a lot of lobbying," said Gilbert, "but we had to go to the Hill and talk to congressmen, senators; we also had to talk to people in the administration, people in the business." In the end they succeeded in fending off the legislation most damaging to Toyota's interests. In addition, though, Gilbert and Berger urged Toyota to adopt a constructive, long-range solution. "You've got to build your cars in the United States," they repeated, until Toyota at last took the advice. "We almost worked our way out of a client!" Gilbert exclaimed. Once the company had built plants — and provided jobs — in the United States, "Most of the issues we handled for them went away, as we told them they would."

The international trade practice expanded through the 1980s, working not only for importers but also for U.S. producers facing increased costs due to protectionist measures. One client, the Coalition of American Steel Using Manufacturers (CASUM), represented hundreds of companies, such as the heavy equipment manufacturer Caterpillar, that used steel in making their products. For years domestic steel producers had succeeded in persuading the government to limit imported steel, which was almost always cheaper than the U.S. product. In 1984, despite its announced commitment to free trade, the Reagan administration imposed a series of restraint agreements on foreign steel products, restricting imports to 18.5 percent of total U.S. production. Steel's vital place in national defense, no less than its political clout, often earned it special treatment in Washington. Nonetheless, the CASUM fought against what it regarded as unfair and costly import restrictions. "We took on the steel industry," said Berger. "That was a great project." Finally, President George H. W. Bush agreed to phase out the restraints, which ultimately terminated in December 1992. This was followed by a new round of steel trade litigation, and new tariffs on many products.

Economic issues, often cloaked in ideology, dominated headlines in the 1980s. The Reagan administration eased antitrust enforcement in order to encourage business expansion. It also sought income tax cuts that the new "supply side" economics predicted would stimulate the economy and, eventually, reduce the federal deficit by increasing taxable corporate profits. The administration also picked up the pace of deregulation in areas like banking, energy, and communications. The breakup of AT&T between 1982 and 1984, for instance, created new opportunities for potential long-distance phone service providers, and for attorneys at Hogan & Hartson like Jay Ricks, Tony Harrington, and Peter Rohrbach, who helped guide communications companies through newly competitive terrain.

That terrain also was expertly charted by William Reyner of the communications practice, who helped Rupert Murdoch establish the Fox television network. It was not an easy feat, for Murdoch was originally an Australian and FCC rules limited the ownership of U.S. television stations to Americans. Other rules then in effect would have prohibited Murdoch, who owned a motion picture studio, newspapers, and other media, from also acquiring a broadcast network. Reyner, assisted by communications associate (now partner) Mace Rosenstein, crafted a complex ownership arrangement that allowed the FCC to approve Murdoch's involvement. Reyner also persuaded the FCC that Fox was not a network under the FCC's rules barring common ownership of networks and film studios — and ultimately won repeal of the rules altogether. At the time of one of Reyner's many victories for Murdoch and Fox, *Broadcasting & Cable* magazine reported a media industry leader as remarking, "Whoever Fox's lawyers were, that's a damned good firm."

Reyner also successfully expanded his regulatory practice to the commercial aspects of media transactions, doing numerous deals with Richard Horan, then a corporate associate and now a partner in the Northern Virginia office. In one marquee deal for Fox and Murdoch, *Time* magazine published an article in June 1994 entitled "Murdoch's Biggest Score," reporting on the frenzied pace of the transaction and explaining that "in the final days, a cadre of briefcase-toting lawyers invaded the Fox studios lot" to get the deal done. When later asked about the description of the lawyers in the *Time* article, Reyner remarked, "I don't know much about the briefcase-toting, you'll have to ask Horan."

In 1982 the administration extended its deregulation policy to the savings and loan industry, allowing the "S&Ls" to broaden their investments beyond home mortgages into riskier commercial real estate and other business ventures. The immediate result was a deluge of work for attorneys like Howard Flack. Flack worked for the SEC for three years after graduating from New York Law School in 1976, then went to a "boutique" firm in D.C. specializing in S&L work. His initial interview with one of that firm's lead partners, Charles Allen, offered a sample of what lay ahead. Allen was on a

J. Warren Gorrell, Jr., showed an early aptitude for corporate practice when he joined Hogan & Hartson in 1979. In 1999 he was named "Deal Maker of the Year" for 1998 by *The American Lawyer* magazine.

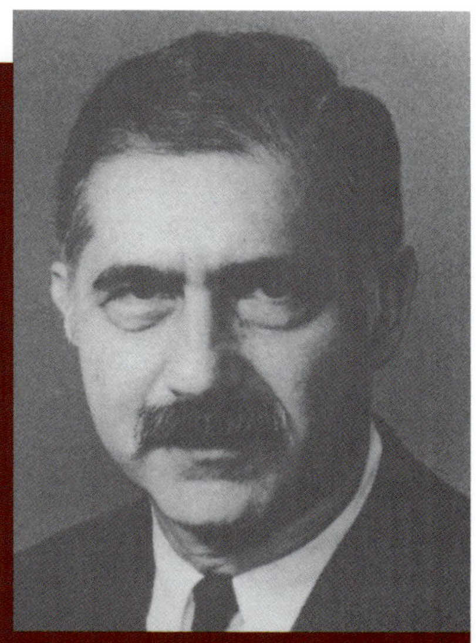

In 1984 Seymour Mintz became of counsel to Hogan & Hartson after thirty-eight years as one of the firm's most influential and respected attorneys. Mintz joined Hogan & Hartson in 1946 and rapidly moved to positions of leadership, serving numerous terms on the Executive Committee. He is widely remembered for his foresight, his judgment, his high standards of ethical practice, and for the enriching influence of his broad intellect and scholarship.

Gerald Gilbert called Mintz "the consummate professional. He treated people with dignity. You knew you were in the presence of a very special person when you were with Seymour." Bob Jeffers regarded Mintz as the firm's "intellectual godfather," while Barrett Prettyman cited Mintz's invaluable guidance and good judgment. "Seymour is not a black-and-white person," said Prettyman. "He can make up his mind, but he will have covered all the gray areas first."

Mintz's sensitivity to the firm's need to change with the times gave powerful impetus to the decision to establish the Community Services Department (CSD) in the late 1960s. Judge John Ferren, who was the CSD's first partner-in-charge, remembered Mintz as "the key member of the firm when I came in 1970. He is a great man — a combination of a tough-minded business man and an altruistic, concerned human being."

In 2003, at age ninety-one, Mintz looked back on the many decisions the Executive Committee had made during the years. When asked which of them had given him the greatest satisfaction, he replied without hesitation, "Three things — the admission of women, the welcoming of blacks, and the elimination of prejudice against homosexuals."

THE OPENING OF HOGAN & HARTSON'S OFFICES IN MCLEAN, VIRGINIA, JUST A SHORT DRIVE FROM DOWNTOWN WASHINGTON, FELT LIKE A MAJOR MOVE TO THOSE WHO FEARED A DILUTION OF THE FIRM'S REPUTATION AS "THE PREMIER WASHINGTON, D.C. FIRM."

conference call when Flack introduced himself. "Look," he told Flack, "I'm on this call but I can still interview you," then handed him a proxy statement. "This is what the call is about, so why don't you thumb through it while I'm on the phone?" After an hour the call and the interview both ended. A week later Flack started working, seven days a week.

Three years later, in August 1983, Flack walked into Allen's office, exhausted and upset. The firm had lots of business. More attorneys had been hired. Flack had just been named a partner. But, he told Allen, "Honestly, it's killing my family life. I really need to be thinking about doing something else." Allen got up from his desk, crossed the room, and shut the door. "Look," he confided, "I don't want to split up this team. What would you think about just moving the entire practice with me?" "Shocked," Flack replied, "that's some offer, but where would we go?" "What about Hogan & Hartson?" Allen suggested. Allen had worked at the firm before leaving to work with the Federal Home Loan Bank Board and then joining the S&L boutique. Spurred to action by the prospect of losing Flack, Allen called Arthur Rothkopf, then on Hogan & Hartson's Executive Committee, and within a few days he and Flack visited the Chanin Building for interviews. Hogan & Hartson was interested in the attorneys' S&L expertise. Allen was a known quantity at the firm, and Flack impressed interviewers with his honesty and his proven capacity for sustained hard work. With little delay, in September 1983 Allen and Flack came in as partners, bringing with them another attorney from the boutique, Steve Ballew.

Jack Keeney and Sherwin Markman stepped in to help the newcomers with a hostile proxy contest that overlapped their leaving the boutique and coming to Hogan & Hartson. After three years of ceaseless grinding, Flack was amazed at the friendly support he encountered. "It was like I had been partners with them forever. They were very embracing." He had been at the firm three months when Bob Odle came around to visit him in his office. It was the week before Christmas. Odle pulled up a chair, sat down, and told Flack, "Look, I just want to tell you everybody is so happy with you, Charlie [Allen] and the group. The Executive Committee couldn't be happier. I hope everything's OK. Is there anything we can do to make your life here better?" There wasn't. Flack, though working extremely hard, had never been happier. They chatted for a few more minutes, then as he rose from his chair, Odle commented, "You work very hard. The Executive Committee wants to recognize you for this in a small way." He handed Flack a substantial bonus check.

Just as Sandy Berger's experience at the State Department had transformed his vision of his career, Howard Flack's experience at Hogan & Hartson crystallized his ideas about how a law firm should be and how important it was to feel connected to the firm. "The firm's showing of its appreciation for my work by word and deed left a major impression on me. I was off and running at Hogan & Hartson."

In contrast to the S&L boutique, Flack found ready access to a wide range of legal support in Hogan & Hartson's tax, securities, employee benefits, regulatory, and litigation practices. He crossed paths often with Peter Romeo, with whom he had worked at the SEC when he was there, and with Bob Waldman, Bob Jeffers, Jim Rosenhauer, Alan Dye, Joe Connolly, Tony Harrington, and George Barsness — all skilled corporate attorneys whose pooled efforts, in the right environment, amounted to more than the mere sum of individual talents. Moreover, the firm's strong background of ethical practice gave even new attorneys the confidence they needed to speak up forcefully when clients strayed from the line of propriety. "It was very easy for us to get support among the others to make sure the client got the best advice and that it stuck," Flack noted.

Hogan & Hartson's atmosphere of mutual support and collegiality did not exempt its attorneys from hard work or long hours. Instead, it meant pitching in for someone who needed help or who had a sick family member or some other personal issue requiring special attention. After all, the help one might give today, one might need tomorrow. Sally Determan experienced that *in extremis* while heading the Community Services Department in 1980. Her eight-year-old son, Steven, was diagnosed with leukemia that year. After four years of treatments and heartbreaking relapses, Steven died in the spring of 1984. During her son's illness, every member of the Executive Committee visited Determan to say, "'Take whatever time off you need. That's what a partnership is for. We cover for each other.' They were wonderful," Determan recalled, picking up a picture of her son that Bob Jeffers's wife, Ginny, had taken before Steven lost his hair to chemotherapy. "It's like this great big family."

Others found that the notion of a team also described Hogan & Hartson's atmosphere of close support. Warren Gorrell played center on Princeton's football team and earned his B.A. in economics magna cum laude. He loved math and thought he would go into business, but getting an M.B.A. seemed, as he put it, "too duplicative" of his undergraduate work, so he went to law school instead. In his final year at the University of Virginia Law School he received offers from Cravath and Davis Polk in New York, as well as Hogan & Hartson. When he chose Hogan & Hartson, a partner in one of the New York firms asked him, "Why would you want to do that?" Like many others, he presumed New York to be the only serious location for a corporate law practice. The question made Gorrell a bit nervous about his decision, but he stuck by it.

With little money and major student loans, Gorrell started working three days after graduation, taking advantage of a program at the firm that allowed full-time pay for half-time work for associates studying for the bar exam. After his initial rotations he took on his first commercial matter, working with Bob Elliott on a redevelopment project for a venerable local institution and a longtime Hogan & Hartson client, the Woodward & Lothrop department store. Stu Ross, a litigator at the firm, then introduced him to another client, a publisher and real estate developer. Gorrell was finding his footing as a corporate lawyer and, just as important, was finding a lot of corporate work in Washington. He enjoyed working with Bob Waldman, Jim Rosenhauer, Richard Poulson, Todd Miller, and others in the corporate and tax groups, and his anxiety over the senior New York lawyer's question faded.

Thomas B. Leary joined H&H in 1983 after a career with a New York firm and, later, as general counsel at General Motors. During the 1980s he served as outside counsel to The Business Roundtable. In November 1999 he was sworn in as a Commisioner at the Federal Trade Commission and began serving a six-year term.

COLUMBIA SQUARE, HOGAN & HARTSON'S WASHINGTON, D.C. OFFICE LOCATION SINCE MAY 1987.

COLUMBIA SQUARE IS LOCATED OVER METRO CENTER, THE EPICENTER OF THE METRORAIL TRANSIT SYSTEM AND OF WASHINGTON, D.C.'S SUCCESSFUL DOWNTOWN REVITALIZATION. THIS ARTIST'S DRAWING CAPTURES THE SUBWAY'S ARCHING SPACIOUSNESS AND GOEMETRIC FLOW.

Gorrell's first major transaction was the 1982 sale of the Guam Oil and Refining Company (GORCO) to international oil trader Mark Rich. GORCO supplied all the petroleum products to the U.S. Department of Defense in the Pacific. Richard Poulson was the partner in charge of the work, but Gorrell was encouraged to play a major role, illustrating one of his reasons for having chosen Hogan & Hartson. "Even though I was a third year associate," he said, "I was asked to take charge, along with Todd Miller on the tax side." GORCO's Texas owners intended to convert all the company's assets to cash and then liquidate, distributing all of the cash to its shareholders through a liquidating trust. But Guam had established a particular court procedure for dissolving a company, and GORCO's owners worried that the large sums of money coming into a Guam corporation and then out to its mainland shareholders might trigger some legal snag and stall the deal.

"I was trying to make sure I really understood how this dissolution and liquidation was going to work," Gorrell recalled, "and I wondered whether the corporation could just amend its charter to terminate its corporate existence rather than going through the formal dissolution procedure." He learned that Guam had originally modeled its corporate code on California's. Further, after a company in California in the early 1900s had done what Gorrell was contemplating GORCO might do, California had amended its law in 1915 to prohibit such transactions. However, Guam had never matched the amendment in its own law. Gorrell figured that GORCO would have one shot, perhaps the only shot, at such a transaction before Guam realized it might want to update its code. "So we did it," he said.

After Robert Kenney secured the critical novations of the supply contracts from the U.S. government, the corporate legal team coordinated the closing of the deal. Gorrell went to Guam and had the papers filed at the end of the day, specifying that the term of existence would end that night. At 12:01 a.m., Guam time, the papers started to move in Texas, and the deal was completed before the next day began in the Pacific. The transaction went through without a hitch. However, Mark Rich had not always conducted his affairs with the conscientiousness that Hogan & Hartson brought to the GORCO deal. In 1983, shortly after buying the GORCO refinery, he fled to Switzerland to evade charges that included tax evasion and illegal oil trading with Iran during the hostage crisis. He gave up his U.S. citizenship, but in 2002, just before leaving office, President Clinton pardoned him, wringing a final hail of denunciation from the storm clouds that hovered, seemingly always, over the controversial Clinton White House.

Hogan & Hartson's practice in the 1980s grew apace with developments in the corporate and commercial worlds. In fact, when faced with the specific needs of a business client instead of a general debate about the merits of expansion, uncertainties about growth seemed to evaporate. In 1984, when client Suburban Bancorp asked Hogan & Hartson to open an office nearby in Bethesda, Maryland, partners John Joyce and Edward Dolan readily did so. The next year Hogan & Hartson opened another suburban office, on the other side of the Potomac River in McLean, Virginia. One day one of the firm's Virginia clients had dropped a broad hint to Bob Odle: "We view ourselves as members of this community," he said, "and we're going to do business with people who have offices in this community." Odle "got the picture," as he said later.

Northern Virginia was then in the midst of an enormous growth spurt, fueled in part by budding technology companies and by defense-related industries drawn to Washington by Reagan administration defense spending. But the real estate market also was thriving in the beautiful, rolling countryside southwest of Washington and east of the Blue Ridge mountains. Odle saw fertile ground for a full-service, multidisciplinary practice in McLean and persuaded Ann Vickery's husband, Ray, to return to the firm to start up the new office. Vickery had begun his career as an associate at Hogan & Hartson, then left to serve in the Virginia legislature.

Ray Vickery opened the office in December 1985 with Langhorne Keith and then-associates Jane Marum Roush and Richard K. A. Becker. While it was one of the first Northern Virginia branch offices of a D.C.-based firm, the McLean office soon established what the *Legal Times* called "its own solid identity" in the Old Dominion. In 1994 Keith served as president of the Virginia Bar Association, and the next year he joined Roush on the bench of the Fairfax County Circuit Court. Roush presided over the trial of Lee Boyd Malvo, one of the notorious snipers who terrorized the Washington area in a series of random shootings in the fall of 2002, and she was widely praised for running a smooth, evenhanded trial and balancing media coverage with fairness.

Fulfilling Odle's vision of a full-service, multidisciplinary office, the Virginia practice expanded through the 1990s under the leadership of Managing Partner Jerry Gilbert. Partners Kenneth Hautman, Richard Horan, Michael Lorenger, and Emily Yinger were interviewed in a June 5, 2000, *Legal Times* article which profiled the office's corporate and securities, employment, litigation, and intellectual property groups. In the years that followed, the office handled many mergers and acquisitions, grew to sixty lawyers, and was named Pro Bono Firm of the Year by the Fairfax Bar Association.

New Yorkers like Dennis Lehr and Arthur Rothkopf did not consider the Bethesda and McLean offices to be major growth initiatives, nor did partners Langhorne Keith and Duncan Klinedinst, who helped open those offices. It was more like a Wall Street firm opening an uptown office and a midtown office. What was so bold about that? Hogan & Hartson had wide and strong capabilities, Lehr felt, "yet when we had opportunities to expand to other cities, the firm would find reasons not to do that."

Thomas Leary came to the firm in January 1983 from the legal department at General Motors, where he had been the attorney in charge of antitrust from 1971 to 1977 and the company's assistant general counsel from 1977 to 1982. A major antitrust suit that General Motors anticipated in the 1970s had never occurred, and with the election of Ronald Reagan it looked like it never would. In the mood of anticlimax that followed, Leary began to feel he was getting, as he put it, "a little bit stale." A recruiter for a legal search firm approached him, not to make an offer but an inquiry. Leary was prominent in the bar association and he might know someone skilled in antitrust who could fit a certain "demographic." The firm in question had an eminent, senior antitrust lawyer, while the other antitrust attorneys were still relatively young. Did he know anyone between those two age groups? "Well, you know," Leary told him, "I might be interested myself." He then learned that the firm was Hogan & Hartson.

After graduating from Harvard Law School in 1958 and before joining General Motors in 1971, Leary had worked at an established New York firm for twelve years. Joining Hogan & Hartson gave him a perspective on how the private practice of law had changed during his years as in-house counsel at GM. It had become much more businesslike, more centralized in its billing, much less like a gentleman's club. It was more openly competitive and more openly meritocratic. His old firm, he said, "didn't keep track of how business originated. The thought was, it's the name of the law firm that attracts the clients. The fact that your roommate happens to be the general counsel of XYZ company and the roommate calls you up with some enormous new matter, well, that's just coincidence." As a young partner in his prestigious New York firm, Leary once had asked a senior partner, "Are you interested in me developing any business?" "Well, quite frankly," his colleague replied, "at your age the kind of business that you could attract we're probably not interested in." So much for initiative.

Leary believed that Hogan & Hartson, for all its adaptation to the new, businesslike efficiency in law practice, "still had retained a fraternal feeling." He recalled what had happened when he and a couple dozen others at Hogan & Hartson had attended a recruiting seminar in the mid-1980s. The two consultants conducting the seminar had asked them to list, in a secret ballot, five of thirty given characteristics they thought most important in applicants to the firm.

Half an hour later one of the consultants returned with the results of the tally. "We have given this test to every major law firm in Washington and a lot of them elsewhere," she said, "but you collectively voted as one of your top five categories a quality we have never, ever seen a major law firm identify — *sense of humor*." "We weren't talking about telling jokes," Leary explained later. "What we were talking about is having an appropriate sense of your place in the world, and a little bit of the humility that goes with it."

John Roberts got a bit more humility than he bargained for when he crossed Lafayette Square in the spring of 1986 to move into his new office in the

Chanin Building. Roberts had clerked for Judge Henry J. Friendly on the Second Circuit Court of Appeals after graduating from Harvard Law School in 1979. Subsequently, he clerked for then-Associate Justice William Rehnquist at the U.S. Supreme Court and served as Special Assistant to U.S. Attorney General William French Smith before moving to the White House in 1982 as Associate Counsel to the President. "I'd been having fun," he said, "but the jobs that I had held didn't really have very translatable skills and I was beginning to feel the need to get a real job as a lawyer. I didn't know quite how to do that, to be honest with you." David Waller, a former Hogan & Hartson attorney, joined H. P. Goldfield (who later joined the firm) and others then working in the White House Counsel's office in recommending that Roberts give Barrett Prettyman a call. The two met, shared their views and visions, and agreed on a goal of developing the firm's appellate work, always a strong point of Hogan & Hartson, into a fully specialized practice.

the U.S. Chamber of Commerce building over an alleyway where the garbage was collected. "A sort of post-White House depression set in," he said. But there was hope, as well as an explanation for the general disrepair. Hogan & Hartson's 230 lawyers had outgrown their space in the Chanin Building and soon would be moving to Columbia Square, just a block from the firm's one-time home, the Colorado Building, which still kept its stolid watch over the junction of 14th and G Streets.

Columbia Square was part of a general revival of D.C.'s downtown between Capitol Hill and the White House that had been under way since the early 1970s. The thirteen-story, 620,000-square-foot building stretched half a block deep along the entire length of F Street between 12th and 13th Streets. Developer Gerald Hines had hired the noted architect I. M. Pei, creator of the National Gallery of Art's East Wing, just seven blocks east on Pennsylvania Avenue, to create a comparably stunning structure for the city's downtown revival.

Roberts was not fussy. He had been a wrestler in high school in Indiana, and as halfback and linebacker on the football team had gotten acclimated to the idea of necessary dishevelment. But his first day in the Chanin Building was, as he recalled it, "one of the more sobering experiences of my life." Unlike most government attorneys, who work in comparatively drab settings, Roberts had grown used to working in offices that ranged from the merely grand to the historic and architecturally splendid. But now his carpet was peeling up and his window faced the rear of

By signing on early as a lead tenant, Hogan & Hartson was able to become a joint venturer without actually having an ownership interest. Bob Odle, Richard Poulson, Todd Miller, and associate Warren Gorrell helped structure and negotiate an arrangement whereby the firm shared in the building's profits in the form of a "rent credit." Hogan & Hartson also was involved in determining certain critical features of the building's interior. The firm's library, for instance, required a reinforced floor to hold the weight of law books and journals. Attractive interior stairwells, not

THE BALTIMORE OFFICE AT HARBORPLACE, NEAR THE CITY'S LIVELY INNER HARBOR.

TY COBB, WHOSE MEETINGS WITH BOB ODLE IN THE SPRING OF 1988 SPARKED THE OPENING OF HOGAN & HARTSON'S BALTIMORE OFFICE IN AUGUST. COBB HAS SINCE SERVED THE FIRM IN A NUMBER OF CAPACITIES, INCLUDING MANAGING PARTNER OF THE DENVER OFFICE.

just fire stairwells, were included to make movement between floors easier. And the building's exterior columns, originally set at twenty-foot intervals, were set instead at thirty-foot distances so that the view from office windows would not be broken. Space also was allocated for a backup day care center to serve children of the firm's employees if their usual child care arrangements were interrupted.

Bob Odle enlisted some expert assistance for this major office relocation. Partner Robert Kenney, Jr., who had started the firm's government contracts practice, helped manage the acquisition of up-to-date computer and telephone equipment. And tax attorney Deborah Ashford, who had helped Odle during the Bethesda and McLean office start-ups, extended her role as his Administrative Associate for an additional eighteen months to cover the move to Columbia Square. Wary of anxieties about change, Odle kept everyone briefed through every step of the project and instituted twice-weekly tours through the construction period up to the final move.

Over the first weekend in May 1987 the firm moved into its new home. On Monday morning everyone reported for work, able to pick up where they had left off on Friday. "Their files were in their file cabinets; their personal belongings in boxes were in their offices," Odle said of the firm's attorneys and staff. With help from employees like Anne Bowen, the firm had successfully engineered what he described as "the single biggest private move in the history of Washington, D.C. It was no small deal." Clifford Stromberg, an attorney in the firm's health practice, had feared along with others that the larger space and the new office configuration would disrupt collegiality. But several months after the move Stromberg found that "it just hasn't worked out that way."[18]

The move also gave Hogan & Hartson a chance to mend fences with Stuart Ross, whose insurance company referrals increasingly had generated conflicts with the firm's representation of other clients. "We all saw this train wreck coming," said Odle. In 1983 Ross left the firm with two associates to set up his own insurance litigation practice. Ross leased some space at Columbia Square and the two firms hung out banners, one from the east tower and one from the west, "Welcome, Ross, Dixon," and "Welcome, Hogan & Hartson."

Centrally situated over the anchor station of Metrorail, the new regional subway that the firm's Jay Ricks, as a Metro Board member and vice chairman from 1968 to 1972, had helped plan, Columbia Square was a new source of pride for Hogan & Hartson. A few years earlier a *National Law Journal* article had characterized Hogan & Hartson's decor as "reminiscent of Mamie Eisenhower."[19] It was one of those embarrassing occasions when, as Bob Odle had said it would, the legal trade press "hung our linen out to dry." But Columbia Square's wide-open, aviary-like atrium and its profusion of interior glass seemed to invite the world to come on in and see its fine, new linen.

The move to Columbia Square had been a precision, clockwork operation, a *tour de force* of planning and foresight. Hogan & Hartson's next major change was, by comparison, serendipitous, even accidental. Bob Odle wanted the firm's Bethesda office, which served principally a single bank client, to develop a multidisciplinary practice like that in the McLean office. The Bethesda office's enlarged capabilities then would become a platform for developing a wider practice in the mid-Atlantic region. In the spring of 1988 Odle contacted a search firm to recruit some attorneys for the anticipated Bethesda expansion. The search firm found Ty Cobb in Baltimore. But Cobb's interest soon took Hogan & Hartson on a path quite different from its intended strategy in Bethesda.

Cobb, distant relative and namesake of the legendary baseball player, had graduated from Georgetown University Law Center in 1978 and then had clerked for U.S. District Court Judge Herbert F. Murray before signing on as an assistant U.S. Attorney in Baltimore. In 1986 he had been one of two candidates for the position of U.S. Attorney, but when the other person was chosen Cobb went to a Baltimore firm where he hoped to develop a white-collar criminal defense practice. The whirling corporate world of the 1980s had spun off a surfeit of such cases, and Cobb exuded enthusiasm for the complex, high-tension, high-stakes drama of the work. To his increasing disappointment, however, the Baltimore firm did not share his ambition and even turned down some cases that he considered promising. When a recruiter called him about joining Hogan & Hartson's Bethesda office, Cobb was ready to listen. But the more he listened, the more he thought he had a better idea.

Litigator Stephen J. Immelt (top) and corporate attorney Michael J. Silver (bottom) exemplified the range of talent that joined Hogan & Hartson's new Baltimore office.

Cobb drove down to Washington in April 1988 to meet with Odle. "There was a lot of personal

While U.S. Attorney in Baltimore in 1973, George Beall earned national respect for his politically courageous prosecution of former Maryland governor, then U.S. Vice President, Spiro Agnew on corruption charges. In 1988 he joined Hogan & Hartson in the firm's new Baltimore office.

[ABOVE] (L TO R) MEREDITH ABRAMS, KATHY STOUT, MARK SAUDEK AND GIL ABRAMSON IN THE BALTIMORE OFFICE'S INFORMATION RESOURCES CENTER. [LEFT] HOWARD FLACK (L) AND TY COBB WERE AMONG THE ATTORNEYS WHO WORKED HARD TO ENSURE THE BEST POSSIBLE START FOR THE BALTIMORE OFFICE.

connection between the two of us," Cobb recalled. "We both grew up in small towns in the West. We were both wearing cowboy boots. We talked for nearly two hours, which was pretty unusual." Before long they were no longer talking about Cobb coming to Bethesda but about Cobb's gathering together a group of young lawyers like Michael Colglazier, J. Clinton Kelly, and Richard Dunne, "young turks, 35 to 40 year olds, with good reputations and work ethics," and starting a Hogan & Hartson office in Baltimore.

As negotiations proceeded through the summer, the word spread, then leaked to the press, that several Baltimore attorneys were about to leave their firms to join a major Washington firm. Cobb didn't want George Beall, his mentor and colleague at the Baltimore firm and a former U.S. Attorney who had supported him for that position in 1986, to find out through the newspapers that he was leaving. So he drove out to Beall's home in the Maryland countryside, took a deep breath, and knocked on the door. Beall was surprised to see him and invited him in. About forty minutes later Beall's wife joined the discussion and, as Cobb put it, "I went into recruiting mode." Far from being hurt or disappointed, Beall, who was on the Baltimore firm's management committee, was understanding and supportive of Cobb's decision. "I went out there feeling like Elmer Fudd and left feeling like Elmer Gantry," Cobb said, contrasting the befuddled cartoon character with the fiery evangelist in Sinclair Lewis's 1927 novel.

Two days later, in what Cobb called "a huge surprise," Beall told him that he, too, would like to go with Hogan & Hartson. To Cobb, Beall was a rare "profile in courage." His father and brother had been United States Senators from Maryland, but Beall's successful prosecution of Vice President and former Maryland Governor Spiro Agnew on tax charges, and his participation in the Justice Department's investigation of President Nixon had, Cobb believed, "virtually killed his political career." Still, Beall had many friends in Washington, and moving to Hogan & Hartson would give him "the opportunity to play on a little bigger stage," Cobb thought.

Hogan & Hartson's Baltimore office opened in the Legg Mason Tower on August 1, 1988, with Beall, Sam Clark, and Kevin Gralley joining Cobb, Dunne, Colglazier, and Kelly. The Baltimore partners and associates added about 10 attorneys to Hogan & Hartson's roster of 235. Later, highly regarded litigator Stephen Immelt also signed on, as did Michael Silver, Duke Lohr, James "Jay" Gede, and Edward Sledge, partners who expanded considerably the office's corporate and securities, energy, and project finance capabilities. The profile of the office was further enhanced by the arrival of Ralph Tyler, a former Deputy Attorney of Maryland, who was able to attract a series of important public law cases to the office.

Bob Waldman was asked by the Executive Committee to spend substantial time in the new Baltimore office to coordinate the development of the firm's corporate practice there. After agreeing to accept the assignment, he discovered that New York and Washington, D.C., where he was a member of the bar, had no reciprocity with the Maryland bar. He would have to take the Maryland bar exam, which focused on civil and criminal procedure. "It was cruel and unusual punishment for a corporate practitioner," he later joked, having passed the exam. "Unlike some of our lawyers who had taken the exam but didn't tell anyone, the whole firm knew I had to do it to carry out the mission in Baltimore." In the end, Waldman was able to devote most of his practice focus to Washington, D.C., because Silver and Lohr, augmented later by the addition of Henry Kahn and Larry Seidman, succeeded in building for the firm a premier national corporate and securities practice from their Baltimore base.

The firm had its skeptics about the new Baltimore office. "Why Baltimore?" was one minority view. But in time most were won over. Washington partners like Austin Mittler, Jim Rosenhauer, Bob Waldman, Arthur Rothkopf, and, of course, Bob Odle spent many days in Baltimore working with their new colleagues to make sure the office would mesh smoothly with the home office in Washington, and that the newcomers would feel both welcomed and supported. "I can't tell you how well Hogan does that," said Cobb. "We had met almost everybody before we launched. When we started it felt like we'd been there forever." That was no accident, even if the office itself had been. Jan McDavid, then chair of the firm's legal ethics committee, succinctly captured the whole experience. "We were looking for Maryland lawyers and we found a Baltimore office."

The firm's new practice areas and offices in the late 1980s required some management adjustments. Odle's management duties had multiplied. In April 1987, at the Executive Committee's request, Odle had assumed overall management responsibility for the firm's various practice groups — lateral recruiting, long-range planning, and development of new practice areas and offices. He spent months examining the firm's many practice groups and mulling over new ways to manage them.

In March 1989 Odle marked ten years as Hogan & Hartson's Administrative Partner. The following month the Executive Committee changed his title to Managing Partner. Odle was humble about what he regarded as an honor and a reflection of the firm's trust and confidence in him. His reassurance to the Executive Committee that, in his view, "the new title is not really a grant of new authority, and I intend to conduct myself accordingly," was correct, strictly speaking. The new title didn't bring any new authority. It didn't have to. The committee effectively had given it to Odle already, in countless major and minor matters over the past decade. The title change formalized what long had been reality.

In April, the same month he was named Managing Partner, Odle submitted a "Future Planning" memorandum to the Executive Committee summarizing

C O N F I D E N T I A L

M E M O R A N D U M

MAY 31, 1989

TO: The Executive Committee

FROM: Bob Glen Odle

RE: Future Planning

During the last several months, we all have devoted considerable attention to the future direction of our firm as we weave our way through the unprecedented restructuring our profession is undergoing. **Our shared objective is to ensure that Hogan & Hartson emerges from the shake-out not only alive and well, but as a preeminent survivor.** Expressed in this memorandum (which clearly is not a definitive strategic plan) are a mix of specific strategies and planning approaches we might follow to reach our shared objective. My purpose is to provide a suggested framework for the Committee's ongoing discussions on these vitally important issues.

In order to plan effectively for the future, we need a clear understanding of the present. Section A below is a broad-brush attempt at asking the pertinent questions about who we are and what's right and what's wrong with the way the firm is run. (Many of these questions have been addressed effectively in recent years, at least in part, by successive Executive Committees and at firm retreats; others have been addressed inadequately, or not at all. For certain, we have never collected our thoughts on the subjects in a single planning exercise.)

Sections B and C are an admittedly biased attempt at prescribing certain courses of action and codes of conduct for the future. These Sections only scratch the surface of what our future thinking and planning should address, and they presume in a fairly obvious way answers to some of the Section A questions. Nevertheless, Sections B and C are a fair representation of of my own current thinking on the subjects addressed. Most particularly, they articulate some of the major principles I attempt to follow in the daily conduct of my responsibilities.

Section D addresses the future planning process per se, and alternative approaches we may wish to consider.

FRANK FAHRENKOPF, A FORMER REPUBLICAN NATIONAL COMMITTEE CHAIRMAN, HELPED GUIDE HOGAN & HARTSON'S LEGISLATIVE AND INTERNATIONAL TRADE PRACTICES IN THE 1980S.

his lengthy study of the firm's management needs. That study had been rigorous and thorough, outlining the guiding principles for what would prove to be, for all of its careful and deliberate progress, an astounding period of expansion for Hogan & Hartson. Key ideas for growth included fostering balance and diversity in practice areas, and being very selective about opening new offices and adding new attorneys and practices. Every addition would need to connect with or add on to something else already existing in the firm, not just to foster intramural cooperation but also to promote the kind of cross-selling that came with a diverse, "one-stop shopping" organization. Odle also noted the necessity of future change in the firm's management structure. For years the Executive Committee consistently had rejected the concept of firm Chairman and Executive Committee Chairman as "an idea whose time had not yet come." But Odle reminded the committee, "As we continue to grow and expand we may find need to revisit these concepts again in the future."[20]

The next month, May 1989, Odle's planning memo was sent to all partners. In June an article titled "The Law Business in the Year 2000," written by Steven Brill for *The American Lawyer*, echoed much of what Odle's memo described: increasingly competitive conditions required new thinking and decisive responses.[21] Partners, for example, were going to have to work harder rather than easing back from daily pressures as they advanced in years and experience. There would be more lateral recruiting, and earnings would be more directly proportional to billings, which would be tracked more closely. Large firms would have to become even larger to serve as "one-stop shops" for international clients with worldwide legal needs.

Brill included Hogan & Hartson among the forty leading contenders to emerge as the nation's "Top Twenty" law firms in the year 2000. Odle intended for the firm to make any final cut. But Hogan & Hartson also valued its traditions and the values they represented, so in his memo Odle recalled Frank Hogan's service ethic of "passionate commitment to the client's cause" while recommending a thorough review to assure success in "the unprecedented restructuring our profession is undergoing."[22] In October 1989 Robert Johnston, a professional administrator, joined Hogan & Hartson as the firm's Director of Administration, a new position analogous to a corporation's chief operating officer. And that month the firm's retreat at Wintergreen resort in Virginia focused sharply on "planning at the practice level."

Following the Wintergreen retreat, the Executive Committee named twenty-one partners to serve as planning directors for the firm's seventeen practice groups, with the litigation group assigned a five-partner committee. Three partners were asked to coordinate planning for three firm-wide practice groups: Jack Keeney for the Community Services Department, Arthur Rothkopf for international practice, and Frank Fahrenkopf for legislative and policy work. After further discussion among the seventeen practice groups, three broad practice areas emerged as a new part of Hogan & Hartson's practice management structure and were placed under the administration of three Practice Area Administrators (PAAs): Commercial (today Business and Finance), under Jim Rosenhauer; Government Regulation, under Phil Larson; and Litigation, under Austin Mittler. Additionally, Ray Vickery and George Beall formally were named Managing Partners of the McLean and Baltimore offices, respectively. The new PAAs' responsibilities were firm-wide and included oversight of associate assignments, recruiting, personnel evaluation, training, ethics, and billing. They also were informally responsible for providing guidance and support to the firm's attorneys as difficult challenges arose. Hogan & Hartson was a firm organizing for rapid transition on a wide stage — wider, as it turned out, than anyone expected.

Hogan & Hartson's practice groups multiplied in response to the globalization of business, the increased sophistication of telecommunications and medical technologies, and evolving national policies concerning antitrust, regulation, health care, and trade. Rosenhauer,

Mittler, Larson, and Larson's successor, Rich Rodin, worked continuously with all of the lawyers in their practice areas to ensure that each area remained integrated, sharing resources, policies and talents, even as the firm grew and expanded to multiple offices and countries. Activities in the firm's Community Services Department also expanded, partly as a result of the firm's now established reputation as a *pro bono* leader, but also because of the energy and talent that the firm's attorneys brought to their CSD cases. Under the successive leadership of Sally Determan, Joseph Hassett, and William Bradford, Jr., the CSD in the 1980s achieved headline successes such as its school desegregation litigation in Prince George's County, Maryland, where Chief Judge Frank A. Kaufman of the U.S. District Court noted the extraordinary contribution of Hogan & Hartson's lawyers. "The commitment of hundreds and thousands of dollars of time," said Judge Kaufman, "not over the course of many years, as is frequently the case, but over the course of less than a year, constitutes, in this court's opinion, an 'exceptional' circumstance in the context of the risk involved."[23] Joseph Hassett and Jack Keeney, the CSD's Senior Associate at the time, tried the case before Judge Kaufman, with assistance from a team that included Hogan & Hartson's Elliot Mincberg, David Tatel, and George Mernick.

The firm's CSD, as well as its reputation for litigation, had attracted Jack Keeney to Hogan & Hartson in 1978, after he completed his clerkship for U.S. District Judge Alexander Harvey in Baltimore. Keeney recalled his first deposition at Hogan & Hartson, "which was attended by Barrett Prettyman, who sat with me all day and offered pointers. I may not have been terrible," he mused, "but in retrospect I could have been a whole lot better. Barrett Prettyman was such a gentleman, he was really good. All he said to me afterwards was, 'Jack, that was very good for a first deposition. Oh, by the way, all those objections the other side made — they were really right.'" During the deposition Prettyman had been totally supportive, never letting on, "but he did want to make sure that I understood," Keeney chuckled.

Pat Brannan was not quite seven years beyond completing her clerkship for Judge John Ferren when she had the opportunity to argue a pro bono case before the U.S. Supreme Court. When vandals defaced the Shaare Tefila synagogue in suburban Maryland in 1982 with spray-painted, anti-Semitic slogans, members of the congregation headed by Kevin Lipson, who would later become a partner in the firm, came to Hogan & Hartson's CSD for help. The eight young men responsible had been arrested and convicted, but this seemed like more than simple vandalism; it felt more like a violation of the members' civil rights. Hogan & Hartson took the case. "A swastika taps into powerful racial issues," said Brannan later. "If someone would have thrown a rock through a window it would have been different."[24] Brannan, Joe Hassett, and Jack Keeney developed a theory designed to establish that such conduct violated federal laws prohibiting racial discrimination. But Shaare Tefila lost in the federal district court in Baltimore and lost the Fourth Circuit appeal, too, which affirmed the district court ruling that Jews were an ethnic group, not a race, and hence not covered under the civil rights laws. The congregation took the next step, to the U.S. Supreme Court, which agreed to hear the case.

Patricia A. Brannan joined Hogan & Hartson in 1980. Her litigation and appellate practice has included several high-profile civil rights and education cases.

Barrett Prettyman helped Brannan prepare for her argument, scheduled for February 25, 1987. For months they conducted rigorous moot court presentations, rehearsing every imaginable hypothetical question that the Justices might ask. Prettyman convinced Brannan to keep her argument free of emotional factors; the Justices themselves would take care of that. Brannan took the advice and the Justices reacted as Prettyman sensed they would. At one point Justice Thurgood Marshall leaned over toward Brannan's opponent and asked, "Do you know what a swastika means?" He answered his own question. "This means death to these people. This is about genocide."[25] On May 18, 1987, the Court unanimously reversed the Fourth Circuit ruling, underscoring for Shaare Tefila and all Jewish people in America that their civil rights would be protected under the nation's civil rights laws.

H&H DADS (L TO R) THOMAS BULLEIT, JEFFREY MUNK AND EDWARD "TED" WILSON.

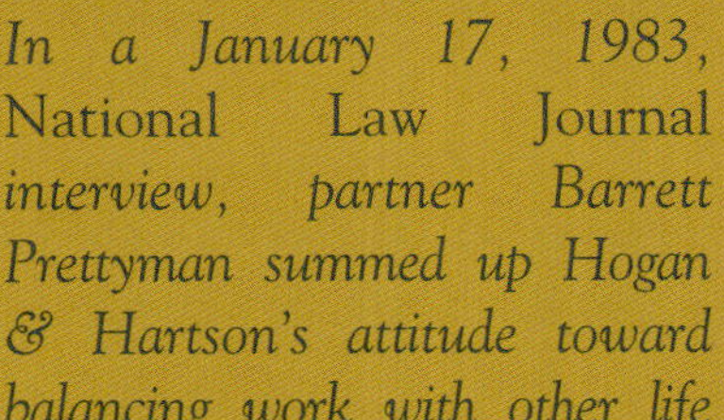

In a January 17, 1983, National Law Journal *interview, partner Barrett Prettyman summed up Hogan & Hartson's attitude toward balancing work with other life goals: "You must do good work, you must get it done on time, you must be professional; but having said that, there's more to the practice of law than that, there's more to life than that." With that heritage as background, Hogan & Hartson has been among the relatively few large firms nationwide consistently singled out for their efforts to help attorneys achieve balance in their personal and family lives.*

The issue is very complex and emotional, especially for attorneys who opt for the challenges and rewards of work in large law firms. Such firms have been caught in a hard squeeze in recent years. On the one hand, sharpened competition between firms has pressured them to respond more efficiently to client demands. Those demands, in turn, have become ever more urgent as a result of raised expectations for speed fostered by new technologies such as e-mail, cell phones, and the Internet. The result: pressure on attorneys to bring in business, turn work around quickly, and log more billable hours.

At the same time, many attorneys have countered with demands for more family time or for just plain relaxing. The result: family leave; dual-tracked billable hour requirements for partnership consideration; on-site backup child care; and flexible or part-time work schedules. Ironically, the same computer and telephone technologies that increase workplace pressures also give many attorneys the flexibility to work outside the office.

The legal profession as a whole is still struggling to find solutions to this highly charged issue. The American Bar Association's Commission on Women in the Profession issued a report in 2001 titled "Balanced Lives: Changing the Culture of the Legal Profession." The commission noted that increasing numbers of male attorneys are seeking more time for activities outside work, such as spending time with their families, but that most of the pressure to balance work and non-work activities still falls on women. Having discovered in the 1970s and 1980s that no one, male or female, really can "have it all," women — who in 1999 comprised about 25 percent of all lawyers and 40 percent of associates in large law firms — are stirring men to join them in a probing reexamination of work and life priorities.

Hogan & Hartson's commitment to balance has opened doors for women — in 2003 women comprised about 41 percent of the D.C. office's attorneys and 28 percent of its partners, more than any other large D.C. firm. That same commitment aims to shatter any "glass ceiling" imposed by a narrow view of how families and careers are best nurtured.

In matters ranging from minority rights to First Amendment cases, from international refugees to the Equal Rights Amendment (ERA), and from workers' pension rights to the preservation of the Wildlife Refuge System, the CSD in the 1980s provided top quality legal representation while creating unique opportunities for attorneys across all practice groups to join forces in shared endeavors. In December 1987, for instance, thirty Hogan & Hartson attorneys began helping the Legal Services Program of the Whitman-Walker Clinic in Washington to staff a once-weekly legal clinic for AIDS patients. The lawyers offered counseling on such matters as estate planning, living wills, health care decisions, powers of attorney, and government benefits. As news of the legal clinic spread, Hogan & Hartson attorneys trained volunteers from other law firms in the city, thereby extending across several law firms' *pro bono* efforts the special bonds and satisfactions usually experienced only in individual firm's own ranks.

Barrett Prettyman often brought to the CSD the good-natured but demanding tutorship that had helped make the firm's appellate practice one of the nation's most accomplished. Attorneys Jack Arness, Dave Hensler, Bob Kapp, Patrick Raher, Pat Brannan, William Bradford, Jay Ricks, and Joe Hassett were among many at the firm who argued cases before appeals courts, including the U.S. Supreme Court, in the 1980s. Prettyman, Allen Snyder, and John Roberts contributed unique insights gained by their prior clerkships for Supreme Court Justices. But as law practice became more and more specialized, so too did the art of appellate argument.

Through a combination of experience, skill, and temperament, some attorneys became specialists in the particular discipline of arguing before the U.S. Supreme Court, where months of preparation boil down to just a few, intense minutes of high-stakes interchange with the Justices. A tightly framed line of reasoning might unravel in a second when snagged in an unexpected line of questioning from a Justice. An argument held too rigidly or pushed too forcefully toward the wrong Justice at the wrong time might fall flat. Or a splendid argument prepared by a superb attorney might just dissolve in a rare attack of nerves. No one could ever count on victory; the best attorneys experienced both wins and losses. But few ever would feel what Barrett Prettyman began to feel when, after about the seventh in a total of nineteen cases he argued before the Court, it occurred to him, somewhere in the middle of every appearance, "Damn, this is fun!"

In 1987 Prettyman and John Roberts worked together on a case for Gwaltney of Smithfield Foods, a client of Patrick Raher at the firm. It involved the Chesapeake Bay Foundation's suit against Gwaltney, a meat-packing company, for violations of the Clean Water Act. Gwaltney had violated "and would continue to violate," the foundation alleged, the terms of its state-issued permit by dumping excessive levels of pollutants into Virginia's Pagan River. Gwaltney of Smithfield's chairman could have settled the case for a relatively small amount of money at the time, said Raher, but on principle he chose instead to fight. The company had exceeded its permitted effluent levels in the past, the chairman admitted, but had since cleaned up its act. Could it properly be held liable for things it was no longer doing because someone thought it might do them again in the future?

On October 5, 1987, Raher, Roberts, and Prettyman entered the Supreme Court to present Gwaltney's case. It was only the second time Raher had ever been in the building. They sat down behind the railing at their assigned table as Raher, who was holding all the briefs, glanced down at them frequently to make sure they all were in order. Prettyman soon would rise and make the argument, but Raher wondered how he was ever going to do it with just the single sheet of paper, folded in thirds, that he held in his hand. Just as everyone was readying themselves for the Justices to enter, Prettyman looked over at Raher. "I have to go to the bathroom," he said. "I'll be right back."

For a single moment Raher froze. "You've got to be kidding me," he thought. Then Prettyman's face broke into a grin. He wasn't going anywhere, but the joke broke the tension and relaxed the team when it most needed it. Prettyman's argument won the case for Gwaltney — "the only victory under that section of the Clean Water Act ever in the Supreme Court," said Raher.

John Roberts's first case before the U.S. Supreme Court also was an unusual one. Irwin Halper, manager of a doctor's group, had been convicted of submitting sixty-five false claims for Medicare reimbursement. He was sentenced to a prison term and a fine of $5,000. However, the federal civil False

Court. "There was no way to have that kind of experience in the private sector," he said. Prettyman supported Roberts's decision. "It's the right thing for him to do at this point in his career," he said. But Prettyman had lived through seven changes of Presidential administration in Washington since joining Hogan & Hartson in 1955, and he may well have figured that he would see John Roberts again.

That opportunity came sooner than Prettyman expected, when he and John Roberts faced each other before the Supreme Court on April 16, 1990, on opposite sides of an argument over the government's allowing private companies to mine certain areas of public lands in the West (*Lujan v. National Wildlife Federation*, 497 U.S. 871). The D.C. Circuit Court had upheld a challenge to the government's decision from the National Wildlife Federation and other parties who felt that mining activities would interfere with recreational uses and aesthetic enjoyment of the lands. The Department of the Interior decided to appeal. Roberts represented the government, while Prettyman argued on behalf of the National Wildlife Federation.

The Justices ruled 5-4 for the government, reversing the D.C. Circuit's decision. Prettyman laughed as he recalled how he "very much resented" losing the case to Roberts. "I had been a kind of mentor to him when he was here at the firm," he said. "But he beat me legitimately. I have gone back and read his opening several times — the six sentences he used to open his argument — and it was as effective as I've ever heard in the Supreme Court, extremely compelling." For his part, Roberts remembered being "staggered by the intensity of Barrett's preparation" when he first joined the firm. "It instills in you an appreciation of how deeply you do have to prepare,

Claims Act allowed the government to impose additional civil penalties for each count of fraud, which ballooned Halper's fines to more than $130,000. The U.S. District Court for the Southern District of New York declined to impose the additional fines, ruling that civil penalties so severe in proportion to the criminal penalties constituted double jeopardy — punishing Halper twice for the same crime — and violated his Fifth Amendment rights. The government appealed, and the Supreme Court asked Roberts to represent Halper. On January 17, 1989, Roberts argued the case, and on May 15 the Court unanimously agreed with him.[26]

Later in 1989 Roberts got another offer he couldn't refuse after President George H. Bush named Kenneth Starr the Solicitor General of the United States, in charge of representing the government's interests before the Supreme Court. Starr, who had known Roberts from the early 1980s when both worked in the Attorney General's office, asked if Roberts would serve as Deputy Solicitor General. Roberts accepted the opportunity, which would allow him to argue as many as eight cases a year before the

The following day, when Berliners began demolishing the grotesque wall that had cleaved their lives and their city for twenty-eight years, Bell, Berger, and Rothkopf could see even more clearly the vast change that Poland was leading. By the end of 1991 the Soviet Union itself was moribund and was replaced in January 1992 by the Russian Federation. The Cold War was over. Now people were free to struggle for security in the new market economies. Bell captured the shock of the change in Poland after January 1, 1990, when all prices were decontrolled and the borders were opened. "Nobody knew when goods were going to reappear, because for a moment there were no goods. Then one day some guy with a truckload of meat just parked right in front of a state butcher shop and started selling meat. It [the market] just exploded. The old way was over."

Hogan & Hartson's work in Poland was, as Sandy Berger put it, "fortuitous," but the firm's appearance in several other countries soon afterward was the result of considerable prior planning and discussion. Bob Odle's May 1989 "Future Planning" memo to the Executive Committee had included a recommendation that the firm move into the international arena as well as expand further in the United States. For several months the memo circulated throughout the firm and was discussed at length at the fall Partner's Retreat. The successful opening of the Baltimore office in August 1988 had eased the anxiety some partners felt about expanding beyond Washington, D.C. It also kindled enthusiasm for venturing overseas in pursuit of an expanded, more versatile corporate and regulatory practice.

Dan Maccoby, managing partner of Hogan & Hartson's London office from 1990 to 2004. The office enjoys a sweeping view of St. Paul's and central London.

"I think it was obvious to everybody that we had to be overseas," said George Carneal, who was on the Executive Committee at the time. However, careful analysis, both of markets and motivations, was required to ensure that expansion occurred in response to client and industry needs. Odle and others said many times that Hogan & Hartson would not grow for growth's sake, nor would it gamble on the theory of "build it and they will come." Instead, the firm's growth followed a very carefully planned strategy, including a balance of local, national, and international clients. At the fall 1989 retreat, those partners with international clients compared notes, some for the first time in a concerted way, and emerged with a plan.

In order to reduce risks and costs, Hogan & Hartson's first effort to establish an office outside the United States was planned jointly with two other law

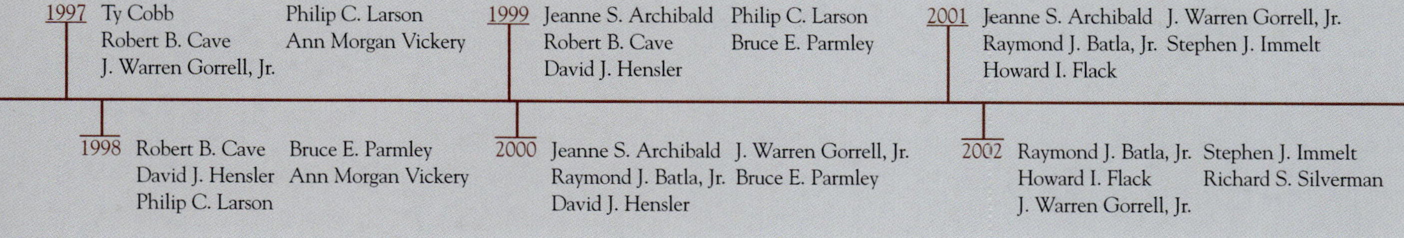

HOGAN & HARTSON'S BRUSSELS OFFICE OPENED IN JANUARY 1991.

firms, Brobeck, Phleger & Harrison and Hale & Dorr. "We were going to dip one toe in the water," Carneal recalled with a smile, but a closer look indicated that the venture might be troubled by several client conflicts. So in June 1990, before the plan was effected, Hogan & Hartson pulled out and decided to go it alone with its own London office, which Daniel Maccoby and Richard Poulson opened in December of that year. Maccoby served as Managing Partner of the new office. Now Hogan & Hartson would be able to serve corporate clients from one of the strongest and most established financial centers in the world.

Hogan & Hartson was not alone in setting sights on Britain and the rest of Europe. Many U.S. law firms opened overseas offices after 1989, partly to follow their clients but also in anticipation of a collapsed Soviet empire and the possibilities that rebuilding and new markets would provide. But even without this stimulus, Europe was moving toward greater centralization and efficiency in trade, travel, and currency. Many saw Brussels, in its relation to European Union members, as similar to Washington, D.C., in its relation to the states — a regulatory and policy center. Sandy Berger thought that many firms had gone to Brussels "because, like Mount Everest, it was there." But Hogan & Hartson's strategy was more focused as well as more realistic. At a time when there was real uncertainty whether the firm would be better pursuing Europe or Asia as its initial international focus, the firm chose Europe. "We had to think very clearly about what our niche was and where our best opportunities would be in a very crowded marketplace," he observed.[1] Hogan & Hartson would concentrate on commercial and corporate work in London and on regulatory work in Brussels.

Randy Miller, a Kansan who had come to Hogan & Hartson from Senator Robert Dole's staff, opened the Brussels office for the firm in January 1991, just one month after the London office opened. Soon he was joined by an experienced communications lawyer from the Washington office, Gerald Oberst. Claud v. S. "Lex" Eley, who had established a Brussels office for another firm before joining Hogan & Hartson, succeeded Miller as Managing Partner.

JOSEPH BELL AND HIS FAMILY MOVED INTO THIS DUPLEX IN FEBRUARY 1991 AND ESTABLISHED HOGAN & HARTSON'S FIRST WARSAW OFFICE IN THE ROOM OVER THE GARAGE.

JOSEPH BELL IN WARSAW, EARLY 1990S.

EXECUTIVE COMMITTEE

2003 Howard I. Flack, Stephen J. Immelt, Richard S. Silverman, Dennis H. Tracey, III, Christine A. Varney

2004 Richard T. Horan, Jr., Peter A. Rohrbach, Richard S. Silverman, Dennis H. Tracey, III, Christine A. Varney

PARTNERS

1989

Edward C. Dolan, Sandra E. Folsom, Howard M. Holstein, David W. Hornbeck, Stephen J. Immelt, Gary J. Kushner, Robert F. Leibenluft, Judith G. Muncy, Rodney R. Munsey, William D. Nussbaum, Edward A. Ryan, John T. Schell, III, Richard S. Silverman

HOGAN & HARTSON SOON MOVED ITS WARSAW OFFICE FROM JOSEPH BELL'S HOME TO A DOWNTOWN SITE THAT IT COMPLETELY RENOVATED. BELOW IS THE ORIGINAL PURCHASE RECEIPT, IN POLISH AND ENGLISH.

RECEIPT

Hereby we confirm the receipt of $100,000 from Joseph C. Bell as a deposit for the purchase of premises on Marszalkowska Street, #6.

Dated: 4/8/91

Signed Zbigniew Herba

They later were joined by Catriona Hatton, a prominent European "competition," or antitrust, lawyer, who succeeded Eley as office Managing Partner in 2002.

By late 1990, after more than a year of *pro bono* assistance to the Polish Ministry of Finance, Hogan & Hartson still had not opened a Warsaw office. Under pressure from World Bank authorities, the Finance Ministry had transferred much of its debt restructuring work to a New York law firm with a longer track record in that specialty. Joe Bell could understand the decision, but it was "a bitter disappointment" nevertheless. Hogan & Hartson maintained a presence in Warsaw, continuing its consulting work with government agencies such as the Ministry of Foreign Economic Relations, the Ministry of Telecommunications, and the Ministry on Ownership Change. Partner Bob Kenney, who had developed a government contracts practice for Hogan & Hartson in Washington in the 1980s, helped a Polish team draft a public procurement bill. But the firm held back from taking the plunge into a formal office opening. A young Polish lawyer, Piotr Kochanski, was excited about the possibility, however, and enthusiastically urged Bell to move forward. In December 1990 Kochanski received an offer to join the Polish foreign service, but he remained hopeful about joining Hogan & Hartson and made a last pitch to Bell. "Well, are you guys going to do something or not?" Bell went to Bob Odle, who took the proposition to the Executive Committee, which decided in January to go ahead with the project.

Just four days after the Executive Committee's approval, Joe Bell returned to Warsaw with his family on February 1, 1991, to head up the firm's office there. The Gulf War was under way and there were threats to U.S. commercial aircraft. "My wife and I flew on separate planes," Bell recalled. "She and my daughter flew on a

1990

Jonathan L. Abram
Deborah T. Ashford
David W. Burgett
Susan S. DeSanti
Isabel P. Dunst
Bruce W. Gilchrist
Janet Pitterle Holt
Stephan E. Lawton
Joan L. Loizeaux
Daniel H. Maccoby
Mark E. Mazo
Elizabeth B. Meers
Randy E. Miller
William L. Neff
Allen L. Schwait
Clyde H. Sorrell
Kimberley E. Thompson
Pamela G. Winthrop

ALEKSANDER GALOS HAS HAD A DISTINGUISHED CAREER IN THE LAW AND PUBLIC SERVICE IN POLAND, AND IS MANAGING PARTNER OF HOGAN & HARTSON'S OFFICE IN WARSAW (ABOVE).

plane that was so empty that they moved everybody into first class." The day after the Bells arrived, the office opened — in the family's rented duplex. Three employees settled into their new beginnings behind three IKEA desks, sharing with the Bells the one phone line into the building. The family's dining room served as the firm's conference room. It was the first time that Hogan & Hartson had practiced domestic law in a foreign country.

Not long afterward the law practice moved into larger quarters, an apartment in Warsaw that the firm purchased. Financing in Poland was still in a formative stage, so Bell carried a suitcase of cash — 2,600 one-hundred-dollar bills — to the settlement. He remembered how workers and craftsmen began renovating the apartment with hand tools, gradually switching over to power tools as their new income, and the supply of available tools, increased under economic reforms. Attorneys, now partners, Maciej Jamka and Aleksander Galos joined Kochanski and Bell in the office. Following a short stint by Jamka as office Managing Partner, partner Steven Ballew began a six-year stint as Managing Partner of that office in 1992.

At the Warsaw office's tenth anniversary celebration in 2001, Aleksander Galos, then Managing Partner, summarized the importance of the help provided by lawyers such as Joe Bell, Bob Odle, Jim Rosenhauer, Bob Kenney, Nevin Kelly, and Ray Batla, who, with American partners-in-residence Steve Ballew and Michael Cheroutes, helped orient their Polish colleagues toward new legal instruments; aided in introducing new standards of client service; brought new technologies that made work more efficient; and gave concrete support to Poland's fresh participation in the modern global economy.[2]

The Iron Curtain's meltdown in Czechoslovakia in 1989 opened many doors for Ray Batla, who had joined Hogan & Hartson in July 1973 after earning his law degree at the University of Texas. Batla's parents were Czech immigrants and, unbeknownst to his Hogan & Hartson colleagues, Texas-born-and-raised Batla had grown up fluent in his parents' native language before learning to speak English. In 1990 he served as a member of the International Observer Delegation to the 1990 National Elections in the newly named Czech and Slovak Federal Republic, the first free elections held there since 1946. In November 1991, assisted by Pavel Bradac, a Czech lawyer who had studied in the United States, Batla

PARTNERS

1991

Gil A. Abramson
George P. Barsness
David F. Grady
W. Michael House
Catherine J. LaCroix
Timothy A. Lloyd
Steven J. Routh

1992

Richard K.A. Becker
Lisa R. Bonanno
Alan L. Dye
Steven P. Hollman
Craig A. Hoover
Steven M. Kaufman
James E. Landry
Walter G. Lohr
John P. Mathis
Thomas F. O'Neill, III
Humberto R. Peña
Michael J. Silver
Maree F. Sneed

opened a Hogan & Hartson office in Prague. Joined by attorneys Jan Tanzer and Milan Lovisek, Batla and Bradac soon were busy with privatization, energy, and airport construction projects. Back in Washington, "We all went, 'Who knew?!'" said Ann Morgan Vickery. "All we knew was that Ray was an energy lawyer from Texas and a great guy."

The enthusiasm for free elections in former Soviet states also carried Hogan & Hartson's Sherwin Markman to unexpected adventure. Markman's ancestors had come to the United States from Ukraine, a Texas-sized country just north of the Black Sea between Poland and southwestern Russia. Markman had joined Hogan & Hartson in 1968 after several years in the Johnson White House as Assistant to the President. Late at night and in the early morning hours he wrote *The Election*, a novel highlighting the electoral college system and a series of improbable, but not implausible, events resulting in the election of an openly racist presidential candidate. *The Election* was hailed by reviewers and was very widely read in the United States, but it wasn't until Markman went to Ukraine in 1989 that he experienced true lionization, when hundreds of people attended a press conference arranged for him there.

Not long afterward an investment group invited Bell to Kiev to discuss a legal services arrangement. Not much came of the Ukrainian connection, Bell noted later, but he did enjoy his *pro bono* work helping to draft a reform plan for the Ukrainian government. "In all naive simplicity, we drafted the reforms," he said. "Bang, bang, bang," and it was done. Bell's Ukrainian hosts took him to a celebration out in the woods, complete with bonfire and singing. The scene was timeless and evocative. "It could have been two hundred years earlier," Bell said, "except that there were motorized vehicles instead of horses out there."

Activities for Hogan & Hartson's London and Brussels offices were planned carefully over several months to achieve specific goals in a relatively predictable environment. The Warsaw and Prague offices evolved more rapidly as part of the firm's

[1] Hogan & Hartson's Prague office: nine windows on the first (middle) floor of a beautifully restored building. [2] Raymond J. Batla, Jr., helped establish Hogan & Hartson's Prague office in 1991. Now based in London as well as in Washington, D.C., Batla is the firm's Managing Partner for International Offices. [3] A view of the Prague office (center left) from Prague Castle. St. Nicholas Church is in the background.

1993

Jeanne S. Archibald	Michael L. Cheroutes	Mary L. Harmon	Kevin J. Lanigan	James E. Showen
Helen C. Atkeson	Dean W. Crowell	Kenneth J. Hautman	Warren H. Maruyama	L. Anthony Sutin
Michael D. Barnes	Mark D. Dopp	Steven E. Keller	Terri S. Reiskin	Donis G. Walker
A. Lee Bentley	Edward C. Duckers	Nevin J. Kelly	Mace J. Rosenstein	T. Clark Weymouth
Rebecca B. Bronson	C. Michael Gilliland	David P. King	David J. Scott	Michael C. Williams

SINCE MARK MAZO JOINED HOGAN & HARTSON IN 1990 TO CARRY FORWARD HIS IDEAS FOR DEVELOPING AN INTERNATIONAL PRACTICE, HE HAS TRAVELED REGULARLY BETWEEN THE FIRM'S WASHINGTON, D.C., AND PARIS OFFICES.

flexible response to events unfolding daily in those capitals. Hogan & Hartson's last European expansion in 1991, in Paris, fell somewhere between these two standards of predictability and was closely linked to the firm's recent hiring of partner Mark Mazo.

Mazo had come to Hogan & Hartson in June 1990 because the firm in which he had practiced for sixteen years proved unable to furnish the legal support he needed in such fields as public company mergers and acquisitions, bankruptcy, insolvency, and federal securities law. He had headed up the corporate practice at his firm and had attracted a major international client, a French aerospace company named Aerospatiale. His goal, he said, was to develop that representation into "a robust, sophisticated, international merger and acquisitions department." Some New York firms expressed an interest, but neither Mazo nor his family wished to move there. So he contacted Hogan & Hartson, and within a few days arrangements were made for him and fellow partner Bill Neff to join the firm.

The timing was both propitious and awkward. Aerospatiale was negotiating a complicated merger, and his old firm could not provide representation because of a conflict with another client. Hogan & Hartson would have no such conflict. That was the propitious part. The awkward part was that Mazo's old firm was angry about his departure and about his taking clients to Hogan & Hartson. The firm held up his move for three weeks, effectively blocking him from doing the crucial merger work for the client.

"At that point," says Mazo, "Warren Gorrell dropped what he was doing and took up the representation of this client for three weeks until I was able to get over there." Working with senior associate, now partner, Bruce Gilchrist, Gorrell left a very favorable impression on the French company. Mazo noted that "the client turned to me and said they felt very comfortable moving all of their business to Hogan & Hartson based not just on my being there, but based on what they saw of the work of others." Even more impressive, and also surprising to Mazo, was the attitude he found in his new colleagues at Hogan & Hartson. "Their approach was: 'What can we do to help you do what you want to do at Hogan?'; it was not: 'Well gee, I'm going out of my way,' or 'Mark, now you really owe me.' It was just how partners treat one another."

That approach meant the world to Mazo at a critical point in his career, and to Hogan & Hartson as it ventured into a wider, international arena. The firm's commitment to mutual support and respect among partners was one of its strongest traditions, not because of any self-conscious boosterism but simply because that was the way the partners always had behaved. The trust they engendered in one another and the quality of work that their cooperation produced were at the heart of all the firm's accomplishments.

Mazo spent much of his first year at Hogan & Hartson working on transactions for Aerospatiale in Paris. He met a law school classmate there, Steven Wolfram, a securities lawyer who told Mazo that his New York firm wanted him to return to Manhattan but that he wished to stay in Paris. Mazo asked Bob Odle and the Executive Committee to consider opening a Paris office for Hogan & Hartson that would be staffed by him and Wolfram. They agreed and brought Wolfram on board

PARTNERS

1994

Scott A. Blackmun
Stanley J. Brown
Thomas N. Bulleit, Jr.
Claudette M. Christian
Robert L. Corn-Revere
Claud v.S. Eley
Kenneth W. Farber
P. Dustin Finney, Jr.
David G. Leitch
Kevin J. Lipson
Evan Miller
Barbara F. Mishkin
Karol Lyn Newman
Timothy C. Stanceu
Stuart G. Stein

1995

Tamara L. Adler
David W. Bonser
Robert P. Brady
Raymond S. Calamaro
Alan S. Cariddi
Jonathan A. Constine
John W. Cook
John M. Gardner
James A. Gede
Patrick F. Hofer
Carol Weld King
M. Gary LaFever
James G. McMillan
Bruce C. Mee
Leslie S. Ritts
Bruce Rogers
Fabrice Rue
Jeffrey G. Schneider
Edward C. Sledge
Jac K. Sperling
Niki F. Tuttle
Craig M. Umbaugh
Richard L.A. Weiner

in 1991 as "European Counsel." By the time Wolfram and the firm parted ways in 1995, the New York firm Mudge, Rose dissolved, leaving its Paris partners looking for a new U.S. law firm with which to affiliate. The Mudge, Rose Group formed their own French law firm and also joined Hogan & Hartson as partners in Paris.

In 2000, the firm attracted partner Winston Maxwell, a well-regarded corporate and communications lawyer, to the Paris office. In mid-2004, following a period of differing views between the firm and the group that joined in 1995, Hogan & Hartson and that group ended their relationship. Working with Winston Maxwell, Mark Mazo, Bill Curtin and other firm lawyers with substantial client interests in France, Hogan & Hartson restructured in Paris to enhance and complement the firm's expanding European practice.

Hogan & Hartson's overseas expansion between 1989 and 1991 was a matter of scope more than scale, of strategy more than size. To be sure, the firm grew larger. Its attorney ranks increased by more than 75 percent, from roughly 170 in 1985 to 300 in 1991. But even more notable were the firm's expectations for the future. Like an aviary, whose dimensions are set not so much by the size or the number of birds but by the fact that they fly, Hogan & Hartson structured itself to encourage far-reaching activities. Its new Washington location in Columbia Square had an arching, spacious feel. Its European offices struck a balance between serving the overseas needs of established clients and pursuing ventures on the frontiers of a new, post-Cold War world. Hogan & Hartson's presence in Britain and on the continent gave the firm a whole new dimension. No longer was it "just" a Washington firm or even a regional U.S. firm but a truly international partnership that stood out from its other Washington competitors.

Even the firm's evolving management structure reflected Hogan & Hartson's new dimensions. The recently implemented Practice Area Administrator system diffused management responsibility effectively from the Executive Committee, through Bob Odle and the three Practice Area Administrators, to the twenty-one partners who had been named "planning directors" for the firm's seventeen practice groups following the October 1989 partners' retreat. These were renamed Practice Group Directors in December 1992, marking the end of the planning stage and the formal implementation of the new system. Involving as many partners as practicable in direct practice management gave them control over the resources they needed, not just to do what they had to do today but to feel confident about what they wished to do tomorrow. Additionally, in December 1992 Sandy Mayo accepted a newly created position with an old title, Administrative Partner, to help the Managing Partner, Bob Odle, with operational duties.

Through all the firm's changes, Hogan & Hartson's Community Services Department offered numerous examples of how the spirit of shared responsibility made for inspired work. John Ferren had set a precedent for the CSD's combination of careful resource management and energetic commitment as the CSD's first partner-in-charge in 1970. As successive partners-in-charge of the CSD, Sally Determan and David Tatel (co-chairs), Joseph Hassett, and William Bradford, Jr., had led the department through the 1980s. In April 1989 Jack Keeney became the CSD's fifth partner-in-charge. Years later he described his initial hopes for the CSD and for himself, "essentially a *pro bono* rainmaker to bring in cases that people would die for; people would go to law school just to work on any one of these cases." That meant bringing in forty or fifty such cases a year, then drawing talent from all over the firm to team up on them. "Fifty different people describing fifty different cases," he said. "They're all going to say that they worked on this really great *pro bono* case and they think it was the most important case in the history of the firm. And you know what? They're all right."

Part of Keeney's job was ensuring the best "mix" of cases for the CSD — the individual with a landlord-tenant problem; a death penalty appeal; the nonprofit organization in need of tax or incorporation counsel; and,

1996

James T. Banks
John W. Borkowski
Colin W. Craik
John F. Dienelt
Robert B. Duncan
Douglas A. Fellman
Richard T. Horan, Jr.
Eve N. Howard
Maciej Jamka
Mark J. Larson
Stephen S. Lawrence
Ellen R. Lokker
Thomas L. McGovern, III
Kornelia Nagy-Koppany
Gerald E. Oberst, Jr.
Linda L. Oliver
Nancy D. O'Neil
Richard S. Parrino
Michael A. Proett
Bruce L. Rogers
Howard S. Silver
Steven B. Steinborn
Jan Tanzer
Ralph S. Tyler
Erik B. Wulff
Emily M. Yinger

In 1989 Hogan & Hartson's Community Services Department helped bring the first discrimination suits against cab companies in Washington, D.C. The plaintiffs achieved a favorable settlement before trial, but not long afterwards Hogan & Hartson attorneys were back in court with continued instances of cab drivers' refusal to pick up African-Americans.

As late as 2003, Hogan & Hartson attorneys and the Washington Lawyers' Committee for Civil Rights and Urban Affairs reported continuing problems with taxi drivers' discrimination against African-Americans in the nation's capital, and concluded that the D.C. Taxicab Commission's efforts to solve this chronic problem had been ineffective. The attorneys have proved as persistent as the problem, however, and have maintained pressure on city officials for better enforcement of the civil rights laws.

By organizing its pro bono work at a departmental level under a full-time partner-in-charge in the early 1970s, Hogan & Hartson created a strong institutional basis on which to follow issues rather than just pursue isolated cases. The Community Services Department's records make for a long memory as well as a sustained readiness to move quickly to address ongoing problems.

COMPETITION FOR TAXICABS IN WASHINGTON, D.C. WAS ESPECIALLY KEEN DURING A MAY 1974 BUS STRIKE.

as the firm put it, "impact litigation," a major discrimination or environmental case, for example, that affected many thousands of persons. Barrett Prettyman addressed the question of whether it was "better to help a hundred homeless people with a lawyer each, or to help ten thousand poor people with a suit that affects their lives?" There was no single answer that fit every situation, but Hogan & Hartson's deployment of 70 percent of its *pro bono* resources toward impact litigation felt like the right proportion, he said.[3] Two examples of impact litigation in the early 1990s were the CSD's involvement in taxicab discrimination in Washington, D.C., and its work to help clear pollution in Arizona's Grand Canyon.

African-Americans in Washington often had complained that taxicab drivers passed them by, only to pick up a white passenger just a short distance away. They also believed that cab drivers would not go into certain neighborhoods in the city, either to pick up or drop off

PARTNERS

1997

Mary Carter Andrues
Robert L. Asher
Donna A. Boswell
Marc H. Bozeman
Charles B. Curtis
Agnes P. Dover
Kenneth Elbert
Kevin D. Evans
Michele C. Farquhar
John P. Fitzgerald
William P. Flanagan
Darrel J. Grinstead
Christopher J. Hagan
Karen M. Hardwick
Melinda R. Hatton
Nancy J. Kellner
J. Hovey Kemp
Laura E. Loeb
Milan Lovisek
Mary Anne Mason
William L. Monts, III
Steven A. Museles
Robert B. Pender, Jr.
Lisa L. Poole
John M. Potter
Gerard J. Prud'homme
Scott H. Reisch
Marissa G. Repp
Richard T. Saas
Lorraine Sostowski
Rose-Ann Sullivan
Susan Tomasky
Albert W. Turnbull
Christine A. Varney
Joseph H. Young

passengers. Drivers reported being afraid of crime, but if they were selecting passengers on the basis of race they were in violation of the city's taxi regulations as well as civil rights laws. Yet no discrimination case ever had been pursued against the city's taxicab companies.

In 1989 Hogan & Hartson's CSD helped six individuals and a church group bring a suit against three D.C. cab companies for alleged discrimination against African-Americans. To bolster the case, the CSD put white and black "testers" on the street to hail cabs and tabulate the results. Some companies did very well, always picking up the first passenger regardless of race. Keeney remembers how one driver almost broke his company's perfect record when he passed a black person and stopped to pick up a white person, but then apologized to the white person and backed up for the passenger he had passed. Despite such instances, the CSD's research confirmed a wider, more general pattern of discrimination.

The taxicab companies advanced a number of arguments in order to avoid a trial — that their drivers were independent contractors, not employees; that the companies did not really own the cabs; and that the companies could not exercise control over, and therefore could not be responsible for, drivers' behavior. But none of the arguments persuaded U.S. District Court Judge Charles Richey, and his reaction persuaded the defendants to take a serious look at settlement. Early in November 1990, just before the trial was set to begin, he approved a consent decree involving payment of damages to the plaintiffs, expanded training for cab drivers, and ongoing, citywide monitoring of the cab companies' compliance. The CSD's work in the matter by Keeney, Craig Hoover, Anthony Sutin, William Flanagan, and several others won Hogan & Hartson an award that year from the Washington Lawyers' Committee for Civil Rights Under Law.

Hoover and Sutin agreed to assist in monitoring the cab companies as part of the consent decree, but the problem was not so easily solved. The case was hardly settled when the CSD brought a second discrimination suit against another D.C. cab company and offered some summer associates from two other law firms an experience they otherwise might have missed. "This was so unbelievable," Keeney exclaimed, recalling the incident. "This was in the *nineties*!" A group of the associates from another Washington firm had gathered outside the Uptown movie theater in an upscale section of Washington after a social outing. Keeney described what happened. "Two black associates couldn't get a cab afterwards. A white associate flagged down the cab. When the driver saw that the black associates were going to try to get in, he uttered epithets and drove off with the door still open." About ten witnesses from the party all remembered the license number of the cab. ("Those summer associates — they were awfully good," said Keeney.) Once again Judge Richey got the case, and once again the cab companies got a message: $10,000 in damages to each of the two associates, plus attorneys' fees and costs.

Hogan & Hartson's *pro bono* work for the Grand Canyon began on New Year's Day 1989 at the Fiesta Bowl, where Notre Dame was playing West Virginia. Jack Keeney and Bruce Babbitt were among the thousands of Notre Dame alumni attending a pep rally before the game. Keeney had worked on Babbitt's presidential campaign the previous year and asked him if he knew of any potential voting rights cases involving Native Americans. Babbitt, a board member of the Grand Canyon Trust, said he didn't know about that but he had "the environmental case of the century" trying to stop the federal Western Area Power Administration (WAPA) from operating the Glen Canyon dam with fluctuating flows that might erode riverbanks and threaten endangered species in the Canyon. Was Keeney interested? "Definitely." Keeney found a pay phone and called Craig Hoover, the CSD's Senior Associate, alerting him that he was likely to hear from the Grand Canyon Trust the next day and "to clear his deck, get ready, and if it comes in, process it, run it through

1998

Edwin P. Aro
L. Weatherly Bentley
Lee E. Berner
Kathryn W. Bradley
Steven A. Cohen
Daniel M. Davidson
Bijan E. Eghbal
Marie-Joseph Experton
Amy B. Freed
Martin J. Hahn
Michael L. Kidney
Robert Leibenluft
Scott R. Lilienthal
Dirk Lontings
Jeffrey A. Lowe
Catherine L. Pinkerton
Douglas A. Pluss
Daniel B. Poneman
Philip D. Porter
Todd D. Schafer
Bruce D. Stocks
Andrew J. Trubin
Ronald J. Wiltsie, II
Zdzislaw Wieckowski

conflicts and get it approved, even while I am on the flight back from Arizona."

Late in September, in a federal court in Salt Lake City, Utah, the Hogan & Hartson team won a resounding victory for their four clients — the Grand Canyon Trust, the National Wildlife Federation, American Rivers, and the Western Rivers Guide Association. WAPA was enjoined from entering into any hydroelectric power contracts pending completion of the appropriate environmental impact studies. Ty Cobb and Steve Immelt, both from Hogan & Hartson's newly formed Baltimore office, comprised the trial team with Craig Hoover and associate Mary Nell McGarity, all assisted by several other attorneys at the firm.

Among them was Patrick Raher, who visited the Grand Canyon with his family the following year. They hiked down the Canyon on their first day and saw its wonders of color and light playing on the layered walls of red-brown and purple-orange rock narrowing toward the Colorado River nearly a mile below. The second morning the Rahers walked along the Canyon's rim to survey the terrain for another hike. But this time "you could not see the bottom," Raher explained. "It looked like somebody had filled up the Grand Canyon with pea soup."

Raher asked a park ranger about it. "That's pollution from the power plant in Page, Arizona," said the ranger. Since Raher had just helped win a case for the Grand Canyon Trust, his son thought he should try to do something about the pollution, too. "His mother agreed with him," Raher recalled, "and I said, 'Yeah, but there's not much I can do about *that*,'" nodding toward the pea soup.

Shortly after Raher returned to work he contacted Bill Rosenberg, then head of the Environmental Protection Agency (EPA) Air Office, about an unrelated matter for the Mercedes auto company. Then, at the end of the conversation, he told Rosenberg about his experience at the Grand Canyon. Rosenberg's response was startling. "You know," he said, "that is really a continuing problem for us, and the reason it's such a problem is that the federal government owns 35 percent of that power plant. We haven't put any pollution control

1991
Pro Bono Publico
Awards

American Bar Association
Standing Committee
on Lawyers' Public
Service Responsibility

ABA
AMERICAN BAR ASSOCIATION

IN 1991 THE AMERICAN BAR ASSOCIATION HONORED HOGAN & HARTSON'S COMMUNITY SERVICE DEPARTMENT WITH ITS PRESTIGIOUS *PRO BONO PUBLICO* AWARD.

PARTNERS

1999

Donna L. Alpi
Barbara Bennett
Carol W. Burton
Nancy A. Clodfelter
Michele Coyle
Edward S. Desmarais, Jr.
Jonathan S. Franklin
Sean R. Gallagher
Aleksander Galos
James R. Ghiselli
Catriona Hatton
Whitney A. Holmes
Henry D. Kahn
Diane A. Koonjy
William J. Kubida
Dirk Leermakers
John R. Lilyestrom
Thene M. Martin
Christopher D. Ozeroff
Christine M. Pallares
Patrick K. Perrin
Mary E. "Beth" Peters
Thomas E. Repke
William J. Roberts
James P. Ruggeri
Lawrence J. Seidman
Peter S. Spivack
Douglas P. Wheeler
Edward C. "Ted" Wilson, Jr.
Michael K. Wyatt

equipment on it because we cannot get any funding from Congress." Raher thought it ridiculous that a power plant partially owned by the government would be polluting a national park. He asked Rosenberg if EPA would hold hearings in Arizona to see what could be done. Rosenberg said he'd be happy to convince the EPA administrator, Bill Reilly, to hold hearings. Working through the CSD, Raher and Jack Keeney worked with the Grand Canyon Trust and found out they had been looking at the problem for years and were eager for some help.

One day an associate in the CSD who was researching the case came to Raher and announced an important find. In congressional hearings leading up to the passage of the Clean Air Act Amendments of 1977, a particular U.S. representative from Florida had questioned EPA officials sharply about the Grand Canyon pollution and had elicited from them a promise that the federal government would retrofit the power plant to reduce its emissions. "The man who asked all those questions is here at Hogan & Hartson," the associate exclaimed eagerly to Raher. "It's Paul Rogers. He was chairman of the committee." Rogers had chaired the Health and Environment Subcommittee of the House of Representatives and was the primary author of the clean air legislation, which included specific requirements for protecting visibility in national parks.

Rogers was the first witness at the March 18, 1991, hearings in Phoenix. He testified that in 1977 the EPA had promised his committee that it would retrofit the Navajo Generating Station with "scrubbers" to reduce sulfur dioxide emissions. Borrowing Iraqi leader Saddam Hussein's widely parodied reference to the 1990-1991 Gulf War as "the mother of all battles," Rogers called the power plant "the mother of all pollution" in the Grand Canyon. It was a perfect "sound bite" for the news media, which gave the hearings national coverage. Rogers's testimony, along with videotape of sulphur dioxide vapors wafting down the Canyon and computer-generated slides illustrating reduced visibility, formed a compelling indictment of the power plant's environmental performance.

But retrofitting to meet 1977 standards at 1991 prices would have cost the power company almost $4 billion, a prohibitive sum. So Raher and other Hogan & Hartson attorneys drew on their past experience to forge a compromise that made everyone a winner. Raher explained to the power company executives that the pollution typically started in September and ran through March, the cool season. Since consumers didn't need as much electricity during those months, wouldn't it make sense for the power plant to perform all its maintenance during that time? If the plant kept one of its three coal-fired boilers shut down on a rotating basis in the cooler months, plant operators could cut pollution by 30 percent while reducing the amount of retrofitting required to meet emission control goals.

The plan, which included the first regulatory action ever taken by the federal government to improve visibility in a national park, proved a great success. President George H. Bush traveled to the Grand Canyon for a September 18 signing ceremony and proclaimed the settlement "a milestone in our implementation of the Clean Air Act and in our efforts to protect one of America's crown jewel national parks."[4] When power company officials contacted Raher in 1995 they reported that they had

Stephen, Patrick and Rosalinda Raher at the Grand Canyon on a clear day, 1990.

2000

Audrey J. Anderson	Celine J. Crowson	Miriam L. Fisher
Matthew T. Bailey	W. Sidney Davis, Jr.	David M. Fox
Douglas L. Beresford	Margaret De Lisser	Gregory G. Garre
Laura Besvinick	David Dunn	Mark D. Gately
Jacqueline P. Cleary	Steven M. Edwards	Jay E. Gerber
Maryanne Courtney	Ira M. Feinberg	Jeffrey S. George

completed the retrofits, that there had been no pollution in the Grand Canyon for the past two years, and that electricity rates had not been raised by as much as a penny. Hogan & Hartson asked for no fee for the service, but the Grand Canyon Trust did compensate Raher. It asked a photographer to take a picture of the Canyon from the site where Raher's son Stephen had first seen the problem in 1990 and had asked his dad if he could help. The picture now hangs on Raher's office wall. Hogan & Hartson also had something to hang on its wall in 1991, for in May that year the American Bar Association honored the firm with its prestigious *Pro Bono Publico* award.

SANDY BERGER JOINED HOGAN & HARTSON IN 1973 AS THE FIRM'S 89TH LAWYER. HE LEFT THE FIRM IN 1977 TO WORK IN THE CARTER ADMINISTRATION AS DEPUTY DIRECTOR OF THE STATE DEPARTMENT'S POLICY PLANNING STAFF. IN 1981 HE RETURNED TO HOGAN & HARTSON AND PLAYED A KEY ROLE IN BUILDING THE FIRM'S INTERNATIONAL TRADE AND LEGISLATIVE PRACTICES. IN 1993 HE SERVED IN THE CLINTON ADMINISTRATION, FIRST AS DEPUTY ASSISTANT FOR NATIONAL SECURITY AFFAIRS, THEN AS THE PRESIDENT'S NATIONAL SECURITY ADVISOR. IN 2001 HE AND ANOTHER FORMER HOGAN & HARTSON PARTNER, ANTHONY HARRINGTON, FOUNDED AN INTERNATIONAL CONSULTING FIRM, STONEBRIDGE INTERNATIONAL LLC, WHICH HAS A STRATEGIC ALLIANCE WITH HOGAN & HARTSON.

During the settlement process, the power plant's largest customer, the Central Arizona Water Conservation District (CAWCD), had challenged the retrofitting rule in the Ninth Circuit Court of Appeals and later filed a petition for *certiorari* in the Supreme Court. Hogan & Hartson's John Roberts worked with Raher, Keeney, and Jim Freeman to prepare a brief in opposition to the cert petition. Their effort was successful and the Ninth Circuit's ruling stood.[5]

Yes, John Roberts had returned to Hogan & Hartson. William Jefferson Clinton's election to the presidency in 1992 had triggered the usual domino-row of appointment changes, displacing Kenneth Starr from his job as Solicitor General and Roberts from his position as Deputy Solicitor General. Roberts missed his work in the Solicitor General's office, recalling that he had left there exactly "at noon on January 20, 1993," in reference to the last possible moment before Bill Clinton's inauguration.

Starr went to another Washington law firm. Roberts considered several options but returned to Hogan & Hartson, which, as he recalled Bob Odle's teasing, "had really grown and prospered in my absence." But despite his disappointment about leaving the "SG's" office, Roberts found that coming back to head up Hogan & Hartson's Supreme Court and appellate group turned out to be "a very easy decision." It also was, he said, "the highest praise that I can give the firm."

PARTNERS

2000 CONT.

William F. Haigney
George F. Hritz
Sandra F. Kinsey
Joseph G. Krauss
S. Gregg Kunzi
Raymond A. Kurz
David L. Lubitz
Stuart Lubitz
Winston J. Maxwell
Scott D. McClure
Jeffrey W. Munk
Peter J. Pettibone
Sharis A. Pozen
John A. Redmon
Jonathan T. Rees
Jai H. Rho
Howard J. Rosenstock
George A. Salter
Jeffrey N. Shane
Jeffrey K. Shapiro
Corine Sheldon
John T. Stough, Jr.
Thomas J. Sweeney, III
James G. Szymanski
Dennis H. Tracey, III
Lyndon M. Tretter
Morris Waisbrot
Nicola S. Walker
Phyllis V. Wan
Howard S. Weber
David F. Wertheimer
Marcia A. Wiss
William H. Wright

But if Clinton's election meant Roberts's return, it also heralded the departure of others. Attorney Christine Varney, who had been chief counsel to the Clinton/Gore campaign, now joined the White House as assistant to the President and secretary to the cabinet. From 1994 to 1997 she served as a federal trade commissioner, then returned to Hogan & Hartson to head the firm's Internet Practice Group. Sandy Berger, who had left the firm once before to serve in the State Department during Jimmy Carter's presidency, now became President Clinton's deputy assistant for national security affairs. After Clinton's reelection in 1996, Berger continued his service through 2000 as the President's national security advisor.

Having been general counsel to the Democratic National Committee, Tony Harrington served as general counsel to the Clinton/Gore campaign. After the election he balanced his practice at Hogan & Hartson with positions as chair of the President's Intelligence Oversight Board and vice chair of the Foreign Intelligence Oversight Board. The White House installed a secure phone line in his Columbia Square office. The phone's distinctive ring usually evoked a special reaction from his neighbors at the firm. "Any time it rang, folks up and down the hall would flutter a bit, even if it was a wrong number," he chuckled.

Harrington and partner Steve Kaufman had logged one of the firm's most successful rides on the 1980s and 1990s telecommunications wave, which generated much securities, mergers and acquisitions, regulatory, and antitrust work. Harrington also was a co-founder of Telecom USA, the nation's fourth largest long-distance phone service provider, and helped bring this company's legal matters to Hogan & Hartson. "We did forty acquisitions for Telecom USA over a period of six years," he recalled, "finally selling it off to MCI in a large cash transaction at the end of 1990. It was one of the largest deals in the industry at the time."

Anthony S. "Tony" Harrington joined Hogan & Hartson in 1968. He worked in the firm's corporate and securities practice and served on the committee, chaired by Bob Kapp, that studied *pro bono* service options and recruited the first head of the Community Services Department. Harrington's practice included several major transactions in the satellite, cable and telecommunications businesses. He served the Clinton administration as chairman of the President's Intelligence Oversight Board and Vice Chairman of the President's Foreign Intelligence Advisory Board. On October 29, 1999, President Clinton nominated Harrington to be the United States' Ambassador to Brazil. With strong bipartisan support in the Senate, Harrington's confirmation occurred in a record time of just 12 days. In 2000 Harrington joined Sandy Berger in founding Stonebridge International and currently is president of that firm.

The firm's media, telecommunications, broadcast, and cable regulatory practices, led by Bill Reyner, Peter Rohrbach, Marvin Diamond, Joel Winnik, Gardner Gillespie, David Saylor, and others, also expanded rapidly in the 1980s and 1990s. The Telecommunications Act of 1996 accelerated the free market trends already set in motion by deregulation in the 1980s. The act aimed to create a regulatory environment compatible with new, fast-paced technologies such as the Internet. It was the first major revision of FCC regulations in sixty years and had the sweeping ambition, as the FCC itself said, "to let anyone enter any communications business — to

2001

Suzanne A. Barr	Max Brauer	Tracy B. Gray	David W. Isbell	Stuart T. Langley
Christopher H. Bartolomucci	Eckhard Bremer	Christian von Hammerstein	Robert Karwowski	Mitchell J. Lazris
David W. Beier	Andrea M. Bruce	Michele S. Harrington	Mark A. Kass	Craig A. Lewis
Peter R. Bisio	N. Thomas Connally, III	Jan Hegemann	Kenneth D. Klein	Carol A. Licko
Jeffrey H. Blattner	Ari Q. Fitzgerald	Mark L. Heimlich	Robert D. Kyle	Paul D. Manca
Christine Bougis	Lewis H. Goldfarb	James A. Hutchinson	Stuart M. Langbein	Stephanie D. Marks

AFTER JOINING HOGAN & HARTSON IN 1974 JANET L. MCDAVID BECAME A NATIONALLY RECOGNIZED AUTHORITY ON ANTITRUST MATTERS. SHE IS PAST CHAIR OF THE SECTION OF ANTITRUST LAW OF THE AMERICAN BAR ASSOCIATION AND HAS ADVISED BOTH REPUBLICAN AND DEMOCRATIC ADMINISTRATIONS ON APPOINTMENTS TO THE FEDERAL TRADE COMMISSION.

let any communications business compete in any market against any other."[6] Partner Joel Winnik typified the firm's success in implementing its long-term strategy of merging strengths in government and private business. Winnik had served in the Office of General Counsel at the FCC before entering private practice in 1979 and then joining Hogan & Hartson in 1985. His client representations included numerous high-profile international communications companies like British Telecom and Japan's Nippon Telegraph and Telephone Corporation (NTT). Hogan & Hartson also represented the radio company Jacor in its acquisition of several radio companies after passage of the Telecommunications Act and represented Clear Channel when it acquired Jacor later. "We go where the stream of technology takes us," said partner Peter Rohrbach, "and it's been a fascinating ride; it's always changing."

The field of antitrust also was changing, and no one in the country tracked those changes more closely than Jan McDavid, who had been active in the American Bar Association's Section of Antitrust Law since 1985. In the early 1990s she was a member of the Section's council and served in successively higher positions, becoming the chair in 1999-2000. McDavid's command of antitrust law and her experience at the intersection of large businesses and the federal government earned her a place on the Clinton administration's transition team for the Federal Trade Commission in 1992. She also served on two Defense Department Task Forces, which advised on antitrust issues related to consolidating the defense industry after an extensive military buildup during the 1980s under Presidents Reagan and Bush.

Through the Reagan, Bush, and Clinton administrations, new ideas about antitrust had changed the way government agencies approached antitrust enforcement. The "law and economics" movement, promulgated most effectively by University of Chicago Law School Professor and U.S. Circuit Court of Appeals Judge Richard Posner, was especially influential. It held that antitrust should be framed in terms of rational, economic analysis instead of social or political notions such as "bigness is bad." As McDavid summarized the view, "We should be focused on protecting competition and not necessarily on protecting competitors. If the Mom and Pop grocery store is not economically rational, then antitrust shouldn't be the crutch that keeps it up."

The "law and economics" school argued that the concentration of a certain industry in the hands of a few large owners does not necessarily constitute an antitrust violation if it results in more efficient production and lower costs to consumers. McDavid recalled that in 1974, her third year of law school at Georgetown, the Supreme Court essentially accepted the "law and economics" position regarding the General Dynamics Corporation's purchase of a midwestern coal company (*United States v. General Dynamics Corp.*, 415 U.S. 486 (1974)). McDavid was particularly interested in the General Dynamics case, but she had no idea that one day the company would be her client at Hogan & Hartson.

PARTNERS 2001 CONT.

David Medine
Gernod Meinel
George Miggel
Robert Mintz
Cynthia A. Mitchell
Helen A. Nastasia
J. Patrick Nevins
David Newmann
Jeffrey D. Pariser
John E. Porter
Steven N. Robinson
Laurent Ruessmann
Justus Schmidt-Ott
Friedrich Tobias Schone
Paul N. Schwartz
Carl-Stephan Schweer
Hans Seiler
David L. Sieradzki
Brent Slosky
David W. Smail
Parker D. Thomson
Shawna R. Tunnell
Christoph Wagner
Christopher J. Walsh
Keith D. Wasserstrom
Edith F. Webster
Robert A. Welp
Marcy J. Wilder
David A. Winter
Heinz Zimmermann

Tom Leary, who had joined the firm's antitrust practice in 1983, served as outside counsel to the Business Roundtable, a private association of chief executive officers formed in 1972 to involve business leaders in discussing national policy matters such as labor, the environment, and regulation. Leary met the general counsel of General Dynamics at a Business Roundtable session, and subsequently the company came to rely on Hogan & Hartson for help with its many defense-related merger activities.

In the defense industry the usual laws of competition required modification. Antitrust issues were especially thorny for military suppliers like General Dynamics because the government necessarily depended on only a few manufacturers for critical products like missiles, submarines, tanks, and fighter planes. The government was not going to buy foreign-made fighter craft, for instance. And military contracts usually included payment of overhead costs, so "if you had a plant, as General Dynamics did with its missile business, that was operating at 30 percent of capacity, the Defense Department was paying for the overhead on the other 70 percent," McDavid explained. Hughes Aircraft Company, another Defense Department missile supplier, had a plant in Tucson, Arizona, that was operating at 40 percent capacity. So in 1992 General Dynamics sold its missile business to Hughes. "They closed the General Dynamics plants," said McDavid, "moved all the business into Tucson, filled the plant up, achieved lower operating costs and overhead, and the Defense Department got more missiles for its dollar."

McDavid was less successful in an effort several years later to consolidate the Navy's submarine manufacturers. The Navy was finding it costly to support submarine production by both the Newport News Shipbuilding Company and General Dynamics and was considering shutting down one of the facilities. But the nature of submarine building complicated that decision. "It takes roughly five years to build a submarine," McDavid explained. "You're welding steel that's five inches thick, using mirrors. These are skills that are honed over a very long time. If you were to close down a submarine yard it would take seven or eight years to restart."

One solution was to consolidate the plants along the same lines as General Dynamics and Hughes Aircraft had followed for their missile businesses. In this case, General Dynamics proposed a $2.6 billion purchase of Newport News Shipbuilding that would have given it about 70 percent of the Navy's shipbuilding budget and control over the manufacture and maintenance of all of the Navy's nuclear-powered ships.[7] But in the end the Defense Department and the Justice Department blocked the purchase and made the Navy keep the two facilities. "It was a real heartbreaker to lose it," McDavid lamented.

If defense industries were in the middle of the crossroads of government and private enterprise, health-related businesses hovered uncertainly around that intersection in the mid-1990s. Jonathan Kahan watched it all take shape, from 1976 when Congressman Paul Rogers, later Kahan's colleague at Hogan & Hartson, authored the Medical Devices Amendments of 1976 (MDA), to President Clinton's ill-fated health care initiative in 1993-1994. The MDA, an amendment to the Federal Food, Drug and Cosmetic Act of 1938, required most medical devices, such as catheters, MRI scanners, and artificial hearts, to go through a premarket clearance process. "Industry needed people who could understand how to get products through the FDA," Kahan explained, "and that's now what I do for a living."

Technological innovation and changing legislation have made it a busy living. By 1996 the U.S. medical device industry marked about $40 billion in sales and employed more than 300,000 people. The FDA Modernization Act of 1997, designed to streamline the regulatory process,

2002

Philip E. Altman	Barry A. Brust	Tomasz Dobrowolski	Scott A. Golden	David F. Hannan	Hywel Jones	David L. Kovacs
Mitchell S. Ames	Lance D. Bultena	Matthew J. Epstein	Neal M. Goldman	Dori A. Hanswirth	Kenneth D. Kastner	Mark L. Landis
Stephen F. Barley	James C. Chen	Mark Fleischer	Daniel E. Gonzalez	Jack A. Horn	Alan Katz	Shalom Y. Leaf
Anthony M. Basich	Jill R. Cohen	Scott Friedman	Ira S. Greene	Linda R. Horton	Stephen H. Kay	Melvin E. Lefkowitz
Stuart A. Barr	M. Jean Connolly	John F. Gaul	George A. Hagerty	Molly F. James	Michael R. Kleinerman	Mitchell Lubart
Robert M. Blue	Jorge Diaz-Silveira	Jeffrey S. Geron	Maureen A. Hanlon	Sten A. Jensen	Michael H. King	Loretta E. Lynch

reflected the increased pressures that a burgeoning industry had brought to bear on federal regulators since 1976. So sweeping were the act's changes that Kahan had to rewrite a book he had authored on the subject only three years earlier.[8] In 2003 Hogan & Hartson represented about six hundred medical device companies, making its practice, said Kahan, "at least double the size of the next largest medical device practice in the country."

Kahan recalled that in the 1980s Bob Odle and the Executive Committee had given him a virtual "blank check" to build the food, drug, and medical devices practice. Over the years he recruited attorneys like Edward Korwek, Howard Holstein, Rodney Munsey, Rick Silverman, Gary Kushner, Robert Brady, Marc Bozeman, and David Fox, specialists in medical devices, food and agriculture, or drugs and biologics like gene therapies. They worked with clients around the world on many different types of products. Most had extensive experience working at the FDA as well as in private industry and with international clients. One of Kahan's clients, for instance, was an Israeli company that made a tiny, capsule-sized camera. After a patient swallowed it, the capsule-camera took pictures all the way through the digestive system — a welcome improvement on earlier, more invasive diagnostic procedures. The company suspended one of them in clear acrylic and gave it as a memento to Kahan, who displayed it proudly on a table in his office.

The complexities of the field increased the range of expertise that the group gathered into its practice. Among its thirty-two lawyers in 2003 were former FDA inspectors, auditors certified in assessing compliance with FDA quality control regulations, and a variety of non-lawyer specialists. Partner Ed Korwek brought to the practice a special combination of skills. He held a Ph.D. in biochemistry and had done postdoctoral work in molecular biology at the National Cancer Institute before returning to school for his law degree.

David Fox served as Assistant Chief Counsel for Enforcement and then as Associate Chief Counsel for Drugs at the FDA before joining Hogan & Hartson in 2000. When Linda Horton joined Hogan & Hartson in 2002 after more than twenty-five years with the FDA, Kahan remarked that with her arrival the firm had transplanted to Columbia Square practically an entire hall of attorneys who once had worked together at the agency. That impression was strengthened by the arrival of FDA veteran Joseph Levitt in January 2004. Both Horton and Levitt had extensive international experience, including negotiations with the European Union, as well as an intimate familiarity with the FDA and its regulation of increasingly sophisticated medical and pharmaceutical technologies. Specialization and size also affected the Practice Group's management, which shared its directorship among Kahan (medical devices), Kushner (food and agriculture), and Brady (drugs and biologics).

The Health Group also benefited from the revolving door between government (Department of Health and Human Services) and Hogan & Hartson. Helen Trilling and Cliff Stromberg joined the group in

JONATHAN S. KAHAN JOINED H&H IN 1974 AND IS NOW CO-DIRECTOR OF THE FIRM'S FOOD, DRUG, MEDICAL DEVICES AND AGRICULTURE GROUP. HE HAS PUBLISHED WIDELY ON UNDERSTANDING AND NAVIGATING FEDERAL REGULATIONS, ESPECIALLY THOSE ADMINISTERED BY THE FOOD AND DRUG ADMINISTRATION.

PARTNERS

2002 CONT.

Slade R. Metcalf
Susan S. Namkung
Andreas Nelle
Neil R. O'Hanlon
Garry J. Pegg
Steven C. Petersen
Stanley Plesent
Laurence H. Pretty
Joseph R. Rackman
Beth L. Roberts
Theodore J. Roper
Jeffrey W. Rubin
Paul D. Sarkozi
Christopher A. Schindler
Andrew R. Shoemaker
Peter W. Smith
Michael Starr
Jolanta Sterbenz
James H. Stevralia
Catherine E. Stetson
Richard L. Stone
Arthur D. Stout
Paul B. Sweeney
Barbara J. Thomas
William Thomson
Oskar Tulodziecki
James K. Trefil
Jose F. Valdivia, III
Paul W. Virtue
Jun Wei
Mark J. Weinstein
Deborah R. Wolfe
Miguel A. Zaldivar, Jr.
Mitchell E. Zamoff

Jon Kahan's talent at recruiting is well exemplified by Rick Silverman (Top) and Gary Kushner, who, at Hogan & Hartson, built one of the nation's leading food and agriculture practices.

the early 1980s, after serving in the department during the Carter administration, and both established very strong practices and reputations. In 1990 HHS Deputy General Counsel Liz Dunst brought her nineteen years of government experience to the firm and helped to recruit two successive Chief Counsels of the Medicare/Medicaid agency, Darrel Grinstead and Sheree Kanner, who arrived in 1997 and 2003, respectively. In 2001 HHS Deputy General Counsel Marcy Wilder, who had responsibility both for medical privacy and research regulation during the Clinton administration, joined Hogan & Hartson, where Donna Boswell (former college professor and Congressional Fellow) had already developed a booming medical privacy practice and Barbara Mishkin (former NIH bioethics expert) had a well-established research regulation client base. The

2003

Dennis Arfmann
A. Cristina Arumi
Christopher H. Bartolomucci
John M. Basnage
Luca R. Bronzi
Jayne P. Bultena
Ying Chen
Mark R. Cheskin
Laurie A. Clarke
Carissa C. W. Coze
William J. Curtin, III
Alexander E. Dreier

OFFICE OF THE UNITED STATES TRADE REPRESENTATIVE

Hogan & Hartson's many overseas offices reflect a burgeoning international trade market and the need for legal services that it generated in the 1990s. On August 12, 1992, President George H. Bush noted the successful completion of negotiations for the North American Free Trade Agreement (NAFTA) by linking it to the end of U.S.-Soviet hostilities. "The Cold War is over," said the President. "The principal challenge now facing the United States is to compete in a rapidly changing, expanding global marketplace." On January 1, 1994, NAFTA went into effect, removing or phasing out most tariffs and other barriers to trade and investment among the United States, Mexico, and Canada.

The following year the World Trade Organization (WTO) was organized to carry forward multilateral trade agreements originally established at the end of World War II under the General Agreement on Tariffs and Trade (GATT). The WTO includes tariff provisions as well as anti-dumping and transparency measures, and provisions concerning intellectual property, telecommunications services, banking, insurance, and securities.

Much of Hogan & Hartson's international trade practice revolves around the complexities of the 30,000-page WTO agreements. The WTO's 150 member nations increasingly look to the WTO to settle their disputes, which have escalated in proportion to the level and sophistication of their trade relations. In just eight years (1995-2003), the WTO handled as many trade disputes as did GATT in its entire forty-seven years (1947-1994).

JEANNE S. ARCHIBALD CAME TO H&H IN 1993 FROM A POSITION AS GENERAL COUNSEL AT THE U.S. DEPARTMENT OF THE TREASURY, WHERE SHE WAS RESPONSIBLE FOR NEARLY 2,000 ATTORNEYS. IN ADDITION TO HER MANAGEMENT SKILLS, SHE BROUGHT MANY YEARS OF INTERNATIONAL TRADE EXPERIENCE GAINED THROUGH POSITIONS IN CONGRESS, AT THE OFFICE OF THE UNITED STATES TRADE REPRESENTATIVE, AND AT THE U.S. TREASURY. SHE CURRENTLY IS HOGAN & HARTSON'S MANAGING PARTNER FOR PRACTICE ADMINISTRATION.

Health Group developed strong teams with other groups, to meet all of the needs of clients in the health sector of the economy. The health antitrust team was strengthened when Bob Leibenluft returned to Hogan & Hartson in 1998 from the FTC, where he had been the Assistant Director for Health Care in the Bureau of Competition. Similarly, the health legislative team was bolstered by the addition of David Beier and John Porter, former Chairman of the House Appropriations Subcommittee on Labor, Health and Human Services and Education, in 2001 and Linda Fishman, former Chief Health Policy Adviser to the Senate Finance Committee, in 2004.

Jeanne Archibald brought an impressive range of experience in international trade when she joined Hogan & Hartson's approximately 350 attorneys in 1993. Archibald had worked for the Ways and Means Committee of the U.S. House of Representatives while in law school at Georgetown and had witnessed the passage of the Trade Acts of 1974 and 1979. In 1980 she accepted a position in the Office of the U.S. Trade Representative (USTR), then in 1986 moved to the Treasury Department. In 1990 she became the general counsel at Treasury, then was recruited by Hogan & Hartson, along with attorneys Warren Maruyama and Clayton Yeutter, to take Sandy Berger's place when he left the firm to join the Clinton administration. "Sandy's shoes were actually very large," joked Archibald about the number of attorneys it had taken to fill them.

Archibald had thought she never would work in a large law firm. "Any friends I had in law school who had done it had no good stories that they were telling about the experience," she said. During her initial interviews at Hogan & Hartson, "I met very nice people but I kept thinking, 'Well, they're just introducing me to the nicest people,' and if I knew which rocks to look under I would find something nasty falling out underneath." But Archibald never found that rock. Like other "lateral hires" at the firm, she found a welcoming and very team-oriented international trade practice that grew rapidly from about seven attorneys when she arrived to nearly forty ten years later. The growth of the trade practice came not only from well-chosen lateral hires such as Ray Calamaro, Lewis Leibowitz, Chris Stokes, and Craig Lewis — all of whom came from other firms — but also from highly talented lawyers who started as associates at the firm and advanced to partnership, including T. Weymouth and Beth Peters.

Trade practice in Washington had broadened in the 1990s from mostly customs and trade policy work to economic sanctions issues and dispute settlement proceedings under NAFTA, the General Agreement on Tariffs and Trade (GATT), and the World Trade Organization (WTO), which, upon its founding in 1995, subsumed the GATT. Section 301 of the Trade Act of 1974, for instance, gave the Office of the USTR authority to investigate the trade practices of other countries and impose sanctions if those practices were deemed "unfair." Archibald had been involved in numerous "Section 301" cases when she worked at

PARTNERS

2003 CONT.

Klaus Goecke
Austen E. Hall
John E. Hayes, III
Paul Hilton
Janice M. Hogan
Jeffrey M. Hurlburt
Jonathan Ivinson
Lori L. Jenkins
Sheree R. Kanner
Michael B. Kaufman
Peter Kohl
Sergey B. Komolov
Alvin F. Lindsay, III
Michael J. Lorenger
Eric J. Lobenfeld
Richard C. Lorenzo
Meredith Manning
Lynda K. Marshall
George Metaxas
Douglas R.M. Nazarian
Philippe Y. Riesen
Ira J. Schaefer
Daniel F. Shea
Julie Ann Shepard
David A. Shuster
David P. Slotkin
Frank T. Spano
Christopher S. Stokes
Thomas L. Strickland
Joy E. Sturm
Gary L. Urwin
Gordon C. Wilson
Wei-Ning Yang

USTR. But in 1995 she found herself on the other side of the table, representing a Japanese automaker facing a sanction by the U.S. government of a 100 percent increase in import duties on its luxury cars. USTR alleged that Japan's regulations regarding the sale of replacement auto parts were structured so as to make it impossible for U.S. parts companies to sell in the Japanese market. Up to that time, the usual Japanese response to U.S. allegations of "unfair" practices was to take a conciliatory approach, making various concessions to USTR in return for the latter's easing of sanction threats.

Archibald regarded that approach not only as a "pretty poisonous cycle" but also as basically unfair to the Japanese client. Under terms of the WTO, to which both the United States and Japan belonged, the United States could not take action on the matter without first obtaining WTO approval. But a WTO decision on the matter could take three years, and USTR was pushing Japan hard, banking on the automaker's reluctance to endure three years' worth of increased import duties pending a WTO reprieve. Archibald counseled her client to make no concessions at all — to "keep playing chicken and see who blinks first," as she put it. Despite the potential risk to the client's interests posed by this approach, Archibald's experience at the government agencies involved and her astute analysis of the dynamics of the matter encouraged the client to take the stand she recommended.

Ultimately USTR blinked first. It won some face-saving "concessions" that the automaker planned to make anyway, such as promising to increase its U.S. investment. But more importantly, the action broke the cyclical pattern of sanction threats and partial concessions, followed by further threats, that had characterized Japanese trade relations with the United States for years.

In the 1990s Hogan & Hartson attorneys continued to work at the center of some of the major cases and transactions of their day. For example, David Saylor from the firm's antitrust group, along with Joel Winnik from the communications group, represented British Telecom in its 1994 merger effort with MCI, and Andy Kilcarr, Jan McDavid, Christine Varney, Tripp Monts, and a team of more than twenty antitrust lawyers also helped Mobil Oil effect a historic merger with Exxon, formerly Standard Oil of New Jersey, in 1999. The merger was the first one bringing back together two parts of the notorious "oil trust," which had been sundered by antimonopoly enforcers in the Progressive era nearly a century earlier. Hogan & Hartson attorneys labored on the Exxon-Mobil merger for an entire year. "People have babies in less time than this," McDavid observed wryly.

Allen Snyder and Christine Varney led the firm's representation of Netscape Communications Corporation in the Justice Department's 1998-1999 antitrust prosecution of Microsoft Corporation, and Hogan & Hartson attorneys continued representing Netscape in its acquisition by America Online in 1999. Also that year, firm partners Nancy Kellner and Richard Becker represented MindSpring Enterprises in its merger with EarthLink Network, creating the country's second largest Internet service provider after America Online.

The firm also began to build an international project finance practice in the mid-1990s, led by Robert

Rep. Robert H. Michel of Illinois (L) and Rep. Delbert Latta of Ohio, June 1981. Rep. Michel joined Hogan & Hartson in 1995 after 38 years in Congress, including 14 years as House Minority Leader.

2004

Robert J. Benson	Yaron Dori	H. Deen Kaplan
Christopher D. Berry	Gregory G. Garre	Elizabeth L. Katkin
Lawrence V. Brocchini	Sean P. Harrison	R. Daniel Keating
Lourdes Catrain	Lorane F. Hebert	Keith D. Larson
Bruce G. Chapman	Sarah Kinnick Hilty	Joseph A. Levitt
Alexander D. Cobey	E. Desmond Hogan	Sanford M. Litvack

ALPHONSO A. CHRISTIAN, II, JOINED HOGAN & HARTSON IN 1972 AND HAS BEEN A PARTNER SINCE 1977, SPECIALIZING IN LITIGATION, ADMINISTRATIVE LAW AND INTERNATIONAL BUSINESS TRANSACTIONS. HE HAS BEEN AN ACTIVE MEMBER OF THE FIRM'S MIDDLE EAST PRACTICE TASK FORCE.

Pender, Claudette Christian, and others. Pender handled many domestic and international project financings over the years for companies such as Sithe Energies, Inc. and AES Corporation.

In 1997 Claudette Christian led an energy project finance team that represented the Brazilian energy company Petrobras in the construction of a 3,100 kilometer, $2 billion pipeline to import gas from Bolivia. The largest infrastructure project in Latin America, the pipeline was under development for forty years and attracted investment and financing from major international energy conglomerates and the multilateral financing institutions. Christian's work on the project expanded to include her involvement in the financing of compressors that would increase the amount of gas that the line can transport.

Christian also represented the Overseas Private Investment Corporation (OPIC) on financing a wireless telecommunications project in Bolivia and on a $1.6 billion project called FLAG — Fiberoptic Link Around the Globe — that was completed in 1997. FLAG, a 17,500-mile undersea fiber-optic submarine cable running from Britain to Japan with landing points in Europe, the Middle East, Africa, and Asia, represented the first project financing of a telecommunications network owned by national telecommunications companies. "I tend to work on large projects," Christian explained, likening them to "Russian novels that go on for hundreds of pages."

Another Hogan & Hartson partner, Alphonso A. Christian, had worked closely with Saudi Arabia's Prince Alwaleed bin Talal bin Abdul Aziz on several major financial transactions since 1986. Born in Beirut and educated in California, HRH Prince Alwaleed brought a worldwide perspective to his investment decisions as well as a record as a hard-working, "straight A" honors business student at Menlo College. The Prince looked to Hogan & Hartson attorneys like Al Christian, Mark Mazo, Dan Maccoby, Jim Rosenhauer, Todd Miller, Dick Poulson, and Bruce Parmley for legal work on such varied matters as a major acquisition of Citibank stock in 1991 (which led to his becoming the largest shareholder); an investment in 1994 in EuroDisney that was widely regarded as a rescue of the then-struggling resort and theme park; a large investment in London's famous Canary Wharf real estate project; and the purchase and restoration of the historic George V Hotel in Paris.

In another example of Hogan & Hartson's wide-ranging practice, Kevin Lipson led a team that included partners Patrick Nevins, Doug Beresford, and Chris Schindler in a lawsuit against El Paso Corporation, a natural gas company. The firm's client, the Southern California Edison Power Company, alleged that El Paso had manipulated the natural gas market in California to create a shortage and trigger an energy crisis that had profound effects on the economy of California and created the climate for the ouster of the state's governor, Gray Davis, who was succeeded by actor Arnold Schwarzenegger. In March 2003, after two years of investigation and hearings before the Federal Energy Regulatory Commission, the Hogan & Hartson team prevailed, gaining a $1.7 billion settlement from El Paso Corporation.

PARTNERS

2004 CONT.

David L. London
Michael S. Long
Brian J. Lynch
Michael F. Mason
Shelly L. McGee
Daniel B. Mestaz
Charles T. Mitchell
Thomas C. Morey
Markus Plesser
H. Keeto Sabharwal
Troy M. Schmelzer
Johannes Schulte
Jonathan M. Sobel
Nicholas G. Stavlas
Joanna R. Swomley
Hanno Timner
Tracey A. Tiska
Jeffrey J. Tolin
Patrick D. Traylor
Ajit J. Vaidya
Kevin L. Vold
Thomas R. Woolsey
Stephen J. Zempolich

Back in Washington, Hogan & Hartson represented Georgetown University when it sold its hospital to MedStar Health in February 2000. The transaction required a team led by Clifford Stromberg from the firm's Health Practice Group and included real estate specialist Bruce Parmley as well as Martin Michaelson from the firm's Education Practice Group. Michaelson had joined Hogan & Hartson in 1973, then left in 1983 to become deputy general counsel, then university counsel, of Harvard University. When he returned to the firm in 1989 he brought a wealth of experience from academia, whose profile, he pointed out, had changed from one of a haven for lone scholars, adding their bits to the store of knowledge, into a "hierarchical, economic enterprise that is accountable in myriad distracting and burdensome ways to far-flung constituencies and governors throughout the nation and the world."[9] Michaelson stepped in to head the firm's higher education practice in 1994, after the Senate confirmed President Clinton's nomination of David Tatel to the D.C. Circuit Court of Appeals.

HOGAN & HARTSON'S MOSCOW OFFICE OPENED IN 1994.

Hogan & Hartson's Moscow office exemplifies the capacity of law and commerce to create new connections across international boundaries. Established in 1994, the firm's diverse practice in Russia and the Commonwealth of Independent Countries now is conducted by fifteen attorneys and legal specialists, including three American partners resident in Moscow. It has included the representation of several Russian enterprises before the United Nations Compensation Commission for claims suffered as a result of Iraq's invasion of Kuwait in 1990; advising a major energy company on its tender for the management of one of the world's largest pipeline systems, in Kazakhstan; and assisting a major Hollywood studio in obtaining the rights to certain life stories for use in the movie, K-19: The Widowmaker, based on the true story of a Soviet atomic submarine.

But no case better dramatized the transition from Cold War to commerce than Hogan & Hartson's involvement in the efforts of the first "commercial cosmonauts," America's Dennis Tito and South Africa's Mark Shuttleworth, to reach the International Space Station (ISS) on a Russian Soyuz-TM34 rocket. Peter J. Pettibone, Managing Partner of Hogan & Hartson's Moscow office, worked with U.S., Canadian, European, Japanese, and Russian officials to address concerns such as training and mission safety for Dennis Tito, who blasted off on April 28, 2001, under a temporary agreement among the officials. Shuttleworth launched nearly a year later, after Pettibone and others from the firm's Moscow office negotiated "space tourist" guidelines acceptable to NASA and other ISS participants. Tito and Shuttleworth each paid the Russian space program about $20 million for the adventure.

Changes in environmental and antitrust policies, evolving technologies in telecommunications and medical fields, and the increased internationalization of business enriched as well as complicated the coordination of Hogan & Hartson's various practice groups in the 1990s. This was particularly true of the firm's legislative practice. Such work always had been a distinctive feature of

HOGAN & HARTSON'S COLORADO SPRINGS OFFICE OPENED IN 1994.

Washington's legal scene and one of the reasons so many out-of-town firms opened offices in the capital. But as Ann Vickery noted, at any given time an attorney from a particular practice group might have some reason to visit Congress or an agency of the executive branch, and when firm attorneys kept bumping into each other, "We thought it probably made sense to coordinate."

past the antiquated notion that legislative practice was not "real law." In 1991 William Michael "Mike" House, three other attorneys, and a lobbyist left their D.C. firm to help reconstitute Hogan & Hartson's Legislative Practice Group, then headed by former Republican National Committee Chair Frank Fahrenkopf. House had been legislative assistant to Congressman James Collins of Texas in the early 1970s and had served as chief of staff to U.S. Senator from Alabama Howell Heflin from 1979 to 1986. During the 1990s Hogan & Hartson's legislative practice added other Capitol Hill veterans like Presidential Medal of Freedom winner Robert Michel, who served thirty-eight years as a U.S. representative from Illinois, including fourteen years as House Minority Leader, and John Edward Porter, who served for twenty-one years as a U.S. representative from Illinois and founded the Congressional Human Rights Caucus. House, Porter, and Michel, together with Jeff Munk, Mike Gilliland, and others, went on to build a lobbying powerhouse in the United States.

[1] MICHAEL CHEROUTES HELPED STRUCTURE THE MULTI-BILLION-DOLLAR FINANCING OF DENVER INTERNATIONAL AIRPORT AND HAS BEEN ACTIVE IN NUMEROUS EUROPEAN PROJECTS AS WELL. [2] JOHN COOK IS NOW MANAGING PARTNER OF THE COLORADO SPRINGS OFFICE. [3] DON WALKER, FIRST MANAGING PARTNER OF THE DENVER OFFICE, BROUGHT THE U.S. OLYMPIC COMMITTEE REPRESENTATION TO H&H. [4] ALSO PICTURED ARE OTHER EARLY PIONEERS IN THE FIRM'S COLORADO-BASED PRACTICE, (L TO R) NIKKI TUTTLE, CRAIG UMBAUGH AND HELEN ATKESON.

It also made sense to consider legislative practice the full-time activity of a separate department rather than just the part-time activity of every department. Like psychiatrists, who sometimes had to fight the perception among their medical colleagues that they were not "real physicians," lawyers had to get

Hogan & Hartson widened its inter-national scope in the 1990s and increased its capabilities in both corporate and government-related matters on the national level. Partners J. Hovey Kemp, Michael Silver, Chris Hagan, and Michael Williams, for instance, helped bring the firm's private equity practice to national prominence. That practice, said Kemp, "allowed the firm to get exposed to pools of capital that are very active in the market and very creative, so if you represent the portfolio company you tend to have a very active practice in mergers and acquisitions, debt financing, IPOs — whatever that company is doing." Additionally, in the course of addressing these issues, it often happens that "the client needs other specialists in the firm — regulatory, environmental, employee benefits, tax, securities lawyers, and sometimes litigation lawyers."

DAVID J. HENSLER JOINED THE FIRM IN 1968 AND HAS BUILT A NATIONAL REPUTATION AS A HIGHLY SUCCESSFUL TRIAL AND APPELLATE ATTORNEY. HE SERVED ON HOGAN & HARTSON'S EXECUTIVE COMMITTEE DURING THE FIRM'S INITIAL EXPANSION INTO EUROPE IN THE EARLY 1990S.

Hogan & Hartson also continued to take care of local clients in Washington, as it had for nearly a hundred years. Attorneys like Vinnie Cohen, Bob Cave, and Harry Jones represented many clients in high-profile civil litigation in the D.C. courts. "White collar" litigation and government investigations also proved to be high-profile affairs, especially after 1978 when Congress, reacting partly to Watergate and partly to long-recognized needs for reform, passed a "special prosecutor" law authorizing the attorney general to seek court-appointed prosecutors, later called "independent counsel," to investigate alleged corruption and abuses of power in government.

Ty Cobb represented officials from the Reagan, George H. Bush, and Clinton administrations, striving wherever possible to avoid publicity for his clients. "It's the ones that nobody knows about that I'm proud of," he said. Allen Snyder also represented officials in the Clinton White House in the mid-1990s when they came under intense and prolonged scrutiny by investigators looking into everything from President Clinton's gubernatorial campaign financing years earlier in Arkansas to the Clintons' real estate transactions, and from the activities of the White House travel office to the President's sexual behavior.

In late 2001 and 2002, Hogan & Hartson responded to the developing corporate crises at Enron, Tyco, and WorldCom. Austin Mittler and Jim Rosenhauer, Practice Area Administrators for the firm's Litigation and Business and Finance Groups, coordinated Hogan & Hartson's diverse corporate and litigation capabilities in a new "corporate governance" initiative. Later in 2002, after the Sarbanes-Oxley Act became law, Hogan & Hartson attorneys worked with their corporate clients to adjust to the post-Sarbanes-Oxley world of new disclosure and accountability standards. The corporate governance practice, under the direction of Stuart Stein, Richard Parrino, and Dennis Tracey, coordinated a multidisciplinary group of attorneys from all practice areas of the firm, advising corporations, boards, and their committees and individual directors on all aspects of corporate and board committee governance and responsibility, and conducting corporate investigations. The firm also expanded its government investigations and white-collar criminal defense and securities enforcement practices. Seasoned attorneys like Loretta Lynch, Sid Davis, Ira Feinberg, Mark Gately, Dan Shea, Elliot Sagor, George Salter, and Dennis Tracey joined Ty Cobb, Joe Hassett, Steve Immelt, Andrew Shoemaker, Doug Fellman, Peter Spivack, and other Hogan & Hartson attorneys skilled in government investigations, white-collar, securities, and professional liability matters. Dave Hensler, who also was involved in some major "D & O," or Directors and Officers, liability matters, observed in 2003, "It's hard to identify any major corporate misconduct case today in which we don't have some involvement."

Not all cases made the evening news, but Hensler recalled one from the early 1990s that had transpired from start to finish under a media spotlight reminiscent of some of Frank Hogan's cases three-quarters of a century earlier. In 1993 Robert Haft sued his father, Herbert Haft, a Washington, D.C., entrepreneur who, with his wife Gloria, had transformed a small pharmacy in Washington, D.C., into Dart Drug, a discount retail chain with six hundred stores in seven states and annual sales of $1.2 billion. Herbert and Gloria had started the business in the 1950s. Their children helped out over the years as the Hafts' enterprises grew to include retail ventures such as Shoppers Food Warehouse and Total Beverage. Robert, the Hafts' oldest son, honed his talents at the Harvard Business School and then launched the multimillion-dollar discount successes Crown Books and Trak Auto.

In April 1993, seventy-two-year-old Herbert reportedly was angered by a newspaper article in which Robert cited the great differences between him and his father and said that when the day came for him to take over, the Dart operation would be run more openly.[10] The Haft family tensions did not begin with that article, but the vehemence of recriminations between family members has puzzled observers ever since. In any event, Herbert's actions after April were clear enough. In June Dart's board of directors dismissed Robert and Gloria and replaced Robert as Dart's president with his younger brother, Ronald. Robert consulted Dave Hensler at Hogan & Hartson.

In mid-August Robert filed suit against Dart for wrongful discharge. Hensler and others at the firm represented him, while a different firm handled Gloria's simultaneous suit against Robert for divorce on grounds of infidelity. Over the many months of preparation for the trial, Robert and the Henslers became quite close, often sharing breakfast together on Saturday mornings. The trial was held in Delaware to help ensure an unbiased jury. Robert proved to be "a brilliant witness," said Hensler. "We got a sensational result." The $34 million award — $38 million when interest was added — was the largest wrongful discharge verdict in U.S. history up to that time. At a post-trial celebration party at the Henslers' home, Robert handed out gifts — a trip to London on the Concorde for Lisa Bonanno and weeklong, all-expense-paid trips to California for Mitch Zamoff, Jon Constine, chief legal assistant Connie Stoskopf, and secretary Feannia Point. Then Robert took Hensler to the front door and showed him his gift — a new Saab convertible. The image conjured a victory more than sixty years earlier, when a grateful Ed Doheny had presented a new automobile to Frank Hogan. In 2004, eleven years after the Haft victory, Hensler was still giving friends "a lift in the gift."

Litigation put the Hafts and Ed Doheny in the news, albeit for very different reasons. But it was the sheer size of their businesses and the amount of money involved that vaulted their cases into the headlines. Neither man sought publicity, but their conspicuous success in business virtually assured it when they went to court. At that point they needed expert litigators. But their businesses had required legal advice all along — advice aimed, among other things, at anticipating future contingencies and avoiding litigation if at all possible. Attorney Robert Swaine of the Cravath,

[1] IN MARCH 1997 THE FEDERAL COURTHOUSE IN WASHINGTON, D.C., WAS NAMED IN HONOR OF JUDGE E. BARRETT PRETTYMAN. [2] HOGAN & HARTSON OPENED AN OFFICE IN NEW YORK CITY IN 1998. [3] HOGAN & HARTSON OPENED AN OFFICE IN BUDAPEST IN 1996.

Swaine & Moore firm once wrote, "The great corporate lawyers of the day drew their reputations more from their abilities in the conference room and drafting documents than from their persuasiveness before the courts."[11] Swaine was referring to the years around 1900, but demand for the legal skills he described only increased as the century passed and company executives developed new ways to do business around the world. Over the years Hogan & Hartson honed its expertise to meet business at the cutting edge of corporate legal practice.

Prentiss E. Feagles joined Hogan & Hartson in 1980 and is director of the firm's Tax Practice Group. He has been centrally involved in the tax aspects of many of the firm's major corporate transactions and now serves as the firm's Managing Partner for Finance.

J. Warren Gorrell, Jr., became Hogan & Hartson's first Chairman in January 2001. Gorrell's emphasis on quality, teamwork and collegiality augured the continuance of Hogan & Hartson's core values into the firm's second century.

[4] Hogan & Hartson's Century City, Los Angeles, office opened in 2001, adding a second L.A. location to the firm's already active office downtown on Grand Avenue established in 1997. [5] The Miami office of Hogan & Hartson opened in 2000. [6] Hogan & Hartson added a Tokyo office in 2000. [7] The firm's office in Boulder Colorado, opened in 1999.

In 1986 the firm had helped a long-standing client, the Pillsbury Company, find a novel way to enhance the value of its holdings in its then-subsidiary Burger King restaurant chain. Working with partner Prentiss Feagles, whom Warren Gorrell unabashedly proclaimed "the best corporate and partnership tax lawyer in America, a tax lawyer who can talk to you and you understand what he's saying," Gorrell and team helped Pillsbury and investment banking firm Merrill Lynch create a new financing structure for the real estate industry. It was called a "master limited partnership," an investment that combines the tax benefits of a limited partnership with the liquidity advantages of publicly traded securities. "Basically what we did was take the real estate underneath franchised Burger King restaurants around the country and put the real estate leases into a public company — a partnership," Gorrell explained. "The rent that came in from operating the restaurants was the income stream

TODD D. SCHAFER'S WORK IN MOSCOW HELPED PLACE HOGAN & HARTSON AT THE FOREFRONT OF A NEW ERA IN POST-SOVIET RUSSIA.

that could then be distributed out to all the public investors."

The Burger King MLP, as it came to be known, was the first publicly traded partnership in the real estate area. "The beauty," Gorrell added, "was that individual investors could get the tax benefits from the partnership structure through a publicly traded security listed on the New York Stock Exchange that they could trade just like stock." The novelty of the arrangement required skillful handling of tax matters and a thorough explanation to the SEC, which Feagles provided. Gorrell was still an associate at the firm — he became partner in the middle of the deal — but he was encouraged by the support and confidence of senior partners like Art Rothkopf and Bob Jeffers, who also worked on the transaction.

Merrill Lynch thereafter called on Hogan & Hartson for some of its most challenging real estate investment banking matters, including finding a way to free investments in real estate limited partnerships from the prohibitive tax consequences of selling. "All investors could do was hold on forever," said Gorrell, "hold on until they died," when at last the investment would receive a tax break — too late. Gorrell, Feagles, and Merrill Lynch investment banker Richard Saltzman devised a way of combining a partnership with a real estate investment trust (REIT) to solve the dilemma. Gorrell described the idea. "You have the public company which is a REIT that is traded on the New York Stock Exchange, and you put a partnership underneath it in which all of the operations would be conducted and all the assets would be held, and that could make acquisitions from other partnerships on a tax advantaged basis."

In 1992 Hogan & Hartson and Merrill Lynch applied the idea to the Oliver Carr Company, a D.C.-based real estate and development firm. The resulting restructuring combined all the partnerships that Carr had formed over the years and raised capital through an initial public offering that succeeded in substantially reducing the Carr Company's debt. "It was revolutionary," observed Gorrell. "Once our team figured out how to do these things, it just opened the capital markets to the real estate industry and enabled our team — partners Bruce Gilchrist, David Bonser, Alan Dye, Eve Howard, George Barsness, and Jim Showen — to end up representing many of the leading REITs and investment banking firms." Hogan & Hartson's growing corporate resources also helped open new paths for the firm to follow, not only internationally but across the United States.

On November 1, 1993, Hogan & Hartson opened an office in Denver, Colorado, as part of the firm's strategy to expand its corporate and commercial practice. Michael Cheroutes, a Denver attorney experienced in publicly financed projects, joined Hogan & Hartson at that time, along with Helen Atkeson, David Scott, and Rebecca Bronson. But there were opportunities for other work as well. Donis Walker, the first Managing Partner of the Denver office, brought his broad-based commercial practice, including the representation of the U.S. Olympic Committee, to Hogan & Hartson. In 1995 Scott Reisch moved from the firm's Washington, D.C., office to Denver to establish an environmental practice there. This group subsequently was joined by Steve Cohen, Niki Tuttle, Craig Umbaugh, Chris Walsh, Whitney Holmes, Ed Aro, and others who helped build the Denver office into a major full-service operation. Ty Cobb moved from Baltimore to become the Managing Partner of the Denver office in 1999 and was succeeded by Tom Strickland in 2004.

In 1994 Don Walker also persuaded a former Colorado Springs colleague, Scott Blackmun, to open a new Hogan & Hartson office in that city. Blackmun, the first Managing Partner of the Colorado Springs office, headed its commercial practice and helped recruit John W. Cook to join the firm to open the office's litigation practice. Cook later became the Managing Partner of the Colorado Springs office.

In 1996 the firm's Los Angeles office opened, with Marc H. Bozeman as Managing Partner. Bozeman's biological product, medical device, pharmaceutical, cosmetic, and food law practice exemplified two of the key Hogan & Hartson growth strategies — "interconnectivity" and "industry focus" — that Bob Odle had outlined in 1989. On the principle that every new partner and practice needed to "add value," and in

Hogan & Hartson's "H&H Academy" has provided a variety of educational programs to firm attorneys since its launching in January 2000. Originally conceived as a way to offer new associates some programmatic legal training beyond what they would learn on the job or in their own reading, the H&H Academy actually began with a much broader mission of keeping all of its attorneys up to date on new developments in the law and in legal practice. Many law firms support such activity, but in the 1990s Hogan & Hartson's Bob Odle and Don Walker aimed at something more substantial.

After partner Barrett Prettyman completed a study of in-house educational programs at comparable firms, Odle and Walker mulled over the possibilities. Then they recommended, and the firm adopted, a model it called the H&H Academy and placed it under the direction of an experienced, twenty-year partner, Pamela G. Winthrop, who devoted all of her time to its operations. Few, if any, firms have decided to assign a partner exclusively to the management of their in-house educational function. As chair of the twenty-five-person H&H Academy Board of Advisors, Winthrop had lots of help, which she needed as the academy sought to coordinate the talents and needs of nearly one thousand attorneys in twenty offices around the world.

Winthrop and the Board of Advisors, which includes about eight associates, quickly decided that the H&H Academy's mission should encompass the needs of its most experienced partners as well as its newest attorneys. During its first year, therefore, its lectures, panel presentations, and structured exercises focused on the theme of "Client Service," while in its second year (2001-2002) it featured a "Focus on Fundamentals" aimed at research and writing skills more relevant to new associates.

Using videotapes, CDs, video-conferencing technology, and the firm's Intranet, the H&H Academy made ninety offerings available to firm attorneys in 2002-2003.

Hogan & Hartson attorneys staff most of the programs. "There's no one better able to teach our attorneys to litigate than our own litigators," Winthrop points out, as an example of the concentrated expertise that Hogan & Hartson enjoys under its own roof. Winthrop's goals for the H&H Academy's future include increasing the involvement of all Hogan & Hartson offices; adding to the academy's growing resource library of presentations; and using technology to make academy offerings even more accessible to the firm's attorneys, who now work in every time zone around the globe.

order to avoid the isolation of partners and offices, the firm determined to add only attorneys and practices that connected with its most valued existing practices. Bozeman and his representations fit nicely into one of Hogan & Hartson's strongest practice areas. Additionally, "industry focus" meant that the firm should organize its practices on an industry basis rather than on a legal expertise basis. Such an approach maximized the value of Hogan & Hartson's diverse capabilities and the marketing of those capabilities to clients.

Hogan & Hartson had become Washington, D.C.'s largest law firm in 1994 when it grew to 324 lawyers. By 1998 it had added about 275 more, totaling approximately 600. Almost one hundred of them worked overseas. Rebecca Bronson, who had helped start the firm's Denver office in 1993, traveled to Moscow the following year to open a new office there. The Moscow office served clients in a host of areas that developed rapidly after the advent of the Russian Federation. It handled telecommunications, natural resources, and aviation matters, including the launching of American Dennis Tito and South African Mark Shuttleworth aboard a Soyuz rocket as the world's first paying "space tourists." Partner Todd Schafer helped place Hogan & Hartson at the forefront of the Russian Federation's transition to a market economy by his representations in numerous major corporate transactions as well as his contributions in several ground-breaking litigation and arbitration matters. And Michael Cheroutes, who

Hogan & Hartson's record of community service includes an eclectic list of assignments its attorneys have undertaken over the years, usually on leave from the firm. In his forty-nine-year career, E. Barrett Prettyman, Jr., completed so many that Bob Odle once described him as "the firm's leading public persona."

In the early 1960s Prettyman had been Special Assistant to Attorney General Robert Kennedy and to President John Kennedy. At the Kennedy administration's request, Prettyman flew to Cuba in the fall of 1962 to help others negotiate the release of 1,113 prisoners taken by Castro's forces following the failed Bay of Pigs invasion. The successful return of the prisoners on Christmas Eve was, Prettyman said, "one of the most emotional moments of my life."

Five years later Prettyman traveled to Vietnam on a fact-finding mission as Special Consultant to Senator Edward Kennedy's Subcommittee (of the Senate Judiciary Committee) to Investigate Problems Connected with Refugees and Escapees. And in 1980 Prettyman and a Hogan & Hartson colleague, Allen Snyder, served as outside Special Counsel to the U.S. House of Representatives Ethics Committee during its investigation of members charged with accepting bribes in an undercover FBI "sting" operation known as "Abscam." Prettyman was in the well of the House on October 2, 1980, when the House, for the first time in one hundred years, voted to expel one of its members, Representative Ozzie Meyers, after his bribery conviction. Prettyman had written the Ethics Committee's majority report favoring expulsion, but then was asked by the head of the minority contingent to write its report, too. "That's the first time I'd ever had the experience of writing a dissent to my own work," he later remarked.

In 1998, at the request of city leaders, including a former colleague, Judge John Ferren, who had taken a leave from the bench to serve as the District of Columbia's Corporation Counsel, Prettyman was asked to take on one of the toughest assignments the then-loosely-managed city government had to offer — Inspector General. Serving for fifteen months, and without pay, Prettyman brought an unprecedented degree of professionalism and commitment to the job, seeking out fraud and corruption, saving the city millions of dollars, and infusing the demoralized IG's office with fresh idealism and energy.

In an era when practice areas have become increasingly specialized, Barrett Prettyman's career illustrates that the benefits of skilled specialization need not come at the expense of general excellence, public service, or personal enthusiasm for new and interesting work.

had played a role in developing the Warsaw office, rendered similar service in the Moscow office.

In 1996 Hogan & Hartson opened its Budapest office, where partner-in-charge Kornelia Nagy-Koppany joined the firm and led the firm's effort in a newly thriving Hungary. Kornelia managed several large-scale privatization matters in Hungary; helped establish the first investment bank in that country; and negotiated a bilateral agreement between the United States and Hungary covering legal status recognition, customs, and tax issues.

"We've got a lot going on here," Odle told the *Legal Times*'s Siobhan Roth in 1998, though he didn't tell Roth that Warren Gorrell, Jeff Schneider, and Mark Landis had set up temporary quarters in the IBM Tower at 57th Street and Madison Avenue in midtown Manhattan six months earlier.[12] Many regarded Manhattan as a kind of frontal cortex in the business world's central nervous system. Establishing an office in New York City, bastion of some of the nation's oldest corporate law firms, took careful planning. By the end of the year, though, the team reported favorable prospects to Odle and the Executive Committee, and in December 1998 the *Legal Times* and the *New York Law Journal* announced that Hogan & Hartson was opening a New York office. Partner Andrew Trubin and associate Amy Davidson Bryant joined the vanguard trio of Gorrell, Schneider, and Landis in the IBM Tower, while Gorrell commuted from Washington to manage several crucial events developing quickly in New York. Christine Pallares soon joined this group in New York.

It was a long way from the temporary space in the IBM Tower to 875 Third Avenue, a move made necessary by a major event — the welcoming in April 2000 of thirty-five attorneys from the former firm of Davis, Weber & Edwards. The firm was a top-ranked New York litigation boutique that was concerned about the competitive "shakeout" that Steve Brill had predicted would hit mid-sized firms hard in the 1990s. "Any firm that could get them would be landing a great group," said a search firm executive in October 1999, when the negotiations with Hogan & Hartson were under way.[13] Howard Weber, Sid Davis, Steven Edwards, Jay Gerber, Dennis Tracey, Morris Waisbrot, David Dunn, Bill Haigney, and others worked closely with Hogan & Hartson to assure a successful launch and transition.

Hogan & Hartson's new partners and colleagues brought into the firm not only extensive litigation experience in New York City but also an active practice in Miami, Florida, led by Laura Besvinick. Mark Sterling, a former Hogan & Hartson partner who had relocated to Miami in 1993 to work with a leading health care company, rejoined the firm to help establish its newest office. Two prominent trial and appellate attorneys, Parker D. Thomson and Carol A. Licko, also joined Hogan & Hartson in Miami. The office's location specially positioned it to serve as a base for Hogan & Hartson's practice group focusing on Latin America, and the firm was successful in attracting a prestigious group of corporate, finance, and litigation lawyers to the Miami office that included Jose Valdivia, Miguel Zaldivar, Daniel Gonzalez, Jorge Diaz-Silveira, and Richard Lorenzo.

as the Practice Area Administrator. The firm's goal in time was to have a full-service IP practice covering litigation, patent, trademark and copyright prosecution, and licensing and other commercial arrangements. In 1993 Kenneth Hautman, head of the firm's Technology Law Group, joined Hogan & Hartson in its McLean office, and in 1999 William Roberts established an office for the firm in Boulder, Colorado. Both McLean and Boulder were centers for technology and "high-tech" business development.

But Miami didn't remain the firm's newest office for long. Just days later, Hogan & Hartson announced the addition of an experienced group of Los Angeles-based intellectual property attorneys including Stuart Lubitz, William Wright, Wei-Ning Yang, and Ying Chen and the addition of a Tokyo office that had been staffed since 1996 by David Lubitz, one of only a few U.S. patent attorneys to achieve qualification as a gaikokuho jimu bengoshi, a special practice status granted to foreign lawyers by Japan's Minister of Justice. David Lubitz attracted Philippe Riesen and a team of attorneys expert in patent, intellectual property, licensing, and general litigation matters. The Tokyo office also illustrated Hogan & Hartson's planned expansion at work, for it resulted from a number of strategic decisions going back several years.

During the 1990s, Hogan & Hartson, whose practices had covered three major areas — business and finance, regulatory, and litigation — carefully built a fourth, intellectual property. The firm created an intellectual property group and named Jim Rosenhauer

In September 2000 the firm attracted William Kubida, now one of five Practice Group Directors (with Kenneth Hautman, Stuart Lubitz, Raymond Kurz, and Phil Porter of its IP Practice Group) to the Colorado Springs office, and Carol W. Burton, also in the IP Practice Group, to the Denver office. Kubida had worked with start-up companies as well as Fortune 100 corporations, including Digital Equipment Corporation, Motorola, and Nippon Motorola. Prior to becoming a lawyer, Burton had been an analytical chemist and had co-founded and served as chief financial officer for a custom microcomputer company. Kubida and Burton greatly expanded the firm's patent prosecution practice.

In 2001 Raymond Kurz, now a Practice Group Director of the Intellectual Property Group, and Celine Jimenez Crowson joined Hogan & Hartson's Washington, D.C., office, bringing with them a long list of publications, an extensive patent and trademark litigation and prosecution practice, and diverse cutting-edge experience in fields ranging from computer hardware and software and Internet technologies to medical devices, pharmaceuticals, and everyday consumer goods. Kurz and Crowson teamed with versatile litigators like Steve Routh, Steve Hollman, and David Kikel, each of whom had spent their entire careers at the firm in supporting the firm's intellectual property litigation practice across the country. The firm continued to expand its intellectual property litigation practice over the years, including the addition in 2002 of highly regarded litigators Laurence Pretty and Bill Thomson in the Los Angeles office and in 2004 of experienced litigators Eric J. Lobenfeld and Ira Schaefer in the New York office.[14]

In June 2000 the *Legal Times* pronounced Hogan & Hartson's growth "staggering" — from three hundred to seven hundred lawyers and from three regional offices to seventeen worldwide in just ten years.[15] Twelve years earlier the firm had worried about the wisdom of opening a single office in Baltimore. Now its offices spanned the globe. Many of Bob Odle's colleagues proclaimed that he had been "the mortar between the bricks" and "the glue" that held the firm together through all that growth. But it also was true that Odle had been the firm's premier brick maker, the person who focused most intently on the sort of growth that started people talking about "mortar" and "glue" in the first place.

Odle had logged thousands of hours "making the rounds" of the firm's now widespread offices, making sure that everyone felt included and appreciated and that the cohesive firm culture, of which his management was the most visible expression, was, as Ty Cobb aptly put it, "imparted to and not imposed on" the firm's many new attorneys. But by early 2000 Odle had to yield to consequences of success. He had helped build a ranch too extensive for him to ride alone. Sandy Mayo's assistance had helped, and in November 1999 Ann Vickery had been named to a new position as Managing Partner of the Washington, D.C., office. But the burden on Odle remained great. "I was one guy," he said, "and the stress and strain of trying to hold it all together was just killing me. I also was aware that there was a growing anxiety in the firm about what was going to happen when I wasn't running the firm anymore." Odle, then sixty-two years old, told the Executive Committee, "Look, by the end of this year we've got to know who's taking over." Jeanne Archibald had been on the committee for only six months when Odle made his announcement. "We were all sitting there going, 'Oh my God,'" she recalled.

Odle had been a member of the Executive Committee back in 1979 when the committee had turned to him to fill the firm's Administrative Partner position. Torn between his desire to pursue his practice full-time and his sense of responsibility about the firm's management, he accepted the committee's call and tried to balance his activities as best he could. By 1989, when his title was changed to Managing Partner, his management responsibilities had crowded out his practice. They took all of his time for the next eleven years. Now Odle and the Executive Committee turned to another of its members, Warren Gorrell, to take over. Gorrell had been involved in the firm's international expansion during his three terms on the Executive Committee and had built a very successful practice in the firm. So it was easy to see why Gorrell shared the same mixed feelings Odle had experienced years earlier about taking time away from his practice.

Gorrell's emphasis on "leadership by example" — the importance of quality and the value of teamwork — lent support to those trying to persuade him to succeed Odle. The firm's corporate practice, like virtually all of its practice groups, was not a solo operation but a team effort, and Gorrell and others had built a very strong team. In fact, in the summer of 2000 Gorrell was able to take a sabbatical, traveling to Kenya and Italy with his family, largely because his team could manage the work in his absence. If he were to head the firm part-time, the Executive Committee suggested, his team could fill in when he was busy with management activities. Still, there seemed to be much more to this transition than simply "taking over" from Bob Odle, and the discussions continued for months. "I spent a lot of time talking to the Executive Committee telling them I really didn't think I should do it," Gorrell said.

Toward the end of 2000 Gorrell bowed — as Odle had twenty-one years earlier — to the larger needs of the firm, but under two conditions. First, he would continue his practice because he enjoyed the work, the clients, and his team, and because he believed he would be a more effective manager if he also was working on transactions and other matters alongside his colleagues. Second, he would manage, as he liked to practice, as part of a team. He, Odle, and the Executive Committee created a new,

IN 2001 PETER RAUE HEADED A GROUP OF 27 ATTORNEYS WHO JOINED HOGAN & HARTSON TO FORM THE FIRM'S BERLIN OFFICE, HOGAN & HARTSON RAUE. HE IS A HIGHLY REGARDED ART CONNOISSEUR WHO WAS AWARDED THE HONORARY TITLE OF "PROFESSOR" BY THE GOVERNING MAYOR OF BERLIN IN 1995 FOR HIS MANY CONTRIBUTIONS TO THE CITY'S CULTURAL LIFE.

"CEO-style," corporate management structure and presented it to the firm in December.

On January 1, 2001, Warren Gorrell became the firm's first Chairman, assisted by a three-member Managing Partner Group with firmwide responsibilities. Jeanne Archibald became the firm's Managing Partner for Practice Administration. She was undaunted by Hogan & Hartson's size, for she had managed about 2,000 attorneys at the Treasury Department. Ray Batla was named Managing Partner for International Offices, and Sandy Mayo, who had assisted Bob Odle for eight years, became Managing Partner for Operations. Soon this team was augmented by two additional Managing Partners — Howard Flack, who oversaw Lateral Hiring and Integration, and Prentiss Feagles, who was placed in charge of firmwide Finance. Odle would serve as Managing Partner-at-Large until his sixty-fifth birthday in November 2002. This Senior Management Group also was assisted by several other partners who performed important responsibilities for the firm in addition to their practices, including Patricia Ambrose and Paul Skelly in labor and human relations and Al Turnbull and Jack Keeney in legal ethics and conflicts.

Gorrell's belief in teamwork was bedrock. "Look at yourself in the mirror," was his message to potential recruits. "If you can't honestly say that you're a team player, self-select. Don't come here, because you won't do well." Hogan & Hartson's Chairman also underscored the limits of the corporate business model for managing a law firm. Hierarchical structure was efficient but limited in its applicability to professionals who valued their autonomy highly and were trained for independent decision-making. "It works extremely well in terms of just operating the firm, from strategic planning all the way through operations," Gorrell observed, "but if we operated like a corporation where maximizing shareholder value — in this case, maximizing profits per partner — was really the only goal, we'd fail in the long run. If money is the glue that holds us together, we'll fail. We have to be successful financially, of course, but as importantly we have to have a work environment that people enjoy being in, where people treat each other with respect and are cooperative."

Even as the Executive Committee was forming a new management structure for the firm in 2000, Hogan & Hartson was negotiating an expansion of its European practice in Berlin, Germany. The opportunity resulted from the very circumstances that Hogan & Hartson was determined to avoid in its own ranks — divisive competition among partners and a dissolving, rather than strengthening, of comradeship under economic pressure. In the spring of 2000 several partners in the Berlin office of the Oppenhoff & Rädler law firm began to look for an environment more supportive of their interests and practices after their firm decided to merge with a British firm.

Christoph Wagner and Christian von Hammerstein had been foreign interns at Hogan & Hartson in Washington, D.C., and both had developed personal friendships as well as professional ties with firm lawyers. Wagner broached the subject of joining Hogan & Hartson with his senior Berlin colleague, Peter Raue, who in turn discussed it with Wolfgang Kuhla, Max Braeuer, Gernod Meinel, and his other partners. Subsequent discussions with Bob Odle and the Executive Committee quickly led to an agreement to open an office, "Hogan & Hartson Raue L.L.P." "Peter Raue," said Bob Odle, "was Mr. Berlin. We could not have found a better-known lawyer in Germany." Hogan & Hartson also gained Raue's expertise as one of Germany's most astute collectors of modern art, complementing the acclaimed judgment of Bob Odle, who had chosen numerous fine paintings for the firm's offices around the world.

The Berlin office of Hogan & Hartson Raue at One Pottsdamer Platz.

Bruce Parmley, a real estate partner who had joined Hogan & Hartson in 1988 and helped negotiate the firm's numerous office leases as it expanded through the 1990s, traveled to Berlin to help close a lease on some prime space in Potsdamer Platz. The once-bustling café district had been crushed by the Berlin Wall that ran straight through it, but now it had returned to life as a thriving commercial center. The negotiations for office space in One Potsdamer Platz proved difficult, though. At one point Gernod Meinel, the Managing Partner of the Berlin office, and Carl-Stephan Schweer grew frustrated and "started to negotiate some frivolous terms," as Meinel recalled it. The result was the incorporation into the formal lease agreement of Hogan & Hartson's rights to build a swimming pool, a putting green, and a driving range on the ninth floor terrace. Of course, these amenities never were built, but Parmley, who participated in the agreement, planned to frame it and put it on his wall — "both the German version and the English translation, because it's not something I'm likely to accomplish again," he said with a broad grin.

Gernod Meinel (L) and Christoph Wagner were among the 27 attorneys who, with Peter Raue, formed Hogan & Hartson's Berlin office in 2001. Meinel is the managing partner of the Berlin and Munich offices.

Meinel was particularly struck by an intuitive decision Bob Odle made at the end of the negotiations to proceed with signing the $15 million, ten-year lease agreement even though none of the twenty-six attorneys expected to join from Oppenhoff & Rädler or the two new attorneys in the group, Eckhard Bremer and Hans Seiler, had yet signed their offer letters. This expression of trust and support from their new firm was the perfect remedy for what had been ailing the German lawyers. "That was quite impressive," said Meinel. "You think, those are people you would like to work with." On January 1, 2001, the same day Gorrell and his new management team started work, Hogan & Hartson's Berlin office opened for business.

Nine months later the atmosphere of post-Cold War warmth and openness that the world had enjoyed for more than a decade chilled suddenly and dramatically. During the DoD/Justice Department investigation of the Newport News transaction, on September 11, 2001, Jan McDavid and the general counsel for General Dynamics were on their way to the Pentagon for a 9:30 a.m. meeting when McDavid received a phone call telling her that a passenger jet had just slammed into the North

Bruce E. Parmley, a real estate attorney, joined Hogan & Hartson in 1988 on the eve of the firm's major expansion effort. He has managed the complex real estate transactions accompanying the firm's astounding growth since 1990 and has served two terms on the Executive Committee.

[ABOVE] HOWARD SQUADRON, 1926-2001, FOUNDED THE FIRM OF SQUADRON ELLENOFF IN 1970. THE FIRM MERGED WITH HOGAN & HARTSON IN FEBRUARY 2002. SQUADRON'S HIGH ETHICAL STANDARDS AND HIS COMMITMENT TO THE ARTS ARE REFLECTED THROUGH THE SQUADRON PROGRAM IN LAW, MEDIA AND SOCIETY AT YESHIVA UNIVERSITY'S BENJAMIN N. CARDOZO SCHOOL OF LAW. [ABOVE RIGHT] HOWARD SQUADRON (R) WITH SENATOR JOSEPH LIEBERMAN.

Tower of the World Trade Center in Manhattan. A tragic accident, most likely. Several minutes later McDavid reached the Pentagon, where she learned that a second aircraft had hit the World Trade Center's South Tower. Thoughts of accidents now darkened into suspicions of hostile attack.

McDavid and her client continued on, deep inside the building, to a soundproof "safe" room several feet thick and protected from electronic eavesdropping, or "bugging." They took their seats around a conference table with several government attorneys and officials. At 9:43 a.m., just minutes after the meeting had begun, they all heard a loud "boom" through the mass of concrete that enveloped the conference room. "I actually assumed it was a bomb," McDavid said later, but at the time no one volunteered any guesses about what was going on outside. Almost immediately someone opened the bolted door and announced that the building was being evacuated.

The conference room was on the Potomac River side of the Pentagon, opposite from where an American Airlines jet had exploded through the building's southwest wall. McDavid and the others packed their briefcases and walked briskly to the exit, then outside into a beautiful late-summer morning. Weatherwise, everything was perfect, sky-blue and crystal-clear. But for those at the Pentagon, and soon for all the world, the day was anything but sunny. Evacuees on the riverside could see smoke from the attack wafting upward into their line of sight as security personnel moved them farther away from the building. From his 13th floor window at Columbia Square, Barrett Prettyman watched it rise, curling upriver like the cumulous exhalation of some exotic menace crashing through America's front door. McDavid noticed baby cribs and strollers from the Pentagon's day care center gathered on the grass near the river as she and her client tried to summon their car. But the roads had been sealed off and the driver could not return to pick them up.

At 10:00 a.m. hijackers of another passenger jet, probably bound for the White House, struggled with passengers who had charged them in the cockpit. The plane crashed into the ground in rural Pennsylvania. McDavid and her colleague were unaware of this attempted fourth attack as they walked around the Columbia Island marina in the Pentagon lagoon, then back to the Lady Bird Johnson memorial between the river and the George Washington Parkway where they managed to hail a cab. The bridges over the Potomac back into Washington were closed, so McDavid headed for General Dynamics' offices in Virginia where she joined others struggling to absorb the morning's calamities, including news of the mounting casualties in the Pentagon explosion. In coming months the impact of new security precautions and regulations reverberated through the nation — and through the legal profession, affecting everything from telecommunications to immigration and international trade. America was locking its doors and windows.

The collapse of the World Trade Center towers raised a difficult problem for the properties' leaseholder, Larry Silverstein, and the nearly twenty property insurance companies involved. Just weeks before the attacks, the companies had "bound coverage" on the behemoth skyscrapers. That is, they had committed themselves to provide coverage on the buildings during the period when the actual policies were being drawn up and issued. But the September 11 attacks intervened. The towers' wholly unexpected destruction presented the insurance companies with a combined $3.5 billion bill, and a hard question: was it $3.5 billion or $7 billion? Had the attacks constituted a single occurrence for the companies to cover, or two? The Hartford, which had agreed to $32 million of the overall coverage on the properties, called on Hogan & Hartson's Hartford Team — Bill Bowman, Sandy Mayo, Pat Hofer, and Jim Ruggeri — to represent its interests in the matter.

The solution to the problem turned out to be different for different companies and hinged on which of two notions had formed the basis of the "bound coverage" agreements. In one, known as the WilProp form after the broker, Willis of New York, the two events would count as one. But in another, issued by Travelers Property Casualty, there was less specificity about how to regard the attacks. The "Travelers" basis left the insurance companies' obligation more of an open question. Hartford had used the WilProp form, which defined the attacks as a single occurrence. In both situations, though, Silverstein sought to obtain the maximum allowable reimbursement, which would result if the attacks were considered as two separate occurrences.

On September 25, 2002, Hogan & Hartson's Bill Bowman and Patrick Hofer obtained summary judgment for Hartford from Judge John S. Martin in the United States District Court for the Southern District of New York. Hofer subsequently left Hogan & Hartson for a position at the U.S. Department of Justice. In July 2003,

FROM HIS OFFICE WINDOW ON SEPTEMBER 11, 2001, BARRETT PRETTYMAN COULD SEE SMOKE RISING FROM THE PENTAGON, WHOSE ROOF TO THE RIGHT OF THE WASHINGTON MONUMENT REFLECTS A LINE OF SUNSHINE IN THE HAZE JUST BELOW THE HORIZON.

World Trade Center Properties, L.L.C., and the Silverstein group appealed to the U.S. Court of Appeals for the Second Circuit. Bill Bowman and John Roberts handled the appeal for Hartford and on September 26, 2003, won the Second Circuit's affirmance of Judge Martin's ruling.

The terrorist attack on the World Trade Center took place during the final months of merger negotiations between Hogan & Hartson and the New York firm

IRA S. SHEINFELD, A NAME PARTNER IN THE HIGHLY-REGARDED FIRM OF SQUADRON, ELLENOFF, PLESENT & SHEINFELD, HELPED EFFECT A SUCCESSFUL MERGER OF HIS FIRM WITH HOGAN & HARTSON IN THE WINTER OF 2000-2001.

Squadron Ellenoff Plesent & Sheinfeld, a full-service New York law firm with more than one hundred attorneys in Manhattan and Los Angeles. The February 2002 merger increased Hogan & Hartson's ability to serve clients in New York and Los Angeles and also created opportunities for Squadron Ellenoff's clients in the international, regulatory, and legislative areas.

Squadron Ellenoff, started in 1970, served national and international clients such as News Corporation, British Sky Broadcasting, Fox Entertainment, and their affiliates in the far-reaching Rupert Murdoch empire. Squadron Ellenoff was known in the legal community particularly as a player in the media and communications, entertainment, technology, and biotechnology industries. The firm's senior partner, Howard Squadron, was also widely recognized for his outstanding legal skills, his moral strength, his commitment to human rights and civil liberties, and his generosity to a variety of arts programs. Ira Sheinfeld, Mark Weinstein, Mitchell Lubart, Jeffrey Rubin, David Kovacs, Slade Metcalf, Ira Greene, Rick Stone, Neil O'Hanlon, and Tony Basich were instrumental in effecting what proved to be a highly successful merger and the subsequent integration of the two firms.

JOHN ROBERTS, JR., JOINED HOGAN & HARTSON IN 1986, LEFT FOR A POSITION IN THE OFFICE OF THE SOLICITOR GENERAL OF THE UNITED STATES IN 1989, THEN RETURNED TO THE FIRM IN 1993. TEN YEARS LATER HE WAS APPOINTED TO A JUDGESHIP ON THE U.S. COURT OF APPEALS, DISTRICT OF COLUMBIA CIRCUIT.

As had been the case in Baltimore in 1988, with Berlin in 2001, and with all of the firm's other offices that opened in between, Squadron Ellenoff's attorneys brought with them to Hogan & Hartson strong commitments to ethical practice, collegiality, and top-quality work. To underscore that commitment, Hogan & Hartson welcomed every new attorney to the firm, one by one, in meetings designed to make sure that their goals and interests, which had justified the merger in the first place, would find useful expression in Hogan & Hartson's practice areas. It was not until April 2003 — more than a year later — that the one hundred integration meetings and resulting implementation meetings were nearly finished. "The worst attribute of a law firm," Howard Flack declared with true conviction, "is when lawyers in the firm feel disconnected, that they're coming to work, sitting in their offices, doing their work, and then going home at night. Nobody's telling them that they're valuable, and I don't mean paying them money. I mean making them feel that they're valuable persons. That's not just my job, management's job. It's every lawyer's job to do that with their fellow lawyers."

In May 2003 John Roberts's appointment by President George W. Bush to a judgeship on the D.C. Circuit Court of Appeals was confirmed by the Senate, and Roberts left the firm. His chambers in the E. Barrett Prettyman Federal Courthouse, named after Barrett Prettyman's father in March 1997, would be next door to the chambers of a former Hogan & Hartson colleague, Judge David Tatel. Between 1993, when Roberts returned to Hogan & Hartson from the Solicitor General's office, and 2003, seven firm attorneys presented arguments in twenty-eight cases before the U.S. Supreme Court. These included successful arguments in 2002 by Roberts for the constitutionality of sex offender registration laws, so-called "Megan's laws," and in 2000 by Jonathan Franklin, formerly senior associate in the firm's CSD and now a partner in the Appellate Practice Group, on behalf of candidates for Congress challenging the constitutionality of a state election law that would have imposed negative ballot labels on candidates who did not support a federal constitutional amendment establishing term limits.

Under the successive leadership of Walter Smith, Jonathan Abram, and Bob Duncan, who succeeded Jack Keeney as partners-in-charge of the Community Services Department, skillful litigation and appellate work also remained a CSD hallmark through the 1990s and into the new century. In 1997, for example, attorneys Jim Hourihan, Scott Reisch, and Cate Stetson led an effort against the U.S. Department of the Interior and the National Park Service on behalf of the National Parks Conservation Association (NPCA), an environmental group, to stop the implementation of a new "vessel

HOGAN & HARTSON LLP

Hogan & Hartson's rich past is more than a history of its legal practice and its lawyers. It is also a history built upon the dedication, teamwork, and commitment to excellence of its senior managers, office managers and administrators, as well as its many staff members. These people have devoted themselves to supporting the interests of the firm and its clients, and have been critical to the remarkable record of success Hogan & Hartson has achieved. Set forth below is a list of the firm's current senior managers, a list of office managers and administrators, and a roster of all current staff personnel who have been with the firm twenty-five years or longer.

Director of Administration ....Robert M. Johnston
Chief Financial Officer ....Joseph W. Cirrito
Chief Information Officer ....William W. Gregory
Controller ....Deborah A. Drummond
Director of Associate Recruitment and Professional Development ....Ellen M. Purvance
Director of Finance..Robert M. Bolton
Director of Human Resources ....Martha K. Williams
Director of Information Resource Center ....R. Austin Doherty
Director of Information Technology .... Michael V. Lucas
Director of Lateral Associate Recruitment and Integration ....Anne R. Bowen
Director of Marketing and Business Development ..Wendy Whitney Taylor
Director of Office Services ....Sandra J. Palumbo
Director of Word Processing ....Leslie A. Burke
Litigation and Conference Center Operations Administrator ....Constance R. Stoskopf
Management Group Director................................Jennifer S. Seibert

Sandra Abé
Viktoria Adamis
Jackie M. Dibnah
Debi L. Groves
Rosemary Helenbrook
Modine E. Hott
Julie A. Johnson
Danielle M. Kopeikin
Piotr Kurcewicz
Susan M. Launer
Olga A. Melekesova
Mayuko Nagashima
Cathy M. Rossow
Jaraslav Scheibal
Britta Teuerle
Mary L. Waters
Edye A. White
Sheila M. Winstanley
Elizabeth R. Wiseman

Carol Acree..........................*Legal Secretary*
Nida Alcala ....*Serials Assistant*
Clara Bell ....*Legal Secretary*
Elaine Borgna ....*Evening Services Manager*
Sharlyn Briscoe ....*Housekeeping Supervisor*
Ildefonso Daguiso ....*Resource Technician*
Judy Dixon ....*Legal Secretary*
John Duvall ....*Administrative Analyst*
Laurette Fletcher.....................*Legal Secretary*
Gayle Hall ....*Legal Secretary*
Lucille Haywood ....*General Office Assistant*
Carol Hedgpeth ....*Legal Secretary*
Linda Heimpel ....*Legal Secretary*
Linda Jones.......................*Expense Supervisor*
Carol Keating........................*Legal Secretary*
Nancy Keller ....*Legal Secretary*
Elizabeth Lamond....................*Conference & Special Events Manager*
Linda Large ....*Legal Secretary*
Susan Lister ....*Legal Secretary*
Nancy Love ....*Legal Secretary*
Gayle Maytan ....*Legal Secretary*
Catherine McGallagher ....*Legal Secretary*
Celestine Morsell ....*Legal Secretary*
Roseanna Nugent ....*Legal Secretary*
Avis Ortner ....*Legal Secretary*
Feannia Point.........................*Legal Secretary*
Briggite Rewa............................*Receptionist*
Sharon Scates ....*Legal Secretary*
Jean Thomas ....*Legal Secretary*
Dianna Thompson...................*Legal Secretary*
Casamira Umana ....*Client Maintenance Manager*
Susan Von Der Osten ....*Legal Secretary*
Catherine Webb ....*Legal Secretary*
Susan Wheeler ....*Legal Secretary*

JONATHAN L. ABRAM JOINED H&H IN 1982. HE HAS SPECIALIZED IN COMPLEX LITIGATION RELATED TO A VARIETY OF REGULATORY ISSUES AND RECENTLY SERVED AS PARTNER-IN-CHARGE OF THE FIRM'S COMMUNITY SERVICES DEPARTMENT.

management plan" allowing dramatic increases in cruise ship and other traffic in Alaska's Glacier Bay without preparation of an environmental impact statement (EIS).

In 1999 the U.S. District Court in Alaska ruled against NPCA and for the Park Service, finding that even though the environmental impacts of the new vessel management plan were "unknown," there was no need for a full-blown EIS. NPCA, again represented by the CSD, appealed to the Ninth Circuit. The following year the CSD team, joined by Mike House, Jeremy Monthy, and the Appellate Practice Group's Cate Stetson, won a unanimous reversal by the Ninth Circuit of the District Court's decision. Cate Stetson, then an associate and in the late months of pregnancy, traveled to Anchorage and impressed the court with a spectacular first appellate argument. On remand, the CSD and Appellate teams obtained an injunction against the "vessel management plan," thus barring increased ship traffic in the Bay pending a full EIS.

Civil rights and human rights also remained high priorities for the CSD, which helped the Washington Lawyers Committee for Civil Rights and Urban Affairs pursue a lawsuit against the Denny's restaurant chain in 1994 triggered by its discriminatory treatment of six African-American Secret Service Agents. The agents had been assigned to protect President Clinton during a visit to the U.S. Naval Academy on April 1, 1993. They had stopped for breakfast with several white colleagues at a Denny's in Annapolis, Maryland. Long after the white agents' food had been served, the African-Americans' orders had not arrived. Eventually they ran out of time and left Denny's without being served.

That very day Denny's had entered into a consent agreement with the U.S. Justice Department following a federal court ruling in California that the restaurant had discriminated against African-American customers there. But the incident in Annapolis suggested that Denny's discrimination problem extended beyond California. "You would never think it would happen to you, especially not in full uniform," said Agent Alfonso Dyson. "I was definitely unprepared. I had let my guard down."[16] Dyson and the other Secret Service Agents sought help from the Washington Lawyers Committee, which in turn requested Hogan & Hartson's assistance to pursue a class action suit. Attorneys Jonathan Abram, Bob Duncan, Craig Hoover, Jack Keeney, William Nussbaum, and Walter Smith were among the thirty-five lawyers and legal assistants Hogan & Hartson assigned to the complex case. The CSD's success was spectacular. With the Lawyers Committee, the CSD negotiated a $17.7 million settlement and won $1.9 million in court-awarded legal fees from Denny's. Hogan & Hartson split the legal fees with the Lawyers Committee, then donated $150,000 of its share to the committee's 25th Anniversary Fund.[17]

In 1999 the CSD succeeded in freeing Wilbert Thomas, an African-American who had been wrongfully imprisoned for twelve years in West Virginia following a rape conviction based on falsified DNA evidence and false testimony, submitted under oath by the state trooper in charge of the police serology lab. "When you're behind bars," said Thomas after his release, "it seems no one will listen to you, not even God." Reuniting Thomas with his two children was, said the CSD's Jonathan Abram, "one of the best moments of my career."[18]

Three years later, in a case that was among the most chilling episodes of civil and human rights violations in recent U.S. history, the CSD joined attorneys from the NAACP and from other law firms to help win the release of thirteen prisoners who had been among forty-six mostly African-American persons arrested in a drug sweep in Tulia, Texas, in 1999. Of the thirty-eight persons convicted, twelve already had served prison sentences and been released. All convictions had been secured through the false testimony of a single police officer, an itinerant man with an unstable and checkered past who had volunteered his "services" to the local sheriff.

The officer's zeal in Tulia earned him the honor of being named Texas's "Lawman of the Year" in 1999. But Hogan & Hartson's Mitch Zamoff had a different opinion, which he expressed to newspaper reporters when the prisoners were released in 2003. The officer, Zamoff said, was "a cancer. The judge diagnosed the cancer two months ago, and now it's time to remove the cancer before it spreads any further."[19] Texas Governor Rick Perry agreed, and on August 23, 2003, following the unanimous recommendation of the Texas Board of Pardons and Paroles, he pardoned thirty-five of the thirty-eight convicted persons.

Cases such as Glacier Bay, Denny's, Wilbert Thomas, and Tulia, Texas, were among many in the CSD that received wide media attention, but no less appreciated were the numerous actions undertaken by the department on behalf of refugees, immigrants, the elderly and disabled, death row prisoners, children and families, and individuals like Linda Lanier. Diagnosed with a life-threatening illness, Ms. Lanier had sought Hogan & Hartson's guidance in 1997 on trust and guardianship matters for her six-year-old son. Later she wrote to Sally Determan and Catherine Guttman-McCabe, who had helped her arrange her affairs. "I was treated as if I were your top client. Most of all you have made a difference in my son's life. I know that my hands are too small right now. They say it takes a village, and you are part of my son's village. Thank you from the bottom of my heart." Service such as this stoked the fires under Hogan & Hartson's commitment to make the law matter, not just to every client but to every attorney, too.

Hogan & Hartson opened a Beijing office in 2003.

Bob Glen Odle, chief architect of Hogan & Hartson's expansion. Odle combined a relaxed personal style, an appreciation of human talents and diversity, and a visionary grasp of modern law practice to guide the firm through a decade of growth that the legal press called "staggering" in its scope and speed.

CLAUDETTE M. CHRISTIAN JOINED H&H IN 1994 FROM POSITIONS AT THE EXPORT-IMPORT BANK AND IN PRIVATE PRACTICE. SHE HAS MANAGED NUMEROUS, COMPLEX INTERNATIONAL TRANSACTIONS IN AREAS OF ENERGY, COMMUNICATIONS, BANKING, AND PROJECT FINANCE AND DEVELOPMENT.

In August 2002 Warren Gorrell, Sandy Berger, and several Hogan & Hartson attorneys traveled to Beijing, China, for the opening of the firm's office there. Hogan & Hartson's decision to establish an office in China reflected that country's increased business interaction with the rest of the world, including business transactions and international trade, especially following China's joining the World Trade Organization in November 2001. Partners Jun Wei and Steven Robinson, members of the firm's Corporate, Securities and Finance Practice Group, co-managed the office.

Sandy Berger had left the White House at the end of Bill Clinton's second term. "I was either going to be governor of New York or be an investment banker or I was going to go back to Hogan," he said. "I never would have even talked to another firm." But the idea of a private strategic advisory firm also appealed to him, so in 2000 he formed Stonebridge International, with himself as chairman and Tony Harrington, former Hogan & Hartson partner and U.S. ambassador to Brazil, as president. In November 1999 the Senate had taken just twelve days, a record time, to confirm President Clinton's nomination of Harrington as U.S. ambassador to Brazil. Now Harrington could add this special experience to his other international credentials.

Stonebridge worked independently around the globe advising clients on major strategic business matters and had a working alliance with Hogan & Hartson. Both opened offices in Beijing at the same time. Beijing became Hogan & Hartson's tenth international site, making a total of nineteen offices, including the firm's nine U.S. locations.[20] In October 2001 Warren Gorrell had said, "I wouldn't be surprised if, in a year or two, we have more lawyers outside of Washington than in Washington."[21] The next year the firm reached a rough equilibrium, with about as many attorneys in the firm's other offices as in Washington, D.C. And in 2004, its centennial year, Hogan & Hartson announced the opening of an office in Munich, its twentieth worldwide and its second in Germany, and an office in Shanghai, its twenty-first worldwide and its second in China. The Munich office opening, led by Berlin partners Jan Hegemann and Johannes Schulte and U.S. partner Steve Ballew, was the firm's seventeenth outside Washington, D.C., and the firm's Shanghai office was the firm's eighteenth outside Washington, D.C., all in just fifteen years. Hogan & Hartson had entered the 1980s as a Washington firm with uncertain aspirations for expansion, then moved into the 1990s as a national firm with a limited international footprint, but committed to further growth. Now it opened the new millennium as an established and thriving international institution.

Hogan & Hartson's relatively rapid growth after 1988 prompted much reflection by its partners, many of whom remembered the firm in what now seemed like distant and different eras from the 1950s through the 1970s. Asked about the effects of all this change on the firm's core values and identity, Bob Odle laughed. "I can tell you I've been hearing this for 35 years," he said. "I was lawyer number 48 on board when I joined the firm, and when we approached 100 lawyers we were wringing our hands and saying, 'Oh, we're getting so big, we're going to lose our warm, cherished culture,' and then, next thing you know, five years later you're 200 lawyers and you're wringing your hands again." Hogan & Hartson, in its centenary year of 2004, seemed more youthful than old as it scanned the widest possible horizon and refitted for journeys yet to come.

It was useful to recall just how much hand-wringing the legal profession had performed over the years, and how much self-scrutiny and introspection it had survived. Still, Odle acknowledged the challenge that increased size and competitiveness — and now a global presence — posed to values of personal contact and loyalty. "That's one of the reasons I was on the road so much," he said. But Odle also had a recipe for sustaining and nurturing the firm's core values. "If you select [attorneys] right, if you deal with problem situations quickly and effectively, if you make your multiple offices feel like they're a part of the main body of the law firm and not some appendage, if you find ways to communicate, you can maintain the essence of this thing that everybody values so much." And no one, he might have added, valued it more or tended it more faithfully than Bob Glen Odle.

"I joined Hogan & Hartson because I felt I could be an individual here," said Claudette Christian, born and raised in St. Thomas, U.S. Virgin Islands. "There are lots of firms that would have offered me the platform that Hogan did, but you become part of the firm and your individuality isn't appreciated, isn't exploited, isn't celebrated. Hogan is quite different; it appreciates my talents and lets me be the best that I can be."

At the turn of the twentieth century Frank Hogan seized an opportunity to be himself and embarked on a remarkable journey as an advocate. Now, one hundred years later, about one thousand attorneys in Hogan & Hartson offices around the world continue that journey in the law together, each adding his or her own special energy to the venture. At the heart of it all, as Bob Odle once put it, is "a pervading spirit of teamwork and cooperation, our genuine affection for one another, and our passion for maintaining a value system that places the highest importance on considerations that go well beyond making money." After a century of growth and evolution, Hogan & Hartson still thrives on its founder's core values, and on the belief — Frank Hogan's binding belief — that the law is the ablest architect of human rights and liberties yet devised, and the surest guarantor of the diversity and dignity that flourish in their protection.

Epilogue
The Next 100 Years

No history of Hogan & Hartson would be complete without recognition of the many partners, associates, and staff whose own individual efforts, though not specifically mentioned in the anecdotes contained in this book, have significantly contributed, and are continuing to contribute, to the firm's reputation, culture, growth, and success. These people reside in offices throughout the United States and elsewhere, some of whom have been with the firm for years, and some for only a few months, but in each case having clearly made their mark on the firm. For many of these, their best years at the firm are yet to come. Though this book and its stories reflect merely a part of our firm's history and it is impossible to describe the important contributions of all of our partners, associates, and staff, one of the book's purposes, apart from celebrating our centennial, is to remind us of who we are and where we came from. Undoubtedly, the next chapters of our story (which have yet to be written) will be filled with vignettes involving many of the people who are at the firm today — their stories have not yet made it to the pages of this book but their impact on the firm will be no less significant.

Some say we only need to look at history to see the future. If the history of Hogan & Hartson over the past one hundred years reveals to us any glimpse of the future, there seems to be no doubt that the future is very bright.

Richard T. Horan, Jr.
Peter A. Rohrbach
Richard S. Silverman
Dennis H. Tracey III
Christine A. Varney

Executive Committee, 2004
Hogan & Hartson L.L.P.

Notes

Chapter 1

1. Jerold S. Auerbach, *Unequal Justice: Lawyers and Social Change in Modern America* (New York: Oxford University Press, 1976), 97.
2. An existing history of Hogan & Hartson, written by a partner and friend of Frank Hogan, Lester Cohen, contains much valuable and interesting information about Hogan and the firm, but inaccurately states the dates of Hogan's first offices, which are documented in *Boyd's Directory*, referred to as the *Washington, D.C. City Directory*, in the Washingtoniana Collection, Martin Luther King, Jr. Library, Washington, D.C. See Lester Cohen, *Frank Hogan Remembered: Reminiscences by Lester Cohen, Retired Senior Partner in the law firm of Hogan & Hartson* (Washington, D.C., 1985), 14, 22.
3. Hogan's work was finished, but Kalbfus's was not. A year later he was summoned before a subcommittee of the House District Committee to explain once more why some property assessments in the District seemed abnormally low. But Kalbfus had come well prepared. He reminded the representatives that the basis for the low assessments was not shenanigans by local assessors but a law passed by Congress itself on July 1, 1902, requiring that all real estate in the District be assessed at two-thirds of its true value. Holding up chapter and verse of the legislators' own handiwork, Kalbfus confessed he was "utterly at a loss to know what Congress meant by this legislation." He had at last slipped loose.
4. *Evening Star*, Washington, D.C., 17 May 1915, 1; ibid., 19 May 1915, 1.
5. Frank Hogan, "Speech before Erie County, N.Y., Bar," n.d. (circa 1928), 10, Hogan and Hartson Archives (hereafter H&H Archives).
6. *Evening Star*, Washington, D.C., 23 May 1916, 1.
7. Ibid, 20.
8. *Evening Star*, Washington, D.C., 27 May 1916, 1.
9. Ellis W. Hawley, *The Great War and the Search for a Modern Order: A History of the American People and Their Institutions*, 1917-1933 (New York: St. Martin's Press, 1979), 74-75.
10. *New York Times*, 5 August 1921, H&H Archives.
11. Ibid.
12. The case normally would have been tried in Washington, D.C., where the alleged conspiracy occurred, but the Justice Department, which thought it had an "open and shut" case, wanted an earlier trial than that allowed by the D.C. docket. Therefore, they sought to have the trial conducted in West Virginia. Chief Justice Taft assisted in the arrangements. *Newark Evening News*, 3 February 1924, H&H Archives.
13. *Parkersburg News*, 19 January 1924, H&H Archives.
14. *The Department of Justice v. The United States Harness Co. et al.*, undated pamphlet, 7, H&H Archives.
15. Ibid, 14.
16. *Hide and Leather*, 9 February 1924, 23, H&H Archives.
17. *Parkersburg News*, 25 January 1924, H&H Archives.
18. *The Department of Justice v. The United States Harness Co. et al.*, 19-20.
19. Margaret Leslie Davis, *Dark Side of Fortune: Triumph and Scandal in the Life of Oil Tycoon Edward L. Doheny* (Berkeley: University of California Press, 1998).
20. "Eulogy by Brother Frank J. Hogan," *Washington Elk* 3, no. 11 (24 August 1923), Scrapbook #2, H&H Archives; Hawley, *The Great War and the Search for a Modern Order*, 76.

21. *Washington Post*, Magazine Section, 10 May 1925, Scrapbook #8, H&H Archives.
22. *Time*, 3 November 1924, Scrapbook #5, H&H Archives.
23. Cohen, *Frank Hogan Remembered*, 39.
24. Hogan, "Speech before the Erie County, N.Y. Bar," 31-33.
25. *Wall Street Journal*, 4 December 1926, Scrapbook #6, H&H Archives.
26. *New York American*, 17 December 1926, Scrapbook #22, H&H Archives.
27. Scrapbook #22, H&H Archives.
28. *New York Times*, 1 March 1927, Scrapbook #23, H&H Archives.

CHAPTER 2

1. Lester Cohen, *Frank Hogan Remembered: Reminiscences by Lester Cohen, Retired Senior Partner in the law firm of Hogan & Hartson* (Washington, D.C., 1985), 49.
2. Richard L. Abel, *American Lawyers* (New York: Oxford University Press, 1989), 81.
3. Frank J. Hogan, "Fresh Fields and Pastures New," speech before the New York State Bar Association, circa 1937, H&H Archives. Hogan probably was including the U.S. Court of Appeals in the District of Columbia, whose name Congress changed (from "the District of Columbia Court of Appeals") in 1937, but which was not formally declared to be one of the eleven judicial circuits of the United States until 1948.
4. Hogan was among 2,000 attorneys nationwide who joined the National Lawyers' Committee of the American Liberty League. This group sought to rein in the administrative authority of federal agencies by requiring judicial review of their decisions. In 1937 Congress passed the Walter-Logan Act for that purpose, but President Roosevelt vetoed it. Rayman L. Solomon, "Five Crises or One: The Concept of Legal Professionalism, 1925-1960," in Robert L. Nelson, David M. Trubek, and Rayman L. Solomon, *Lawyers' Ideals/Lawyers' Practices: Transformations in the American Legal Profession* (Ithaca: Cornell University Press, 1992), 144-73, 161.
5. The Court's shift toward the New Deal after the failure of Roosevelt's effort to restructure it has recently been disputed by historian Marian C. McKenna in *Franklin D. Roosevelt and the Great Constitutional War: The Court Packing Crisis of 1937* (New York: Fordham University Press, 2002).
6. The Honorable John Warner, U.S. Senator from Virginia, telephone interview with Adrian Kinnane, 29 April 2003 (hereafter Warner Oral History). Senator Warner married Mellon's granddaughter and was an attorney and partner at Hogan & Hartson between 1960 and 1968.
7. Walter Lippman, "Today and Tomorrow," *New York Herald Tribune*, 5 March 1936.
8. In *Mapp v. Ohio* (1980), Justice Black finally found a way both to hold and to resolve his doubts about Fourth Amendment protections. Placing the Fourth Amendment next to the Fifth Amendment, against self-incrimination, he saw that "a constitutional basis emerges which not only justifies but actually requires the exclusionary rule." That is, evidence unlawfully seized could not be used against the accused, not because it violated the Fourth Amendment alone but because it amounted to a violation of the Fifth as well.
9. Frank Hogan, "A Rendezvous with the Constitution," speech before the American Bar Association, Boston, MA, 26 August 1936, H&H Archives.
10. *Res Ipsa Loquitor* 1, no. 3 (March 1939), Georgetown University Law School, Washington, D.C.
11. Frank Hogan, "A Tribute to a Washington Boy," speech before the National Council of the Boy Scouts, Washington, D.C., 16 May 1941, H&H Archives.
12. Cohen, *Frank Hogan Remembered*, 88.
13. He got one anyway, displacing the simple stone slab in his honor outside the National Archives building. On May 2, 1997, President Clinton dedicated the FDR Memorial, an attractive, park-like series of low-rise granite inscriptions and bronze statues near the Lincoln Memorial recalling the struggles and triumphs of the Depression and World War II and Roosevelt's thoughts about them.
14. William M. Kiplinger, *Washington is Like That* (New York: Harper and Brothers, 1942), 123-24.

15. David Brinkley, *Washington Goes to War* (New York: Alfred A. Knopf, 1988), 119-20, 109.
16. Marc Galanter and Thomas Palay, *Tournament of Lawyers: The Transformation of the Big Law Firm* (Chicago: University of Chicago Press, 1991), 20-36, 36.
17. Ibid., 35.
18. Martin Mayer, *The Lawyers* (Westport, Conn.: Greenwood Press, 1967), 308.
19. *Interview with E. Barrett Prettyman, Jr., Esquire*, by Robert H. Kapp, Esquire, 6 June 1996, 71-72, Oral History Project, United States Courts, District of Columbia Circuit, The Historical Society of the District of Columbia Circuit.
20. Warner Oral History. The name of the defendant, "Willy Jones," is fictional.
21. Gail Starling Marshall, "Personal Reminiscences of Hogan & Hartson, 1972-1986," H&H Archives.
22. *Jay Ricks, an Oral History*, interview by Max Paglin for The Cable Center, August 1987 (www.cablecenter.org/library/col).
23. Austin Mittler, interview by Adrian Kinnane, Washington, D.C., 21 April 2003.
24. Hogan, "Fresh Fields and Pastures New."

CHAPTER 3

1. *Washington Post*, 5 April 1968.
2. *Washington Post*, 6 April 1968.
3. *Report of City Council Public Hearings on the Rebuilding and Recovery of Washington, D.C. from the Civil Disturbances of April, 1968*, Government of the District of Columbia, City Council, Washington, D.C., 10 May 1968.
4. George J. Benston, *Conglomerate Mergers: Causes, Consequences, and Remedies* (Washington, D.C.: American Enterprise Institute for Public Policy Research, 1980), 9.
5. *Fortune* Editors, *The Conglomerate Commotion* (New York: Viking Press, 1970), 8.
6. Arthur Herzog, *Vesco: From Wall Street to Castro's Cuba: The Rise, Fall, and Exile of the King of White Collar Crime* (New York: Doubleday, 1987).
7. Memorandum, The Community Relations Study Committee to The Executive Committee, 8 September 1969, 6-7. Courtesy of John Ferren, personal files.
8. Several years later the period for circulating a case among the firm's partners was lowered to four days.
9. Robert Vesco's biographer claims that Vesco's $200,000 "campaign contribution" in 1972 was used to finance the Watergate break-in. Herzog, Vesco, 172.
10. John Sirica, *To Set the Record Straight: The Break-in, the Tapes, the Conspirators, the Pardon* (New York: W. W. Norton & Company, 1979), 206-9.
11. Lee Loevinger, "A Washington Lawyer Tells What It's Like," *The George Washington Law Review*, 1969-1970, 531-45, 533.
12. Jay E. Ricks, "Some Interesting Experiences With People Who Changed the Communications Landscape," H&H Archives, 2002, 8.
13. *Teleprompter Cable Communications Corporation v. FCC*, 565 F2d 736, 742 (D.C. Cir 1977).
14. *Hughes Tool Company v. Trans World Airlines*, 409 US 363 (1973).
15. Barrett Prettyman, Jr., *Death and the Supreme Court* (New York: Harcourt, Brace & World, 1961).
16. *Interview with E. Barrett Prettyman, Jr., Esquire*, by Robert H. Kapp, Esquire, 6 June 1996, 71-72, Oral History Project, United States Courts, District of Columbia Circuit, The Historical Society of the District of Columbia Circuit.
17. *Garrison v. Patterson*, 391 US 464 (1968).
18. *Vermont Yankee Nuclear Power Corporation v. National Resources Defense Council*, 435 US 519 (1978).
19. *NAACP v. Claiborne Hardware Company et al.*, 458 US 886 (1982).
20. *International Controls Corporation v. Hogan & Hartson*, No. 77 Civ. 5764, 1979 U.S. Dist. LEXIS 10275, at *23 [1979 Transfer Binder], Fed. Sec. L. Rep. (CCH), ¶97, 183 (S.D. N.Y. 21 August 1979).
21. Memorandum to the Executive Committee, 26 June 1970. In Jeffers's personal files.

CHAPTER 4

1. Gerald S. and Deborah H. Strober, *"Let Us Begin Anew": An Oral History of the Kennedy Presidency* (New York: HarperCollins, 1993), 139-40.
2. Richard L. Abel, *American Lawyers* (New York: Oxford University Press, 1989), 188.
3. Charles's statement recalled by Samuel "Sandy" Berger in interview with Adrian Kinnane, May 13, 2003.
4. Robert L. Nelson and David M. Trubek, "New Problems and New Paradigms in Studies of the Legal Profession," in *Lawyers' Ideals/Lawyers' Practices: Transformations in the American Legal Profession*, ed. Robert L. Nelson, David M. Trubek, and Rayman L. Solomon (Ithaca: Cornell University Press, 1992), 1.
5. Michael J. Powell, "Developments in the Regulation of Lawyers: Competing Segments and Market, Client, and Government Controls," *Social Forces* 64, no. 2 (December 1985): 281-305.
6. Marc Galanter, "The Legal Malaise; or, Justice Observed," *Law & Society Review* 19, no. 4 (1985): 537-56, 542.
7. Lewis H. Goldfarb currently is a partner in the New York office of Hogan & Hartson L.L.P. and a member of the firm's Litigation Group.
8. Galanter, "The Legal Malaise; or, Justice Observed," 539.
9. *Legal Times*, 21 May 1990.
10. *Missouri v. Jenkins, 495 U.S. 33* (1990). As the remedy costs ballooned to nearly $200 million annually, Missouri continued its challenges in court. In 1995 the case once again reached the Supreme Court, where Chief Justice Rehnquist delivered a 5-4 majority opinion essentially reversing key parts of the remedy.
11. Dividing the fees, however, proved the truth of Vincent Cohen's observation that "money is a very destructive force." The firm's management had to work hard to prevent perceived inequities in distributing the windfall from eroding morale. Harold M. Hyman, *Craftsmanship and Character: A History of the Vinson & Elkins Law Firm of Houston, 1917-1997* (Athens, Ga.: University of Georgia Press, 1998), 506-8.
12. Jeffrey Williams, *Manipulation on Trial: Economic Analysis and the Hunt Silver Case* (Cambridge: Cambridge University Press, 1995), 1-3, 29-63.
13. Jay E. Ricks, "Some Interesting Experiences With People Who Changed the Communications Landscape," H&H Archives, 2002, 2.
14. Robert Goldberg and Gerald Jay Goldberg, Citizen Turner: *The Wild Rise of an American Tycoon* (New York: Harcourt Brace & Company, 1995), 249-50.
15. Reese Schonfeld, *Me and Ted Against the World* (New York: Cliff Street; HarperCollins, 2001), 116.
16. Ricks, "Some Interesting Experiences," 3.
17. Ibid., 4.
18. Ibid.
19. *The National Law Journal*, 17 January 1983.
20. Bob Glen Odle, "Future Planning," confidential memorandum to the Executive Committee, May 31, 1989, H&H Archives.
21. Steven Brill, "The Law Business in the Year 2000," *The American Lawyer*, June 1989, 5-26. Brill's article in turn reflected the analysis of scholars like Marc Galanter and Thomas Palay, who saw in the partner-associate "leverage" system, often referred to as the "Cravath" system for the New York firm that developed it, an ultimately untenable model for law firm growth, for it responded more to the firm's own need to grow than to the market's actual demand for legal services. See Marc Galanter and Thomas Palay, *The Tournament of Lawyers: The Transformation of the Big Law Firm* (Chicago: University of Chicago Press, 1991).
22. Odle, "Future Planning."
23. *Vaughns v. Board of Education of Prince George's County*, 598 F. Supp. 1262, 1286 (D. Md. 1984). Quoted in Joseph M. Hassett, *Community Services Department Report of Activities: 1981-1985*, September 1985, 5.
24. Quoted in Robert Safian, "Making Waves — If Not Rain — At Hogan & Hartson," *The American Lawyer*, April 1968, 140.
25. Ibid.

26. *United States v. Halper* raised as many problems as it solved, for civil fines had become an important tool in the enforcement of certain criminal statutes, notably securities and drug laws. In 1996 the U.S. Supreme Court revisited its *Halper* ruling in another case, *United States v. Ursery*, in which it upheld the government's seizure of Guy Ursery's house after he was convicted of using it to grow and process marijuana.

CHAPTER 5

1. Karen Dillon, "Hogan & Hartson Picks Its Own Niche in Europe," *The American Lawyer*, September 1990, 6.
2. Aleksander Galos, "Remarks at the 10th Anniversary of the Warsaw Office," H&H Archives.
3. Quoted in Cameron Barr, "Doers and Talkers," *The American Lawyer*, July/August 1990, 51-59.
4. Hogan & Hartson, *CSD 1991 Annual Report*, 6.
5. Hogan & Hartson, *CSD 1993 Annual Report*, 17.
6. http://www.fcc.gov/telecom.html.
7. http://www.globalsecurity.org/military/industry/general_dynamics.htm.
8. Jonathan S. Kahan, *Medical Device Development: A Regulatory Overview* (Lowell, Mass.: Parexel, 2000).
9. Martin Michaelson, "Beneath the Surface: The Practice of Law at U.S. Colleges and Universities," *Change: The Magazine of Higher Learning*, May/June 2003, 11-15.
10. Rachel L. Dodes, "The Haft Family Rebuilds After an E-commerce Shootout," *Business Forward*, May 2001.
11. Robert Swaine, *The Cravath Firm and Its Predecessors, 1819-1947*, vol. 1 (New York: Ad Press, 1946), 371. Quoted in Marc Galanter and Thomas Palay, *The Tournament of Lawyers: The Transformation of the Big Law Firm* (Chicago: University of Chicago Press, 1991), 6.
12. Siobhan Froth, "Hogan Joins the Big Boys," *Legal Times*, 19 October 1998.
13. Vanessa Blum, "Hogan Courting Big Apple Firm," *Legal Times*, 25 October 1999.
14. Hogan & Hartson, Press Release, New York, 1 December 2003.
15. Vanessa Blum, "In With the Old," *Legal Times*, 26 June 2000.
16. *Washington Post*, 24 May 1993, A4.
17. In 1995 Hogan & Hartson partner and former CSD head William Bradford, Jr., explained the history and rationale for shifting the cost of plaintiffs' attorney fees to defendants in cases such as civil rights suits when the plaintiffs prevail. See Bradford, "Private Enforcement of Public Rights: The Role of Fee-Shifting Statutes in Pro Bono Lawyering," in Robert A. Katzman, ed., *The Law Firm and the Public Good* (Washington, D.C.: The Brookings Institution, 1995), chap. 6.
18. *Legal Times*, 25 October 1999.
19. *Washington Post*, 17 June 2003, A8.
20. Hogan & Hartson closed its Bethesda office on 20 June 1998.
21. Claudia MacLachlan, "One Step Forward," *Legal Times*, 22 October 2001.

Photo Credits

Photos and images not otherwise credited are from the Hogan & Hartson archives, or have been provided by Hogan & Hartson partners and offices.

Institutional Collections:

Georgetown University Library, Washington, D.C.
2, 3 (L), 6, 11 (top)

Getty Images USA
38 (bottom), 79, 144

The Library of Congress, Prints and Photographs Division
5, 11 (bottom), 12, 21, 36, 43 (top)

National Archives and Records Administration (NARA II), College Park, MD
7 (L), 18 (R), 39, 42, 43 (bottom), 44 (top), 46 (L), 47 (bottom), 48, 54, 56, 59 (top), 66, 67, 68 (R), 69 (top), 75, 85, 99 (bottom), 102 (R), 105, 106, 109, 110 (L, R), 132, 140

Washington *Evening Star* Photo Collection, Martin Luther King Jr. Library, Washington, D.C.
37, 45, 74 (bottom), 81, 97, 108, 151

Washington Historical Image Collection, Martin Luther King Jr. Library, Washington, D.C.
ix, 3 (center), 6 (R), 7 (L), 38 (top), 41 (R), 50, 57 (R), 65, 116 (center)

Courtesy of:

Ambassador Anthony Harrington
145

The Bar Association of the District of Columbia
52

Brooks Blunck and Chase Photography, Bethesda, MD
58

Benjamin N. Cardozo School of Law, Yeshiva University
166

Doug DeMark Photography
103

The Honorable John M. Ferren
77

Mike Flanery, Denton, Texas, and his Texas Courthouse collection
96

Patrice Gilbert, photographer, and *The Washington Lawyer* magazine
89 (bottom)

The Honorable Stanley S. Harris
46 (R)

Commissioner Thomas B. Leary and the Federal Trade Commission
115

The family of Edward A. McDermott
69 (bottom)

The National Hospice and Palliative Care Organization
104 (bottom)

The Honorable John Roberts, Jr.
168

The Honorable David S. Tatel
101

History Associates Incorporated:

Garry Adelman
iii, 3 (R), 13, 57 (L), 62, 95 116 (top and bottom), 117, 118, 119, 128, 129, 159, 162, 167 (top)

Adrian Kinnane
51 (R), 61, 87 (top), 156 (L), 161

L

M